The
Munros
SCOTLAND'S HIGHEST MOUNTAINS

This book is dedicated to the memory of Alan Sands,
Bookseller and Mountaineer.

First published in Great Britain in 1996 for Lomond Books Ltd.
14 Freskyn Place, East Mains Industrial Estate,
Broxburn EH52 5NF
www.lomondbooks.com

Produced by Colin Baxter Photography Ltd.

Reprinted 1996, 1997, 1999, 2000, 2002, 2003, 2004, 2005, 2009.
Revised 1998, 2006, 2011.

Information used in the creation of the maps was kindly supplied by the
Macaulay Land Use Research Institute in Aberdeen and the Royal Commission on the
Ancient and Historical Monuments of Scotland (LCS88 Photography).

Colin Baxter Photography Ltd. gratefully acknowledges permission granted
by Neil Wilson Publishing Ltd., Glasgow, to reproduce those route summaries that
are also published in *The Munro Almanac* by Cameron McNeish.

ISBN 978-1-84204-082-9

Printed in China

Photography:

© Colin Baxter 2011:
Pages 1, 6, 9, 14, 24, 26, 27, 28, 43, 48, 60, 62, 65, 71,
72, 78, 84, 89, 90, 93, 94, 97, 98, 102, 106, 114, 116, 123,
124, 129, 131, 137, 140, 158, 165, 174, 195, 212, 219

© Alan Gordon 2011:
Front Cover, Back Cover and Pages 23, 31, 34, 51, 69, 75, 76, 83, 86, 100,
112, 121, 132, 143, 144, 148, 151, 154, 157, 160, 162, 169, 172, 179, 180, 184,
188, 192, 200 (Scotland in Focus), 203, 205, 207, 209, 210, 217, 221, 223

© David Paterson 2011: Pages 47, 52, 58, 186, 191, 216

© R G Elliott (Scotland in Focus) 2011: Pages 152, 215

© Alex Gillespie 2011: Pages 55, 81

© Alan O'Brien 2011: Pages 126, 183

© Jerry Rawson 2011: Pages 41, 66

© Chris Townsend 2011: Pages 39, 171

© Rab Anderson 2011: Page 146

© Jeremy Ashcroft 2011: Page 18

© Laurie Campbell (Scotland in Focus) 2011: Page 109

© R Weir (Scotland in Focus) 2011: Page 37

Front cover photograph: Sgurr na Ciste Duibhe and Sgurr nan Spainteach from Saileag.
Back cover photograph: Sunrise from The Saddle.   Page 1 photograph: Ben Nevis.

The Munros

SCOTLAND'S HIGHEST MOUNTAINS

Cameron McNeish

LOMOND
www.lomondbooks.com

KEY TO ALL ROUTE MAPS

Start of route
Route and direction of travel
  as in route summary
Munro
Other mountain or top
Main road
Minor road
Track
Other footpath
Railway
Parking
Youth hostel
Buildings
Woodland

Munro   ▲ BEN KLIBRECK
Other mountain ▴ Ben Rinnes
Chapter areas   *Ullapool Hills*

0   10   20   30mls
0 10 20 30 40 kms

© 2006 Wendy Price Cartographic Services.

CONTENTS

THE MUNROS

The Munros, the 283 mountains in Scotland over 3000ft (914m) in height, are enjoying an unprecedented popularity. Since the centenary of *Munros Tables*, the list of 3000ft mountains first compiled in 1891 by Sir Hugh Munro of Lindertis, it has become fashionable to climb the hills, with an increasing number of people stoically ticking their way through the list. I completed my first round of the Munros during the centenary year in 1991 and became Munroist No. 913. Since then, well over three thousand other hill walkers have added their names to the list.

So what's the appeal? Physical exercise has become much more popular in recent years. The completion of the Munros offers a tremendous challenge. As well as the physical exertion involved, there is also the aesthetic appeal of magnificent scenery, the skills to be learned, the camaraderie of like-minded souls and the bonus of visiting parts of Scotland that you would otherwise probably ignore.

When Sir Hugh Munro compiled his tables he could scarcely have realised the consequences. I wonder what he would think today if he knew that his surname had become a generic term for mountains over 3000ft? I wonder what he would think of the legions of people who refer to themelves as Munro-baggers rather than walkers, climbers or hikers? What would he think of those poor souls who have suffered premature dementia because of a continued struggle to climb mountains for the prime purpose of ticking them off in a book? Or if he heard his name taken in vain as the afflicted souls struggle up their umpteenth Geal Charn in snow, sleet and wind for the pleasure of following their compasses all the way back down again?

But despite the disadvantages of being a Munro freak, the game undoubtedly has good points. The walker or climber who has never wavered from the single-mindedness of the Munro challenge will have travelled the length and breadth of the Scottish Highlands, enjoying considerable exercise in the most beautiful of surroundings. He, or she, will have become familiar with some truly magical places and many magnificent hills – hills which the car-borne visitor will never see. Some favourites flash to mind – Seana Bhraigh, the 'old high slopes' up in the empty quarter beyond Inverlael; the castellated form of An Teallach, the forge, in shape and form one of the most appealing mountains in the land, and of course for sheer, rugged, majestic splendour, the spectacle that is the Cuillin of Skye.

The other attractive feature of the Munro challenge is the sheer volume of experience that is gained. I know of many hillwalkers who are purely fair weather climbers. Several of them have many years' experience in climbing and walking in Scotland, but the vast majority of their activities have been enjoyed in good weather. To my mind this only makes then half a walker. It really is the foul weather and winter conditions which are the givers of experience. Climb hills in good weather and all you really gain is some exercise and a good view. This is fine but it doesn't prepare you for the day when the conditions will change rapidly and you are suddenly faced with an adventure of epic proportions!

In the course of climbing 283 Munros you will inevitably be faced with more than a fair share of nasties. By the time you have completed the round you will be well prepared for almost every eventuality you can encounter in the British hills. Your navigation will have reached a high level of expertise, you will have a pretty shrewd idea of what the

Ben Cruachan, Ben Laoigh and Stob Binnein

weather is likely to do by watching the clouds and sensing the wind, you will have become a competent scrambler if not a rock climber, and it is more than likely that you will have picked up a fair degree of experience in snow and ice. All in all, it's not a bad game, a favourable excuse, if one is needed, for going to the hills and wild places.

Even after all these years there are still those who dislike the idea of Munro-bagging, suggesting that people shouldn't need that form of motivation to head for the high places. While the critics may be absolutely right, there is little doubt that virtually everyone who climbs all 283 of the Munros has scored a pretty high achievement, an achievement that will have been made worthwhile by a host of mountain memories that will never diminish.

This book is *not* intended to be packed away in your rucksack for quick reference. I hope it will be used to glean information on the mountains and the routes, and I believe the photographs portray the grandeur and beauty of the hills in a way which has not previously been achieved and which will encourage readers to get out there.

I therefore hope the text of this book fulfills two main functions:

1. To offer a choice of route up the mountains, and in particular, ways of combining several Munros together to make a satisfying day out. It would also serve the purpose of spreading the load on the hill, taking the more adventurous away from the popular honey-pot routes.

2. To form a good, substantial read which can motivate and inspire people to go out and climb the hills in question. Many people climb the hills without actually getting to know them, climbing and descending them by the shortest possible route. I would hope this book will introduce them to different aspects of the hills' characters, in a more holistic way.

One of the difficulties Sir Hugh Munro discovered when first compiling his list was determining what should constitute a mountain summit, or a top, and what, in terms of distance and loss of height, distinguished one mountain from another. Many mountains have several tops, some even appear as a small range of hills. The debate on what tops should be Munros, ie separate mountains, has raged on for the past century. The most recent changes took place in 1997, when the Scottish Mountaineering Club promoted eight mountains to Munro status and deleted one from the existing list, following a re-survey by the Ordnance Survey.

The demoted Munro was Sgor an Iubhair in the Mamores, which was considered to have too small a re-ascent to merit continued inclusion. The new Munros were Stob Coire Raineach on the Buachaille Etive Beag ridge; Stob na Broige on Buachaille Etive Mor; Stob Coire Sgreamhach on Bidean nam Bian; Spidean Coire nan Clach on Beinn Eighe; Tom na Gruagaich on Beinn Alligin; An Stuc in the Ben Lawers group; Sgurr na Carnach on the Five Sisters of Kintail ridge and Sgor an Lochain Uaine on the Braeriach to Cairn Toul ridge in the Cairngorms.

All the usual route-planning information is included in sidepanels – distance of recommended routes, height climbed, translation and pronunciation of hill names, etc – but always bear in mind that this is not intended as a basic guide to be slavishly followed, but simply as a tool to help when planning days or weekends away.

Finally, it's important to remember that it is not the ticking off of 3000ft mountains that is important, but the 'being there' which really matters. Even if you don't reach the summit, the mountains will always be there for another day.

CAMERON MCNEISH

Cairn Toul, Sgor an Lochain Uaine, Carn na Criche and the River Dee from Ben Macdui, Cairngorms National Park

MUNRO HEIGHTS, NUMBERS AND CHECK-LIST

No.	Name	Height	DATE	No.	Name	Height	DATE
1	Ben Nevis	1344m/4409ft	....	35	Meall Garbh	1118m/3668ft	....
2	Ben Macdui	1309m/4295ft	....	36	Sgor Gaoith	1118m/3668ft	....
3	Braeriach	1296m/4252ft	....	37	Aonach Beag (Badenoch)	1116m/3661ft	....
4	Cairn Toul	1291m/4236ft	....	38	Stob Coire an Laoigh	1116m/3661ft	....
5	Sgor an Lochain Uaine	1258m/4127ft	....	39	Stob Coire Easain	1115m/3658ft	....
6	Cairn Gorm	1244m/4081ft	....	40	Monadh Mor	1113m/3652ft	....
7	Aonach Beag	1234m/4049ft	....	41	Tom a' Choinich	1112m/3648ft	....
8	Aonach Mor	1221m/4006ft	....	42	Carn a' Choire Boidheach (White Mounth)	1110m/3642ft	....
9	Carn Mor Dearg	1220m/4003ft	....	43	Sgurr Mor (Fannaichs)	1110m/3642ft	....
10	Ben Lawers	1214m/3983ft	....	44	Sgurr nan Conbhairean	1109m/3638ft	....
11	Beinn a' Bhuird (North Top)	1197m/3927ft	....	45	Meall a' Bhuiridh	1108m/3635ft	....
12	Carn Eige (Eighe)	1183m/3881ft	....	46	Stob a' Choire Mheadhoin	1105m/3625ft	....
13	Beinn Mheadhoin	1182m/3878ft	....	47	Beinn Ghlas	1103m/3619ft	....
14	Mam Sodhail	1181m/3875ft	....	48	Beinn Eibhinn	1102m/3615ft	....
15	Stob Choire Claurigh	1177m/3862ft	....	49	Mullach Fraoch-choire	1102m/3615ft	....
16	Ben More	1174m/3852ft	....	50	Creise	1100m/3609ft	....
17	Ben Avon (Leabaidh an Daimh Bhuidhe)	1171m/3842ft	....	51	Sgurr a' Mhaim	1099m/3606ft	....
18	Stob Binnein	1165m/3822ft	....	52	Sgurr Choinnich Mor	1094m/3589ft	....
19	Beinn Bhrotain	1157m/3796ft	....	53	Sgurr nan Clach Geala	1093m/3586ft	....
20	Derry Cairngorm	1155m/3789ft	....	54	Bynack More	1090m/3576ft	....
21	Lochnagar (Cac Carn Beag)	1155m/3789ft	....	55	Stob Ghabhar	1090m/3576ft	....
22	Sgurr nan Ceathreamhnan	1151m/3776ft	....	56	Beinn a' Chlachair	1087m/3566ft	....
23	Bidean nam Bian	1150m/3773ft	....	57	Beinn Dearg (Ullapool)	1084m/3556ft	....
24	Sgurr na Lapaich	1150m/3773ft	....	58	Beinn a' Chaorainn (Cairngorms)	1083m/3553ft	....
25	Ben Alder	1148m/3766ft	....	59	Schiehallion	1083m/3553ft	....
26	Geal-Charn (Loch Pattack)	1132m/3714ft	....	60	Sgurr a' Choire Ghlais	1083m/3553ft	....
27	Binnein Mor	1130m/3707ft	....	61	Beinn a' Chreachain	1081m/3547ft	....
28	Beinn Laoigh (Ben Lui)	1130m/3707ft	....	62	Beinn Heasgarnich	1078m/3537ft	....
29	An Riabhachan	1129m/3704ft	....	63	Ben Starav	1078m/3537ft	....
30	Creag Meagaidh	1128m/3701ft	....	64	Beinn Dorain	1076m/3530ft	....
31	Ben Cruachan	1126m/3694ft	....	65	Stob Coire Sgreamhach	1072m/3517ft	....
32	Carn nan Gabhar (Beinn a' Ghlo)	1121m/3678ft	....	66	Braigh Coire Chruinn-bhalgain (Beinn a' Ghlo)	1070m/3510ft	....
33	A' Chralaig	1120m/3674ft	....	67	An Socach (Glen Cannich)	1069m/3507ft	....
34	An Stuc	1118m/3668ft	....				

68	Meall Corranaich	1069m/3507ft	....
69	Glas Maol	1068m/3504ft	....
70	Sgurr Fhuaran	1067m/3501ft	....
71	Cairn of Claise	1064m/3491ft	....
72	Bidein a' Ghlas Thuill (An Teallach)	1062m/3484ft	....
73	Sgurr Fiona (An Teallach)	1060m/3478ft	....
74	Na Gruagaichean	1056m/3465ft	....
75	Spidean a' Choire Leith (Liathach)	1055m/3461ft	....
76	Stob Poite Coire Ardair	1054m/3458ft	....
77	Toll Creagach	1054m/3458ft	....
78	Sgurr a' Chaorachain	1053m/3455ft	....
79	Glas Tulaichean	1051m/3448ft	....
80	Beinn a' Chaorainn (Glen Spean)	1049m/3442ft	....
81	Geal Charn (Loch Laggan)	1049m/3442ft	....
82	Sgurr Fhuar-thuill	1049m/3442ft	....
83	Carn an t-Sagairt Mor	1047m/3435ft	....
84	Creag Mhor	1047m/3435ft	....
85	Ben Wyvis (Glas Leathad Mor)	1046m/3432ft	....
86	Chno Dearg	1046m/3432ft	....
87	Cruach Ardrain	1046m/3432ft	....
88	Beinn Iutharn Mhor	1045m/3428ft	....
89	Meall nan Tarmachan	1044m/3425ft	....
90	Stob Coir' an Albannaich	1044m/3425ft	....
91	Carn Mairg	1041m/3415ft	....
92	Sgurr na Ciche	1040m/3412ft	....
93	Meall Ghaordaidh	1039m/3409ft	....
94	Beinn Achaladair	1038m/3405ft	....
95	Carn a' Mhaim	1037m/3402ft	....
96	Sgurr a' Bhealaich Dheirg	1036m/3399ft	....
97	Gleouraich	1035m/3396ft	....
98	Carn Dearg (Loch Pattack)	1034m/3392ft	....
99	Am Bodach	1032m/3386ft	....
100	Beinn Fhada (Ben Attow)	1032m/3386ft	....
101	Ben Oss	1029m/3376ft	....
102	Carn an Righ	1029m/3376ft	....
103	Carn Gorm	1029m/3376ft	....

104	Sgurr a' Mhaoraich	1027m/3369ft	....
105	Sgurr na Ciste Duibhe	1027m/3369ft	....
106	Ben Challum	1025m/3363ft	....
107	Sgorr Dhearg (Beinn a' Bheithir)	1024m/3360ft	....
108	Mullach an Rathain (Liathach)	1023m/3356ft	....
109	Aonach air Chrith	1021m/3350ft	....
110	Stob Dearg (Buachaille Etive Mor)	1021m/3350ft	....
111	Ladhar Bheinn	1020m/3346ft	....
112	Beinn Bheoil	1019m/3343ft	....
113	Carn an Tuirc	1019m/3343ft	....
114	Mullach Clach a' Bhlair	1019m/3343ft	....
115	Mullach Coire Mhic Fhearchair	1018m/3340ft	....
116	Garbh Chioch Mhor	1013m/3323ft	....
117	Cairn Bannoch	1012m/3320ft	....
118	Beinn Ime	1011m/3317ft	....
119	Beinn Udlamain	1011m/3317ft	....
120	Ruadh-stac Mor (Beinn Eighe)	1010m/3314ft	....
121	The Saddle	1010m/3314ft	....
122	Sgurr an Doire Leathain	1010m/3314ft	....
123	Sgurr Eilde Mor	1010m/3314ft	....
124	Beinn Dearg (Atholl)	1008m/3307ft	....
125	Maoile Lunndaidh	1007m/3304ft	....
126	An Sgarsoch	1006m/3301ft	....
127	Carn Liath (Loch Laggan)	1006m/3301ft	....
128	Beinn Fhionnlaidh (Affric)	1005m/3297ft	....
129	Beinn an Dothaidh	1004m/3294ft	....
130	The Devil's Point	1004m/3294ft	....
131	Sgurr an Lochain	1004m/3294ft	....
132	Sgurr Mor	1003m/3291ft	....
133	Sail Chaorainn	1002m/3287ft	....
134	Sgurr na Carnach	1002m/3287ft	....
135	Aonach Meadhoin	1001m/3284ft	....
136	Meall Greigh	1001m/3284ft	....
137	Sgorr Dhonuill (Beinn a' Bheithir)	1001m/3284ft	....
138	Sgurr Breac	999m/3278ft	....
139	Sgurr Choinnich	999m/3278ft	....

		DATE				DATE
211	Beinn Mhanach	954m/3130ft	248	Meall Buidhe (Glen Lyon)	932m/3058ft ....
212	Meall Dearg (Aonach Eagach)	953m/3127ft	249	Beinn Bhreac	931m/3054ft ....
213	Sgurr nan Coireachan (Glen Dessarry)	953m/3127ft	250	Ben Chonzie	931m/3054ft ....
214	Meall Chuaich	951m/3120ft	251	A' Chailleach (Monadh Liath)	930m/3051ft ....
215	Meall Gorm	949m/3113ft	252	Bla Bheinn (Blaven)	928m/3045ft ....
216	Beinn Bhuidhe	948m/3110ft	253	Mayar	928m/3045ft ....
217	Sgurr Mhic Choinnich	948m/3110ft	254	Meall nan Eun	928m/3045ft ....
218	Creag a' Mhaim	947m/3107ft	255	Moruisg	928m/3045ft ....
219	Driesh	947m/3107ft	256	Ben Hope	927m/3041ft ....
220	Beinn Tulaichean	946m/3104ft	257	Eididh nan Clach Geala	927m/3041ft ....
221	Carn Bhac	946m/3104ft	258	Beinn Liath Mhor	926m/3038ft ....
222	Meall Buidhe (Knoydart)	946m/3104ft	259	Beinn Narnain	926m/3038ft ....
223	Sgurr na Sgine	946m/3104ft	260	Geal Charn (Monadh Liath)	926m/3038ft ....
224	Bidein a' Choire Sheasgaich	945m/3100ft	261	Meall a' Choire Leith	926m/3038ft ....
225	Carn Dearg (Monadh Liath)	945m/3100ft	262	Seana Bhraigh	927m/3041ft ....
226	Stob a' Choire Odhair	945m/3100ft	263	Stob Coire Raineach	925m/3035ft ....
227	An Socach (Glen Ey)	944m/3097ft	264	Creag Pitridh	924m/3031ft ....
228	Sgurr Dubh Mor	944m/3097ft	265	Sgurr nan Eag	924m/3031ft ....
229	Ben Vorlich (Loch Lomond)	943m/3094ft	266	An Coileachan	923m/3028ft ....
230	Binnein Beag	943m/3094ft	267	Sgurr nan Each	923m/3028ft ....
231	Carn Dearg	941m/3087ft	268	Tom na Gruagaich (Beinn Alligin)	922m/3025ft ....
232	Carn na Caim	941m/3087ft	269	An Socach (Glen Affric)	921m/3022ft ....
233	Beinn a' Chroin	940m/3084ft	270	Sgiath Chuil	921m/3022ft ....
234	Luinne Bheinn	939m/3081ft	271	Carn Sgulain	920m/3018ft ....
235	Mount Keen	939m/3081ft	272	Gairich	919m/3015ft ....
236	Mullach nan Coirean	939m/3081ft	273	A' Ghlas-bheinn	918m/3012ft ....
237	Beinn Sgulaird	937m/3074ft	274	Creag nan Damh	918m/3012ft ....
238	Beinn Tarsuinn	937m/3074ft	275	Meall na Teanga	918m/3012ft ....
239	Sron a' Choire Ghairbh	937m/3074ft	276	Ruadh Stac Mor	918m/3012ft ....
240	A' Bhuidheanach Bheag	936m/3071ft	277	Sgurr a' Mhadaidh	918m/3012ft ....
241	Beinn na Lap	935m/3068ft	278	Carn Aosda	917m/3008ft ....
242	Am Basteir	934m/3064ft	279	Geal Charn (Drumochter)	917m/3008ft ....
243	Meall a' Chrasgaidh	934m/3064ft	280	Beinn a' Chlaidheimh	916m/3005ft ....
244	Beinn Chabhair	933m/3061ft	281	Beinn a' Chleibh	916m/3005ft ....
245	The Cairnwell	933m/3061ft	282	Beinn Teallach	915m/3002ft ....
246	Fionn Bheinn	933m/3061ft	283	Ben Vane	915m/3002ft ....
247	Maol Chean-dearg	933m/3061ft			

BEN LOMOND
AND THE ARROCHAR ALPS

The Munros:

Ben Lomond Ben Vane Beinn Ime Beinn Narnain
Ben Vorlich Beinn Bhuidhe

Dominating the wild eastern shore of Loch Lomond, the view from the summit of the Ben is in turn dominated by the craggy outline of The Cobbler and its higher cousins of the Arrochar Alps. This is a tight clutch of high individual hills, all fine peaks in themselves, which tend to be steeper and more rugged than most other hills in the Southern Highlands. There is a wonderful sense of history in these hills and Arrochar is indisputably one of the early centres of climbing development in the country. This was entirely due to The Cobbler, the lowly yet extraordinary peak which most hill-goers would put amongst their top dozen hills. The Munroist who ignores the wonders of The Cobbler, at 883m (2899ft), is the undoubted loser. The best base for the Arrochar Alps is either Arrochar itself or Tarbet, and for Ben Lomond, there is a Youth Hostel at Rowardennan and bed and breakfasts, guest houses and hotels in Drymen and Balmaha.

Ben Lomond (184), 974m/3195ft

Ben Lomond, the beacon hill. Glasgow's hill. This, the most southerly of all the Munros, has indeed been a beacon to generations of Clydesiders, summoning them from the urban sprawl of Scotland's biggest conurbation to the gateway that it represents on the very edge of that old geological fault, the Highland Boundary.

Dominating the eastern shore of Loch Lomond, Ben Lomond rises from a skirt of forestry into a mountain of some grandeur, and when glimpsed through the trees which surround Loch Katrine in the north east, the great north-east face can look positively Alpine.

The summit itself is formed by a fairly short, level ridge, curving gently round the head of the north-east corrie. To the north it falls away into a high plateau of extensive moorland which falls steep-sided towards Loch Lomond, while to the south it throws out a

Route Summary: Follow the signposted path from the Rowardennan car park up through the woods to the lower slopes of the S ridge. Climb to the ridge and follow it N to the summit cone. An obvious path leads to the summit

Map: OS Sheet 56

Access Point: Rowardennan Hotel, GR360983

Distance: 11km, 914m ascent

Approx Time: 5-6 hours

Translation: beacon hill

Pronunciation: Low-mond

Ben Lomond from the east across Loch Ard

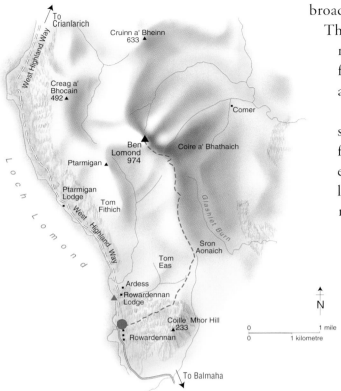

broad and bulging ridge for some distance.

The normal route of approach follows this ridge, approaching it through the forest from Rowardennan following a well-used and well-maintained footpath.

Eventually the path zigzags up the final slopes to reach an 800m long curved ridge from which cliffs fall away to the north-east. The summit cairn and view indicator lie at the north-west culmination of this ridge and in clear conditions the views are dramatic. The tops of the Arrochar Alps and Crianlarich hills appear to choke the northern end of Loch Lomond, a real jumble of peaks that clearly contrast with the flatlands in the south – the Highlands and the Lowlands, with Ben Lomond looming as the very edge of the Highlands.

Route Summary: From Inveruglas take the Hydro road to Coiregrogain (Route A), cross the bridge and climb the ESE ridge of Ben Vane to summit. Drop down to the bealach to the W and take a SW line to climb to the bealach N of Beinn Ime's summit slopes. Climb S to the summit. Now descend S to the Bealach a' Mhaim and climb slopes of Beinn Narnain. From the summit ridge descend N to the footpath in the glen and return to Coiregrogain

Map: OS Sheet 56: GR277099, GR255085 and GR272067

Access Point: Inveruglas

Distance: 20km, 1550m ascent

Approx Time: 6-8 hours

Translation: middle hill; butter hill; hill of the notches

Ben Vane (283), 915m/3002ft, Beinn Ime (118), 1011m/3317ft, Beinn Narnain (259), 926m/3038ft

Although it looks fairly innocuous from Loch Lomondside, Ben Vane is an incredibly steep hill. The Scottish Mountaineering Club's guide to the Munros suggests its south face climbs up to the small summit plateau at a continual angle of 45 degrees, for a full 600 metres. You'd have to be daft to climb the hill from this side but even the normal route of ascent from Coiregrogain above Inveruglas is comparatively steep and sustained and in winter conditions its ascent can be particularly testing.

Rising up from Coiregrogain in a tumble of crags and slabby buttresses, Ben Vane is caught up in a clutch of neighbouring Munros with Beinn Narnain and Beinn Ime to the south and west and the long craggy ridge of Ben Vorlich in the north. Covered in snow and under a blue winter sky it's easy to see why this little group of hills is known as the Arrochar Alps.

Because of its central position, Ben Vane is often climbed along with Beinn Ime and Beinn Narnain (with The Cobbler thrown in for good measure) in a big 23 km hill hike around the head of

Coiregrogain. There's about 1500m of climbing involved. A high bealach separates the rough western slopes of Ben Vane from Beinn Ime, and another bealach south of Beinn Ime, the Bealach a' Mhaim, also connects to The Cobbler and the other Munro, Beinn Narnain. The Bealach a' Mhaim also connects with a rather pleasant Corbett called Beinn Luibhean that rises above the Rest and Be Thankful road. Ben Vorlich is sequestered from the rest of the Arrochar Alps by the great gulf that cradles Loch Sloy.

There is now a good footpath paralleling the main A82 all the way to the car park and visitor centre just north of Inveruglas.

To the west of Ben Vane, a high bealach separates the hill from Beinn Ime and involves a fair descent and re-ascent to reach the summit slopes of Ime, a hill that is more often climbed together with The Cobbler in the south. This fact becomes clear as you struggle up Beinn Ime from that high bealach. The badly eroded footpath that runs up Ben Vane vanishes and instead a rather sketchy path leads towards Ime's north ridge.

It's a straightforward descent to the bealach that separates Beinn Ime from The Cobbler and Beinn Narnain and it's always good to lie among the rocks for a while and just soak it in before tackling the 300m climb to Beinn Narnain, the last summit of the day, with its wonderful views down Loch Long to the Kyles of Bute and across to the jagged peaks of Arran.

Pronunciation: byn vain; byn eem; byn narnyn

NB: Parking at the foot of the Hydro Board road is discouraged. Park in car park opposite Loch Sloy Power Station to the north

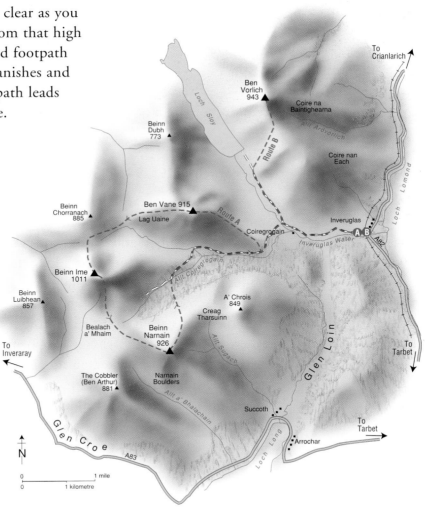

The Arrochar Alps from Ben Vorlich

Ben Vorlich (229), 943m/3094ft

Route Summary: Just before you reach the Loch Sloy dam leave the track and climb steep slopes in a NE direction to gain the summit ridge (Route B). Follow this ridge N for a little over 1km to the summit cairn. Return the same way

Map: OS Sheets 56 and 50: GR295124

Access Point: Inveruglas to Loch Sloy Dam

Distance: 10km, 900m ascent

Approx Time: 4-6 hours

Translation: hill of the bay

Pronunciation: byn voarlich

Ben Vorlich is a solitary hill which boasts no single line of ascent. Some folk climb Vorlich from Inveruglas, others by its big eastern corrie, while many climb it from the road leading to Loch Sloy. However you climb it, it offers a long, hard pull up steep slopes and it's always good to reach the long ridge, even though, as you'll quickly discover, this is fairly undulating in itself. It's not until you reach the final stretch to the summit that you'll come across any real erosion and I can safely say that Ben Vorlich is one of the least damaged hills I have walked on. I'm sure this is simply because there is no single route of ascent, the load has been well and truly spread, to the benefit of the hill. The most popular ascent routes are by the steep slopes north-east of the Loch Sloy dam or from Ardlui via Coire Creagach.

Beinn Bhuidhe (216), 948m/3110ft

This is an isolated mountain which rises near the head of Loch Fyne between Glen Fyne and Glen Shira. The hill itself is a long triple-topped ridge with its highest point roughly in the middle. Although you can't really get decent views of it from the south, it does appear as a fairly steep-sided cone from Ben Oss in the north-east. As vehicles are only allowed up the Glen Fyne road on official business (push bikes are allowed), park in the loop road between the A83 and the old Fyne bridge and continue on foot to Inverchorachan, then take to the slopes due west, climbing up a fairly steep and wooded gully above the house.

Follow the south bank of the stream to its source, then bear north-west up steep grass and bracken into the upper corrie. Climb one of the gullies to the ridge. The summit cone and trig point are about half way along the ridge.

Route Summary: Park in the loop road between the A83 and the old Fyne Bridge. Continue on foot to Inverchorachan, past Glenfyne Lodge, then take to the slopes in a rough WNW direction, following a small stream that flows down from a gully. Follow the S bank of the stream to its source then bear NW up steep grass and bracken into the upper corrie. Climb one of the gullies to the ridge. The summit cone is about half way along the ridge. Return the same way.

Map: OS Sheet 50: GR203187

Access Point: Glen Fyne, GR228160

Distance: 20km, 940m ascent

Approx Time: 6-7 hours

Translation: yellow hill

Pronunciation: byn voo-ee

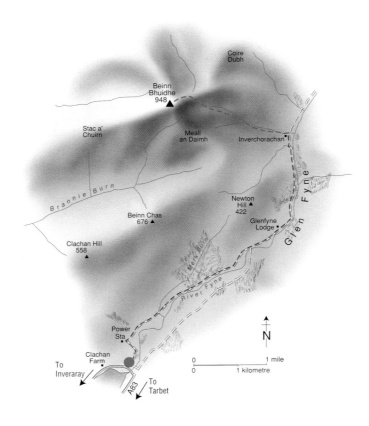

THE CRIANLARICH HILLS

The Munros:

Beinn Chabhair   An Caisteal   Beinn a' Chroin
Cruach Ardrain   Beinn Tulaichean   Ben More   Stob Binnein

The long pass of Glen Falloch runs from the head of Loch Lomond to Crianlarich, rising from the magnificently wooded lower glen to an increasingly wilder landscape characterised by windblown Scots pines. To the east of the road rise the lower slopes of a mountain range dominated by no fewer than seven Munros and fourteen tops, the highest group of hills in Britain south of Tayside. The best base is Crianlarich which has a Youth Hostel, a hotel and several bed and breakfast establishments.

Beinn Chabhair (244), 933m/3061ft, An Caisteal (147), 995m/3264ft, Beinn a' Chroin (233), 940m/3084ft

Like its close neighbours An Caisteal and Beinn a' Chroin, Beinn Chabhair is best climbed from Glen Falloch by its long north-westerly ridge. Most folk are disinclined to drop down into the low bealach that separates Beinn Chabhair to climb all three in one trip and tend to leave An Caisteal and Beinn a' Chroin for another day. But, as is so often the case, the ascent of all three summits in one day is not only feasible, but quite practical.

To Killin

To Tarbet

Benmore Farm
Sron nam Forsairean
Crianlarich
Keilator Farm
A85
Dismantled Railway
Route C
Ben More 1174
Bealach-eada-dha Beinn
Meall na Dige 966
Stob Binnein 1165
Stob Coire an Lochain 1066
Creagan Liatha
Benmore Glen
Benmore Burn
Grey Height 666
Stob Coire Bhuidhe 855
Stob Garbh 960
A82
Glen Falloch
River Falloch
Route B
Sron Gharbh 708
Coire Eich
Meall Dhamh
Cruach Ardrain 1046
Stob Glas 815
Beinn Tulaichean 946
Inverlochlarig Burn
Derrydarroch
Twistin Hill
Allt Arnan
Route A
Stob Glas 708
Coire a' Chuilinn
An Caisteal 995
Beinn a' Chroin 940
Ishag Burn
Allt a' Chuilinn
Stob Creag an Fhithich
Lochan Beinn Chabhair
Beinn Chabhair 933
River Larig
Parian Hill 663

0   1 mile
0   1 kilometre
N

Derrydarroch Farm makes a good starting point, with a handy parking place on the A82. Behind the farm a slanting path climbs up through some birch and hawthorn and eventually runs out beside the tumbling Allt a' Chuilinn burn where something of the rugged grandeur of Beinn Chabhair is first seen, a steep face made up of rocky outcrops and grass terraces. Those of an adventurous disposition will be happy to thread their way up this broken face to the summit, but most tend to head south-west to an obvious bealach on the north ridge. From there a path twists its way through outcropping crags and tiny lochans to the summit, perched precariously on top of its own little crag.

Like Beinn Chabhair, An Caisteal and Beinn a' Chroin are made up of rocky outrops above lower grassy slopes and their dual ascent offers a fine day's hill walking. An Caisteal can be attacked directly from Glen Falloch from where the prominent tor which gives the hill its name is easily identified, but the best approach is from Derrydarroch Farm from where the hill can be climbed by either of the ridges which flank the corrie of the Allt Andoran.

Linking An Caisteal with Beinn Chabhair is much easier than you might expect – a fairly long, but simple descent down into a narrow bealach and then a short but stiff climb up to the col between Caisteal and Beinn a' Chroin. Beinn a' Chroin has two tops separated by a 60m drop – its western top, the next one on the route, is the start of a short rocky ridge which leads to the more distant, eastern top. Until recently, and according to all the Munro guidebooks, this eastern top was considered the highest, but the Ordnance Survey now admit there has been some confusion about which of the two peaks is the highest because of the way contours and spot heights are shown.

According to the Ordnance Survey there is a 940m spot height on the eastern peak, but no spot height on the western one. However, there is a 940m contour line on the western peak which implies, but does not guarantee, that the land within it is likely to be higher than 940m. The OS have told me they plan to add an extra spot height of 942m on future editions of their 1:10,000, 1:25,000 and 1:50,000 scale maps of the area. So, the Munro is officially the western top, not the eastern top as everyone thought, although I suspect most Munro-baggers will have climbed both tops anyway.

From the western summit return to the col before the last scramble up to An Caisteal, the castle. From the summit it is an easy descent back to Derrydarroch via Twistin Hill and the slopes of Sron Gharbh.

Route Summary: Cross the River Falloch by its bridge and pass Derrydarroch Farm to follow a slanting path to the Allt a' Chuilinn (Route A). Cross the burn and climb to the obvious bealach between Stob Creag an Fhithich and Beinn Chabhair. From the bealach a faint path twists its way to the rocky summit. Descend steep slopes in a NE direction to another bealach and from there climb ENE to the col between An Caisteal and Beinn a' Chroin. Climb the steep NW slopes of Beinn a' Chroin, zigzagging left then right to avoid the steepest of the crags. Once you've visited the summit cairn, descend to the bealach again then climb the steep SE ridge of An Caisteal. Descend N via the Twistin Hill ridge and just before the ascent to Stob Glas descend steep slopes W to the Allt Andoran where open slopes take you back to Derrydarroch

Map: OS Sheet 50

Access Point: Opposite Derrydarroch Farm on the A82

Distance: 15km, 950m ascent

Approx Time: 5-7 hours

Translation: possibly hill of the hawk; the castle; hill of danger

Pronunciation: byn chav-aar; aan kastail; byn a chroin

Route Summary: From the car park cross the field and go through the underpass below the railway (Route B). Cross the River Falloch by a bridge and continue on the Land Rover track for about 1.6km. Opposite the corner of the forestry plantation drop down to the river and cross it by a footbridge. Climb E now to the summit of Grey Height. Continue in a SSE direction and follow the ridge to Meall Damh. Descend to a high bealach and then climb steep slopes to the first of Cruach Ardrain's twin summits.

The true summit lies a short distance to the NE across a shallow dip. To continue S to Tulaichean return SW past two cairns and descend to a grassy ridge. Follow crest of this ridge S to Beinn Tulaichean

NB: Beinn Tulaichean can also be climbed from Inverlochlarig in the S

Map: OS Sheets: 50, 51, 56 and 57

Access Point: Car park on S side of A82 opposite Keilator Farm

Distance: 15km, 1067m ascent

Approx Time: 5-7 hours

Translation: stack of the high peaks; hill of the hillocks

Pronunciation: kroo-ach ar-dran; too-lach-an

Cruach Ardrain (87), 1046m/3432ft, Beinn Tulaichean (220), 946m/3104ft

The ascent of Cruach Ardrain and its southern neighbour, Beinn Tulaichean, is ideal for a winter day, especially if you get blue skies, sunshine and snow-covered tops. They can be climbed from the south, from Inverlochlarig Farm where Rob Roy Macgregor spent his last years. There isn't a lot to recommend an ascent from this side though. From the farm long grassy slopes are climbed in a north-west direction to the ridge just south of Beinn Tulaichean's summit. From here it's a straightforward walk along a broad ridge to Cruach Ardrain.

The ascent of the hills from Glen Falloch starts just south of Crianlarich in a car park opposite Keilator farm. Across a rather boggy field a Land Rover track runs under the railway and climbs up the length of Coire Earb beside the infant River Falloch. This route follows the track for about 1.6km until you're opposite the corner of the forestry plantation. Just below you a footbridge crosses the river and easy slopes lead to the crumpled summit of Grey Height.

From here, a path climbs over the bumps and knolls of the ridge that leads to Meall Dhamh where, after a short descent, the slopes of Cruach Ardrain begin to steepen appreciably towards its north-west summit, a subsidiary top that's adorned by two small cairns. The true summit lies just across a shallow col. Beinn Tulaichean can be easily reached from here – return past the twin cairns and descend south-west to a grassy ridge from where it's an easy stroll to the summit of a Munro that is more like another subsidiary top of Cruach Ardrain!

For a slightly different descent route, leave the Tulaichean/Cruach Ardrain ridge slightly early to skirt the southern slopes of Cruach Ardrain towards the col between the Munro and another of its outliers, Stob Glas. From the col the long and gentle slopes of upper Coire Earb drop down to the river where you can pick up the Land Rover track that will take you back to the start.

Route Summary: Leave the farm and bear right towards the ridge of Sron nam Forsairean (Route C). Follow this to the summit. Descend S from Ben More, then SW following an indistinct ridge to the flat Bealach-eader-dha Beinn. Climb Stob Binnein from here by its N ridge

Ben More (16), 1174m/3852ft, Stob Binnein (18), 1165m/3822ft

These hills are the Castor and Pollux of the Scottish Highlands, heavenly twins joined together by a high bealach. The highest peaks south of the Tay, they are clearly visible from mountain vantage points throughout the Southern and Central Highlands. Although Ben More is the higher of the two, Stob Binnein is the more shapely, its long and elegant slopes rising from long, sweeping ridges to a tiny tabled summit.

Ben More and Stob Binnein

Ben More's northern slopes sweep down virtually continuously from its summit all the way to Glen Dochart and I vividly recall as a teenager sliding down almost all the way back to Benmore Farm. I think we descended from the summit in under an hour. Care is needed though, for a hanging corrie, immediately below the summit facing north-west, has a steep upper section which is liable to avalanche in snowy conditions – sadly it's been the site of several fatalities so avoid it if you can.

Follow the Sron nam Forsairean ridge virtually all the way from Benmore Farm to the summit. It is a long and strenuous climb and it's a welcome descent from the summit down to the flat Bealach-eader-dha-Beinn. Stob Binnein is climbed from here by way of its north ridge. An alternative route, avoiding the long pull up the Sron nam Forsairean, follows the Benmore Burn southwards. From the headwaters of the burn take a diagonal line across the slopes to the spur of Creagan Liatha. Climb to the top and follow the ridge to Stob Coire an Lochain. Follow the south-south-east ridge of Stob Binnein to the summit, and then climb Ben More by way of the Bealach-eader-dha-Beinn.

Map: OS Sheet: 51

Access Point: Benmore Farm, GR414257

Distance: 15km, 1600m ascent

Approx Time: 6-8 hours

Translation: big hill; hill of the anvil

Pronunciation: byn moar; stop binyan

THE TYNDRUM HILLS

The Munros:

Beinn Laoigh   Beinn a' Chleibh   Ben Oss   Beinn Dubhchraig

These hills can be reached from Glen Falloch but a better approach is by the River Cononish just south of Tyndrum. From this approach Beinn Laoigh (Ben Lui) in particular is seen to best advantage, probably the most Alpine-looking mountain in the Southern Highlands. Its great NE corrie, Coire Gaothaich, holds snow until well into the spring. Unfortunately, extensive gold mining has hideously disfigured what was once a most scenic walk up to Cononish Farm.

Beinn Laoigh (Ben Lui) (28), 1130m/3707ft, Beinn a' Chleibh (281), 916m/3005ft

I've often heard Beinn Laoigh, or Ben Lui, described as the 'Queen of Scottish Mountains', a sobriquet which describes the regal lines of this, one of the most beautiful mountains in the country. The approach down Glen Cononish is without doubt the most aesthetic. Some 8km from the Tyndrum/Crianlarich road the route climbs up into the eastern corrie and then on to the north-east spur which leads to one of the two summits of the hill. These two summits drop twin spurs which enclose a high round-bottomed corrie, 300 metres deep. At the back of this high corrie, a central gully splits the wall, a route which offers a classic snow climb in winter, often topped by an equally classic cornice. A word of warning – it's also a route which is frequently avalanched.

A shorter and less aesthetic route, which seems to satisfy most Munro-baggers with little inclination towards rock scrambling or snow climbing, leaves a car park on the A85 in Glen Lochy. In low river conditions stepping stones lead across the river where a path follows the Eas Daimh through the conifers. (Don't try and cross the river when it is in spate.) After 400m or so cross the burn and follow the path to the stile in the fence which leads to the open hillside. It's an easy climb up to the broad north-north-west ridge to the summit of Beinn Laoigh. Wide slopes lead down south-west to the col at the head of the Fionn Choirein and another broad ridge leads to the summit of Beinn a' Chleibh. Return to the bealach and descend the slopes of the Fionn Choirein back to the forestry fence.

Route Summary: Cross the river and follow paths on the E side of the Eas Daimh (Route A) through conifer forest to a stile in the fence that leads to open hillside. Climb NNW ridge of Ben Laoigh to N top then along the corrie rim to the summit cairn. Descend SW to the bealach at the head of Fionn Choirein and follow the gently rising ridge to the flat-topped summit of Beinn a' Chleibh. Return to the bealach and descend steep slopes back to the forestry fence

Map: OS Sheet 50: GR265264; GR251256

Access Point: Glen Lochy, GR239278

Approx Time: 4-7 hours

Distance: 12km, 1006m ascent

Translation: hill of the calf; hill of the chest

Pronunciation: byn loo-ee; byn a chlayv

Ben Laoigh from just below the summit of Ben Oss

Ben Laoigh (left) and Ben Oss (right) from the air

Route Summary: Leave Dailrigh in Strathfillan (Route B) and follow rough road on S side of river to a bridge over the railway. Head W and cross the Allt Coire Dubhchraig. Follow path through woods to open hillside and continue SW up grassy corrie to the shoulder of Beinn Dubhchraig. Follow broad stony ridge to summit. From Dubhchraig follow ridge NW and W to Ben Oss

Map: OS Sheet 50

Access Point: Dailrigh, GR344290

Distance: 20km, 1006m ascent

Approx Time: 5-7 hours

Translation: loch outlet hill; black rock hill

Pronunciation: byn oss; byn doo-craig

Ben Oss (101), 1029m/3376ft, Beinn Dubhchraig (175), 978m/3209ft

Although overshadowed by the beauty of Beinn Laoigh, these two hills offer a high knobbly traverse with stunning views down the length of Glen Falloch to the Crianlarich hills and Loch Lomond. From the south Ben Oss appears as a fine pointed peak and Beinn Dubhchraig more rounded but presenting a craggy, well-broken face, but from the north-east, the usual approach, Oss presents steep slopes above Coire Buidhe while the summit of Beinn Dubhchraig sits over the wide and open Coire Dubhchraig above recent forestry plantations. Just below the conifers, as a form of consolation, ancient remnants of the pine woods of Caledon stand proudly, wind-blown, twisted and gnarled. This wood, the Coille Coire Chuilc, fills the confluence of the River Cononish and the Allt Gleann Auchreoch.

Our route begins at Dailrigh, the King's Field, in Glen Fillan, commemorating a battle between the MacDougalls of Lorn and the forces of Robert the Bruce in 1306. The route to Beinn Dubhchraig follows

The Crianlarich Hills from Ben Oss (Ben More on the far left and Ben Chabhair on the far right)

the track across the railway line then a path into the pines of the old Caledonian Forest. Follow paths on the north-west side of the burn to the edge of the wood where a stile crosses a deer fence and continue south-west up the wide, grassy slopes of the corrie to reach the upper ridge of Beinn Dubhcraig just north-west of the summit, which is easily reached from here along a broad rocky ridge. From the summit return along this ridge and continue steeply westwards down to the col. From here the route follows a wide ridge over a knobbly summit and then onwards in a south-west direction to the true summit of Ben Oss. It is possible to descend immediately north into Glen Cononish but the ground is steep and broken in places. It's probably best to return over the knobbly summit and back on to Beinn Dubhcraig where the north ridge can be followed back down to the lower reaches of Glen Cononish, where the track returns to Dailrigh.

THE CRIEFF AND LOCH EARN HILLS

The Munros:

Ben Vorlich   Stuc a' Chroin   Ben Chonzie

These three mountains lie just to the north of the Highland fault line which runs from the southern shores of Loch Lomond to Stonehaven just south of Aberdeen. As such they form something of a dividing line between the Central Highlands and lowland Scotland and needless to say, the best views are to the north and west. Ben Vorlich and Stuc a' Chroin, because of their proximity to the Central Belt, are very popular hills indeed and tend to suffer the ravages of sponsored walks and the like. Ben Chonzie is far less popular, having a reputation of being one of the less interesting of the Munros. Nevertheless, because of its position it can catch some bad weather and offer a challenging walk. In good summer weather it makes a delightful evening stroll.

Ben Vorlich (165), 985m/3232ft, Stuc a' Chroin (182), 975m/3199ft

Not to be confused with Ben Vorlich which frowns down on the head of Loch Lomond, this Perthshire Ben Vorlich nevertheless shares the same name origin. It comes from the Gaelic Mur-Bhalg, meaning sea-bay, and refers to small bays in the lochs which sit at their respective feet. Ardvorlich, at the beginning of this hill walk, is therefore Ard-Mhurlaig, the Promontory of the Sea-bay, and is the home of the Stewarts of Ardvorlich, an ancient family who have held these lands for some 400 years.

For many years a stone was kept in Ardvorlich House, the Clach Dhearg, or the Red Stone, which was believed to have miraculous properties. If you dipped it in a pail of water and moved it three times sun-wise around the pail, the water would then contain healing powers which could be used to treat sick cattle. So famous was this stone that it attracted people from all around the area, who came with their own buckets to carry home some of the miraculous water which had been swilled over the stone. It was said that the stone had been brought back to Ardvorlich House in the fourteenth century after a crusade.

Beyond the house, away up Glen Vorlich lie the high slopes of Ben Vorlich. Take the private road from the east gate of Ardvorlich House on the south side of Loch Earn. There are few parking places so be careful where you leave your car so that you don't

Route Summary: Follow the track past Ardvorlich House on to the open hillside in Glen Vorlich. Follow the track to the foot of Coire Buidhe and then the SE side of the corrie to reach the NNE ridge of Ben Vorlich and the summit. Follow the line of fence posts down to the Bealach an Dubh Choirein and take the steep path which avoids the obvious steep, and loose buttress. From the cairn at the top of the buttress head S to summit of Stuc a' Chroin. Descend via the Bealach an Dubh Choirein and Coire Buidhe

Map: OS Sheets 51 and 57

Distance: 17km, 1200m ascent

Approx Time: 5-6 hours

Access Point: Ardvorlich, GR633232

Translation: hill of the bay; peak of danger

Pronunciation: byn vorlich; stook a kroin

Ben Vorlich from above Balquhidder, rising behind the slopes of Meall nan Oighreag

interfere with passing vehicles. As you enter through the gates of the estate follow the road south, past the farm, where a signpost points to the right. Cross a stone bridge, and find another sign, this time pointing to the left. The track now wanders up through Glen Vorlich, a lovely spot with a tree-lined burn and good views opening up across Loch Earn towards the mighty Lawers hills.

Just over 2km further on a wooden bridge crosses the Allt a' Coire Buidhe. The real walking begins now, a stony footpath that heads right across the bare moorland and begins to climb onto the steeper and stonier north-north-east ridge of Ben Vorlich itself. Recently resurfaced, the footpath continues upwards to the 100m long summit ridge which is crowned by a small cairn. The OS trig point at its north-west end indicates the true summit.

Most walkers will want to add the ascent of Stuc a' Chroin, Vorlich's neighbouring Munro, to their day's climb. While the ascent of Stuc a' Chroin from Ben Vorlich is straightforward enough, it does involve some fairly loose scrambling from the adjoining Bealach an Dubh Choirein. The steeper ground can be avoided by ascending in a south-west direction from the Bealach, avoiding the obvious rocky buttress by traversing about 15m to the right (north-west) and following a steep path up through some broken rocks. The direct route up the north-east buttress offers some fine scrambling for those used to such things, but is definitely not for the inexperienced.

At the top of the buttress you'll reach a small cairn and the summit of Stuc a' Chroin is only about 180m away along a line of fence posts.

To return to Ardvorlich from Stuc a' Chroin, simply descend to the Bealach an Dubh Choirein and then traverse north-west across a grassy hillside to reach another bealach at the head of Coire Buidhe. Descend the east ridge of the corrie to regain the footpath in Glen Vorlich.

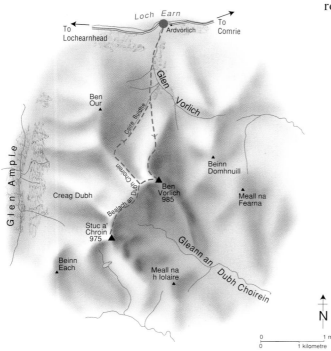

Looking north from Ben Chonzie towards Schiehallion and the Grampian mountains

Ben Chonzie (250), 931m/3054ft

Ben Chonzie is a relatively isolated lump, the highest point in a huge area of hill and moorland between Strath Earn and Loch Tay. It's a big sprawling hill, lacking any notable feature other than its long, broad southern ridge and its eastern corrie. The mountain's flat summit rises well above the surrounding hills, but its northern slopes drop down into the wonderfully lonely upper reaches of Glen Almond and that massive empty quarter of hilltop and ridge that lies south-east of Loch Tay. An ascent from that direction could be the culmination of a pretty wild walk.

A shorter, less remote route, links Chonzie with a neighbouring Corbett, the 789m Auchnafree Hill, and gives an excellent horseshoe-shaped high-level route of about 18km around the head of Loch Turret.

From Invergeldie in Glen Lednock take the right of way up the west side of the burn. At a track junction just beyond a gate take the right hand track and follow it across the burn and east-north-east up the hillside then north-east to the broad summit ridge. Follow the fence north-west then north-east to the summit. Return the same way.

Route Summary: Take the right of way up the W side of the burn. At a track junction take the right hand track, cross the burn and head ENE up the hillside then NE to broad summit ridge. In bad weather you can follow the line of fence NW then NE to the summit. Return the same way

Map: OS Sheets 51 and 52

Access Point: Invergeldie, GR743272

Distance: 14km, 670m ascent

Approx Time: 3-5 hours

Translation: possibly hill of moss

Pronunciation: byn ee hoan; locally honzee

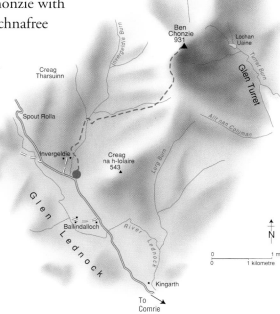

RANNOCH AND GLEN LYON

The Munros:

Schiehallion   Carn Gorm   Meall Garbh   Carn Mairg
Meall nan Aighean (Creag Mhor)   Stuchd an Lochain   Meall Buidhe

With the exception of Schiehallion, these hills tend to be flat topped, heather clad and featureless, although Stuchd an Lochain's Lochan nan Cat is rather fine. Having said that, the western end of Loch an Daimh, below the steep slopes of the Corbett Sron a' Choire Chnapanich, has a quality of wilderness unequalled in the Southern Highlands. For that reason I would recommend a long link around the head of the loch when climbing Stuchd an Lochain and Meall Buidhe.

Schiehallion, a superb cone when seen from Rannoch-side, has been tamed by a newly aligned footpath built by the John Muir Trust. My first visit to the hill was on a multi-day Trans-Scotland walk from Oban to Montrose and we climbed Schiehallion immediately after traversing the Carn Mairg hills. I have also climbed it from Tempar, to the north-west. Both of these routes were far preferable to the trudge up from Braes of Foss.

Aberfeldy makes a good base for this group, although Fortingall is closer to the hills. Local legend claims that Pontius Pilate was born in Dun Geal, an old fort not far from Fortingall, where his father was on a mission of peace between Caesar Augustus and Metallanus, King of Scotland. There is a Youth Hostel in Killin.

Route Summary: The new John Muir Trust route follows the track W from the car park at Braes of Foss (Route A). This was once one of the most eroded footpaths in the Highlands but the new track takes a zigzag course up the E ridge of the mountain. Higher up the ground becomes stony and the faint track climbs a series of rocky shelves to the tight, rocky summit ridge. Continue on the ridge to the summit. Either descend by the upward route or continue over the summit and descend in a WSW direction to the head of Gleann Mor. Follow the stream down the length of the glen leaving it eventually to climb back over Schiehallion's E ridge to pick up

Schiehallion (59), 1083m/3553ft

Walking this hill with Hamish Brown a few years ago he commented that he wished people would begin to act more like goats rather than sheep. He was criticising the fact that everyone tended to climb hills by the same route, rather than discover their own way to the summits. The large car park at Braes of Foss positively encourages walkers to take the same route, with disastrous erosion of the old footpath. Much of the mountain is now owned by the John Muir Trust and all their skill and ingenuity have been tested to the full as they have attempted to repair the path.

The Trust has wisely avoided a large patch of peaty ground and the new track follows the route of a very old path that tackles the mountain's east ridge directly. After some zigzags it reaches a more level section of very stony ground and then it becomes quite sketchy. The route continues east, over a series of rocky shelves to the narrower summit ridge. The cairn sits on top of a large rocky block.

I can offer two alternative routes. From Braes of Foss follow the track south into Gleann Mor. From the end of the track cross the slopes to the riverside and explore the length of the glen (with some searching you can find some old cup-and-ring markings). From the upper glen follow the burn north-west to the building at the end of the Tempar track. Climb Schiehallion by its western slopes.

The other, simpler, route follows the Tempar Burn from the Braes of Foss/Kinloch Rannoch road up towards the bothy at GR699546. Leave the track just north of the bothy and climb the west slopes of the hill, which become increasingly rocky as you ascend.

the track at Aonach Ban. Follow the track back to Braes of Foss

Map: OS Sheet 51: GR714548

Access Point: Braes of Foss, GR750559 or Tempar, GR691575

Distance: 8km, 753m ascent

Approx Time: 3-5 hours

Translation: Fairy Hill of the Caledonians

Pronunciation: shee-haal-yan

Carn Gorm (103), 1029m/3376ft, Meall Garbh (186), 968m/3176ft, Carn Mairg (91), 1041m/3415ft, Meall nan Aighean (Creag Mhor) (169), 981m/3218ft

My abiding memory of my first traverse of these hills, on a Trans-Scotland walk from Oban to Montrose, was of a series of high plateau-like hills with little to commend them. Return visits, especially on skis, have changed my opinion.

From the top of the forest steep moorland and grassy slopes lead to Carn Gorm and the beginning of a long, broad and easy ridge walk to An Sgorr (which can be avoided by a traverse across its north-west slopes) and the flattish summit of Meall Garbh. The north-west top is the highest. A long line of fencing now leads past a tiny lochan to a wide bealach before the slopes begin to rise towards

Route Summary: (Route B) Follow the Invervar Burn to the top of the forest, then steep grassy slopes W then N to the summit of Carn Gorm. Follow broad ridge NNE to An Sgor and the summit of Meall Garbh. Follow the march fence to Meall a' Bharr then E and SE to Carn Mairg. Follow ridge E of summit to Meall Liath then S on

From Creag Mhor summit above Glen Lyon, looking east across Strath Tay

a wide ridge around the head of Gleann Muillin to Meall nan Aighean (Creag Mhor)

Map: OS Sheet 51: GR635501, GR646517, GR684513, GR695496

Access Point: Invervar, GR666483

Distance: 18km, 1387m ascent

Approx Time: 7-8 hours

Translation: blue hill; rough hill; hill of sorrow or boundary hill; hill of the hind (big rock)

Pronunciation: kaarn gor-om; myowl gaarv; kaarn mairg; myowl yan yaan (crayk vore)

Meall a' Bharr at 1004m. The ridge now descends and narrows considerably for its ascent of Carn Mairg and its great cairn. The slopes north-east of Carn Mairg lead down into Gleann Mor and form a front to an unusual view of Schiehallion: no fine conical shape from this angle, but a long whalebacked ridge rising to its western summit.

The route from Carn Mairg to Meall Liath is fairly obvious but you can avoid the latter top by turning south down grassy slopes from the bealach. These slopes lead to a wide col, a deer-infested place in summer, then on to the broad ridge of Creag Mhor. The summit is the rock-capped north-east top called Meall nan Aighean. Finally, descend due west to the grassy ridge on the south side of the Allt Coire Chearcaill and follow this ridge back to the footpath above Invervar.

Route Summary: From the dam climb the steep grassy hillside S to reach the ridge above Coire Ban. Follow fence posts W to Creag an Fheadain, then SSW to Sron Chona Choirein then W and NW to summit of Stuchd an Lochain. Continue W to Meall an Odhar, drop down its SW slopes to a wide bealach and climb the S slopes of the

Stuchd an Lochain (197), 960m/3150ft, Meall Buidhe (248), 932m/3058ft

Most walkers combine these two hills by climbing Stuchd an Lochain, returning to their starting point by the Loch an Daimh dam, climbing Meall Buidhe and returning by the same route. A circuit of Loch an Daimh starting and finishing at the dam makes a superb circular walk and adds an excellent Corbett, Sron a' Choire Chnapanich, 837m (2746ft), to the itinerary.

Stuchd an Lochain can also be climbed from Cashlie at the western end of the Stronuich Reservoir in Glen Lyon via the Allt Cashlie which leads to the plateau between Sron Chona Choirein and the summit, but this route of ascent lacks the character of the north side of the hill.

Better to start from the Loch an Daimh dam, where a faint path climbs grassy slopes southwards to reach the ridge above Coire Ban. A line of fence posts can be followed westwards to Creag an Fheadain from where a descent into a bealach is followed by an easy climb to Sron Choma Choirein. A broad mossy ridge now leads round the cliffs above Lochan nan Cat to the summit. It seems that in 1590, a local laird, Mad Colin Campbell of Meggernie, took a perverse delight in climbing the hill and chasing a herd of goats over the edge into Lochan na Cat. Apparently the shepherd only just escaped a similar fate!

From Stuchd an Lochain a descent down a broad ridge leads to a col then an easy climb to Meall an Odhar whose south-west ridge leads down to a rather wet and boggy bealach. From here climb almost due north to the Corbett of Sron a' Choire Chnapanich, the Nose of the Lumpy Corrie.

Steep slopes drop down to the head of Loch an Daimh, a place of great atmosphere which I would never have associated with these southern hills. It feels as remote a spot as any, hemmed in on three sides by high, steep hills, with the long slim trench of Loch an Daimh creating a funnel for the wind.

Steep slopes lead to Meall Cruinn and a long tramp over high moorland leads to Meall Buidhe. From here follow the rim of the Glas Choire to just before Meall a' Phuill before dropping southwards to pick up the broad ridge of Druim Chaluim and the return to the dam.

Corbett, Sron a' Choire Chnapanich. From the summit head N for a short distance and descend the very steep NW slopes to the Feith Thalain. From the W end of Loch an Daimh climb steeply to Meall Cruinn and follow the rolling moorland in a rough NE direction to Meall Buidhe. Descend back to the dam via Meall a' Phuill and the Druim Chaluim

Map: OS Sheet 51

Access Point: Loch an Daimh, GR510436

Distance: 20km, 1070m ascent

Approx Time: 6-8 hours

Translation: peak of the small loch; yellow hill

Pronunciation: stoochk an lochan; myowl boo-ee

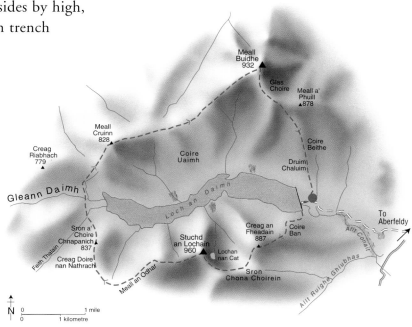

THE LAWERS GROUP

The Munros:

Meall Corranaich   Meall a' Choire Leith   Meall Greigh   Meall Garbh
An Stuc   Beinn Ghlas   Ben Lawers   Meall nan Tarmachan

This is one of the most popular mountain walking areas in Scotland, owing to the proximity of the Central Belt and the fact that there is easy access to the hills from the National Trust for Scotland car park on the Lochan na Lairige road. Because of the rich calcareous soil of this area, caused by the very friable schist, Arctic-Alpine plants grow here in profusion and the whole area is a National Nature Reserve. Lawers is the highest point in a long and easy winding ridge which aids the walker, while the Tarmachan ridge, particularly in winter conditions, offers a traverse of great character.

A complete traverse of the Lawers massif is a long and arduous expedition (25km, 2500m ascent), but is well worth while, especially if you can arrange for a car to be left at the NTS car park to return you to your starting point on Loch Tayside. Most walkers, though, are content to tackle these hills in two, or even three groupings.

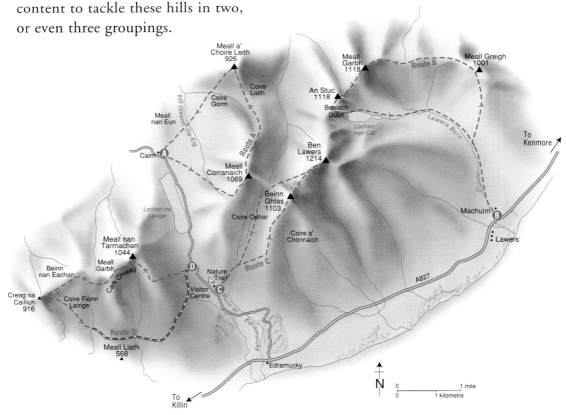

Ben Lawers from the east

Meall Corranaich (68), 1069m/3507ft,
Meall a' Choire Leith (261), 926m/3038ft

Start this walk just north of the Lochan na Lairige, near the prominent cairn above the road. Leave the road and take to the rough hillside, to reach the upper Allt Gleann Da-Eig. Follow the stream's shallow corrie in a south-east direction and climb the slopes above its source to reach the narrow south-west ridge of Meall Corranaich. Follow the ridge north-north-east to the summit and then beyond, down a broad grassy ridge to where the ridge bifurcates to form two ridges enclosing the high Coire Gorm. Follow the right-hand ridge, the north one, passing close to the edge of the steep Coire Liath. Beyond the corrie lip the ridge narrows to a col and then broadens out to form the flattish summit of Meall a' Choire Leith.

Descend the south-west slopes of Meall a' Choire Leith, cross the stream in Coire Gorm and the Allt Gleann Da-Eig, cross open, peat-hag ridden ground and pass through the shallow col immediately south-east of Meall nan Eun. From there it's a short drop back to your starting point.

Route Summary: Leave road just N of Lochan na Lairige (Route A) and cross rough moorland SE over peat hags. Reach the Allt Gleann Da-Eig and follow it uphill to SW ridge of Meall Corranaich. Leave the summit and head N down the easy angled ridge. Keep to the NNE ridge, drop to a col then follow ridge on the flat topped summit plateau of Meall a' Choire Leith

Map: OS Sheet 51: GR616410, GR612439

Access Point: Summit of Lochan na Lairige Road

Distance: 13km, 720m ascent

Approx Time: 4-6 hours

Translation: notched hill or hill of lamenting; hill of the grey corrie

Pronunciation: myowl kora-neech; myowl kora lay

Meall Greigh (136), 1001m/3284ft,
Meall Garbh (35), 1118m/3668ft, An Stuc (34) 1118m/3668ft

While the western hills of the Ben Lawers range can all be climbed from the NTS car park, access to the other three Munros has always been more difficult because of car parking problems in Lawers village.

The owner of the Ben Lawers Hotel has excavated a car parking

Route Summary: From Lawers follow the side road to Machuim Farm (Route B). Beyond it, follow the track on the E bank of the Lawers Burn. Climb due N to Meall Greigh on easy grassy slopes. Follow W ridge to Meall Garbh. This ridge is broad and featureless and navigation can be tricky in misty weather. Follow ridge around the head of Coire na Cat to the very steep N slopes of An Stuc. This ascent can be tricky in winter conditions and even in summer requires some mild scrambling. The S slopes of An Stuc are easier and lead to the Bealach Dubh and a steep gully down to Lochan nan Cat. Follow the N shores of the loch to the path beside the Lawers Burn, back to the start

Map: OS Sheet 51

Access Point: Lawers on the A827. At the time of writing the owner of the Lawers Hotel is happy to allow hill-walkers to use the hotel car park provided they buy a pint or pot of tea or coffee at the end of their walk

Distance: 15km, 1240m ascent

Approx Time: 6-8 hours

Translation: hill of horse studs; rough hill; the peak

Pronunciation: myowl gray; myowl garv; an stook

area large enough to take about a dozen vehicles. He doesn't make a charge, but expects hill-walkers to buy a drink or a pot of tea at the end of their walk. Sounds perfectly reasonable.

From Machuim Farm, the Lawers Burn offers a long and curving route all the way to Lochan nan Cat and a path runs alongside it. This path gives access, after about 2km, to the south ridge of Meall Greigh. As you tramp west now, you will see Ben Lawers rising above its archetypal hanging corrie and lochan, and you can trace your skyline route over Meall Garbh and the shapely An Stuc.

Continue up the grassy shoulder of Meall Garbh, turning onto its north-east ridge which narrows as you approach the summit and the small cairn. An easy descent follows to the col below An Stuc, the next top on the round, where steep, badly eroded slopes lead to the small table of a summit. These slopes have caused problems in winter conditions when great icy sheets often form but in normal summer conditions the ascent is an easy scramble.

Beyond the summit, easier slopes drop down to the Bealach Dubh where you can follow a steepish gully down to Lochan nan Cat in the corrie below. Follow the north shore of the lochan to reach the Lawers Burn path again, loping back to Lawers village with the thought of a refreshing drink before you head for home.

Route Summary: Follow the nature trail as it climbs beside the Burn of Edramucky (Route C). After 1km or so the path leaves the burn and climbs onto the SSW ridge of Beinn Ghlas. Follow this ridge to the summit. From the cairn follow a linking ridge NE to Ben Lawers. Return to the col below Beinn Glas and descend NW to the bealach at the head of Coire Odhar. Take the path back to the outward route

Map: OS Sheet 51: GR636414

Access Point: NTS Centre on the Lochan na Lairige road between Loch Tay and Glen Lyon

Distance: 10km, 930m ascent

Approx Time: 4-6 hours

Translation: green-grey hill; hill of the loud stream

Pronunciation: bin glas; ben law-ers

Beinn Ghlas (47), 1103m/3619ft, Ben Lawers (10), 1214m/3983ft

Ben Lawers rises aloof from the green farmlands that fringe the northern shores of Loch Tay. The usual route to the summit leaves the NTS car park and after 500m crosses the Burn of Edramucky to its east bank where the path climbs up towards Coire Odhar. In summer this is a green and lush place, the haunt of meadow pipits and skylarks.

About 500m further on the path climbs in a north-east direction to reach the south ridge of Beinn Ghlas. An easy walk along the ridge takes you to the summit. Beyond here the broad ridge continues in a north-east direction, drops to a high bealach then climbs the summit slopes of Ben Lawers.

Return to the high bealach you've just climbed up from and follow the path that runs round the foot of Beinn Ghlas to the wet bealach above Coire Odhar. From there it's an easy climb to Meall Corranaich on a wet and rather boggy path. Alternatively, just follow the path that runs back down Coire Odhar to meet up with your outward route.

Ben Lawers across Lochan nan Cat

Meall nan Tarmachan (89), 1044m/3425ft

The Tarmachans represent a long switchback of a ridge that is at times chronically tortuous, often high above steep cliffs the like of which you won't find in all Breadalbane. Another bonus is that this walk starts nearly 550m (1800ft) above sea level, at a point just north of the NTS Visitor Centre where a bridge crosses the Allt a' Mhoirneas. From here make your way west over the rising moorland to reach the south ridge of Meall nan Tarmachan. The going is fairly rough here but once the ridge is reached life becomes more bearable. Follow the ridge north over its prominent knoll and follow a distinct grassy rake up below and then through the crags to reach the Tarmachan ridge itself just slightly north of the summit of Meall nan Tarmachan. Climb to the summit and then enjoy this winding ridge above the cliffs of Cam Chreag, over Meall Garbh, Beinn nan Eachan and finally Creag na Caillich, which sits above a long line of steep cliffs. To reach the Coire Fionn Lairige and the return to the starting point you'll have to backtrack a few hundred metres to the col between Caillich and Beinn nan Eachan. From here you can safely drop down into the corrie and pick up a Land Rover track which takes you back to the start.

Route Summary: Leave the bridge, cross the rough moorland and pick up the S ridge of Meall nan Tarmachan (Route D). Climb easy grass slopes to a prominent knoll. Turn NW and climb various raked terraces to the ridge just N of the summit of Meall nan Tarmachan. Follow the ridge SW

Map: OS Sheet 51: GR585390

Access Point: Bridge over Allt a' Mhoirneas, GR603382

Distance: 13km, 740m ascent

Approx Time: 4-6 hours

Translation: hill of the ptarmigan

Pronunciation: myowl nan tar-mach-an

THE MAMLORN HILLS

The Munros:

Meall Ghaordaidh   **Creag Mhor**   **Beinn Heasgarnich**
Ben Challum   **Sgiath Chuil**   **Meall Glas**

In many ways these hills which surround the lonely western extremity of Glen Lochay are undistinguished mountains, lacking any really distinctive feature. Nevertheless, they offer a degree of wildness and remoteness lacking in the less subtle delights of Ben Lawers, Beinn Laoigh or Ben More. All the hills are accessible from Glen Lochay but Ben Challum is more usually climbed by the less scenic route from Strath Fillan. Likewise, Meall Glas and Sgiath Chuil can be climbed from the south. Killin makes a convenient base for ascents of all the hills.

Route Summary: From Duncroisk, go through the gate by the road and follow the very muddy footpath that runs through fields on the W side of the Allt Dhuin Croisg. Follow this muddy footpath as it climbs higher past some old shielings. Cross a fence by a stile onto open hillside and continue on the track until you reach an old sheepfank on the skyline. From here leave the track and take a NW line up the broad and undulating ridge to more rocky slopes just below the summit. Weave a route around the rocks and climb more steeply to the summit trig point that sits inside a large circular cairn. Descend by the same route

Map: OS Sheet 51

Access Point: Duncroisk in Glen Lochay

Distance: 7km, 823m ascent

Approx Time: 3-5 hours

Translation: Possibly rounded hill of the shoulder, arm or hand

Pronunciation: myowl jirdee

Meall Ghaordaidh (93), 1039m/3409ft

Meall Ghaordaidh is a blunt nose that rises above the rough moorland of the long ridge from the Lairig Breisleich to the Lairig nan Lun between Glen Lochay and Glen Lyon. The usual route is from Glen Lochay, but the route from Glen Lyon is marginally more attractive, thanks to two rocky spurs, Creag an Tulabhain and Creag Laoghain. This route follows the Allt Laoghain high into its corrie and grassy slopes lead to the summit cairn. A better route crosses the river near Cashlie and follows the line of the Allt Chiorlaich to a bealach just west of Meall Na Cnoc-laraich. From its summit there is a short descent, then a climb up a broad ridge to the Munro.

From Glen Lochay, a long trudge from Duncroisk follows grassy slopes, with some rocky outcrops near the summit ridge. A more rewarding way to climb Meall Ghaordaidh is to make it part of a high-level traverse between Glen Lochay and Glen Lyon, using two cars. From the summit, head north-east via Beinn nan Oighreag, then north along the ridge

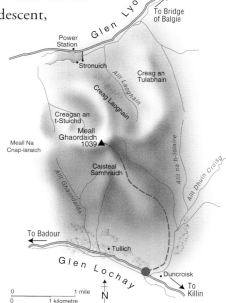

Ben Challum from its southern top

above the Lairig Breisleich; the ridge dwindles out above the Lochan na Lairig road (the high level road that runs past the Ben Lawers Visitor Centre) as it descends to Bridge of Balgie.

Creag Mhor (84), 1047m/3435ft,
Beinn Heasgarnich (62), 1078m/3537ft

Creag Mhor, Beinn Heasgarnich, and Beinn Challum, can all be ascended from upper Glen Lochay although Ben Challum is more usually climbed by its less scenic route from Strath Fillan in the south. Most folk are content climbing just two, Creag Mhor and Beinn Heasgarnich.

Creag Mhor forms the blunt apex of three distinct ridges. Climb the steep Sron nan Eun nose of Creag Mhor first, by way of a hydro road that zigzags uphill from Batavaime. From the top, the ridge levels out towards the summit. Beyond the summit follow the easier north-west ridge for a short distance before descending directly to the col. Heasgarnich's west ridge rises somberly above – over 900m of steep climbing up to the Stob an Fhir-bhoga top. A good zig-zagging track makes fairly easy work of it and from the subsidiary top it is an easy walk north over a couple of humps to the summit. Descend by the Allt Badour to the hydro road parallel to, but at a higher level than, the glen track.

Route Summary: Cars are not allowed up Glen Lochay beyond the gate at GR465364. Follow the track SW as far as Batavaime (Route A, p.42) where a hydro track climbs up towards Sron nan Eun. Leave the end of the track and climb up to the subsidiary top. Follow the ridge NW to the summit of Creag Mhor. Descend by the NW ridge then down grassy slopes due E to the Bealach na Baintighearna. From the col climb the prominent W ridge of Benn Heasgarnich that leads to its S top. Follow the ridge N to the summit. Descend roughly SSE to the Allt Bad Odhar which can be followed to the hydro track above Badour. Follow this E back to above the start

Map: OS Sheets 50 and 51

Access Point: Glen Lochay, GR465364

Distance: 20km, 1250m ascent

Approx Time: 7-9 hours

Translation: big rock; peak of the roaring waterfall of the horses

Pronunciation: craig vore; byn heskarneech

Route Summary: From the remains of St Fillan's Chapel follow the track uphill and cross the West Highland railway line (Route B). Take to the untracked hillside in a NE direction. There is a very sketchy path. Go over grassy slopes, then flatter ground and a slight knoll where fence posts to your right show the direction uphill. Where the fence posts end walk a short way, past a

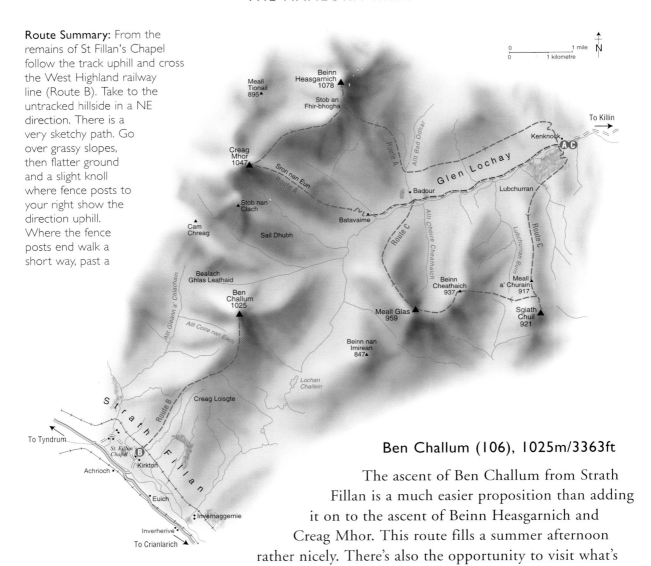

small cairn, a short distance beyond is the S top. The summit lies to the N but descend slightly W from the S top for a few metres to a ridge that descends gradually then gives a steep pull to the large summit cairn. Return by the same route

Map: OS Sheet 50

Access Point: Kirkton Farm in Strathfillan

Distance: 11km, 914m ascent

Approx Time: 4-6 hours

Translation: Calum's peak

Pronunciation: byn hallum

Ben Challum (106), 1025m/3363ft

The ascent of Ben Challum from Strath Fillan is a much easier proposition than adding it on to the ascent of Beinn Heasgarnich and Creag Mhor. This route fills a summer afternoon rather nicely. There's also the opportunity to visit what's left of St Fillan's Priory, just beside the Kirkton farmhouse.

Immediately opposite the Priory ruins the path to Ben Challum climbs up past a couple of old graveyards, crosses the railway line then wriggles up through and over bracken-covered hillocks past the rocky outcrops of Creag Loisgte. The south ridge of the hill is better formed than the map suggests and it's an easy climb to the south summit of the hill. In misty weather just follow the fence posts.

This southern top can be confusing in the mist for you have to descend slightly west to gain a short, rocky ridge, which in turn descends to the high bealach between the two tops. From there it's an easy to climb to the summit from where the views can be spectacular, with Ben More and Stobinian dominant in the south and the Bridge of Orchy close by to the north.

Sgiath Chuil (270), 921m/3022ft, Meall Glas (199), 959m/3146ft

Lying in a broad wedge of high, undulating moorland between Glen Lochay and Glen Dochart, Sgiath Chuil and Meall Glas can be climbed from either glen. Glen Dochart may be more accessible but Glen Lochay, especially in its upper reaches, feels distinctly wild and remote, a much better place to start and finish a mountain walk. A gate at Kenknock bars further vehicular progress along Glen Lochay. A layby is big enough for several cars.

A bridge crosses the river close to the road end at Kenknock. A forestry track switchbacks up the hill to the top of a big water pipeline. It is a short climb to the long north ridge of Sgiath Chuil which narrows over the subsidiary top of Meall a' Churain then leads to the summit of Sgiath Chuil, a fairly undistinguished top, although there is a hint of promise in some rocky outcrops on its south and west flanks. That promise is short lived though, as you have to retrace your steps towards Meall a' Churain. At the low point on the summit ridge descend westwards where steep slopes fall away into the bealach between Meall a' Churain and Beinn Cheathaich.

On the other side of the bealach, slopes lead to Beinn Cheathaich and the best part of the route as the ridge forms a gentle curve around the head of Coire Cheathaich before rising to Meall Glas. Descend by the north-west ridge then north-east down into Glen Lochay. Cross the river by the footbridge at Badour and take the track back to Kenknock.

Route Summary: Cross the River Lochay by the footbridge just W of Kenknock (Route C). Follow the forestry road up the hillside to the top of a water pipe. Climb grassy slopes SW to the long N ridge of Meall a' Churain. Pass its small cairn and continue S to the rocky summit of Sgiath Chuil. Return almost to Meall a' Churain, descend steep slopes W to the bealach between Meall a' Churain and Beinn Cheathaich. Climb steepening slopes W to the Beinn Cheathaich ridge, follow it SW to a small cairned top, continue along the broad curving ridge round the rim of Coire Cheathaich to the summit of Meall Glas. Descend by the NW ridge and follow it NE into Glen Lochay

Map: OS Sheet 51

Access Point: Kenknock in Glen Lochay

Distance: 17km, 1200m ascent

Approx Time: 4-7 hours

Translation: grey-green hill; back wing

Pronunciation: myowl glas; skeea-chool

Meall Glas (right) and Beinn Cheathaich above Glen Lochay

THE BRIDGE OF ORCHY HILLS

The Munros:

Beinn Dorain   Beinn an Dothaidh   Beinn Mhanach
Beinn Achaladair   Beinn a' Chreachain

Although geographically these hills are in the Southern Highlands, most walkers feel that they are entering the Highlands proper once they drive up the long winding pull out of Tyndrum towards Bridge of Orchy with the immaculate conical shape of Beinn Dorain filling the horizon. To add credence to that feeling, as soon as you set foot on these hills you become aware that they are generally rockier and steeper than their heather- and grass-clad cousins of the Southern Highlands. In effect Beinn Dorain, Beinn an Dothaidh, Beinn Achaladair and Beinn a' Chreachain form a gentle curve with Beinn Mhanach in their grasp, with Dothaidh, Achaladair and Chreachain showing broken and cliff-girt faces to the flat wilderness of the Rannoch Moor.

Bridge of Orchy, with its hotel and bunkhouse, is the obvious base, but there is a greater choice of accommodation in Tyndrum.

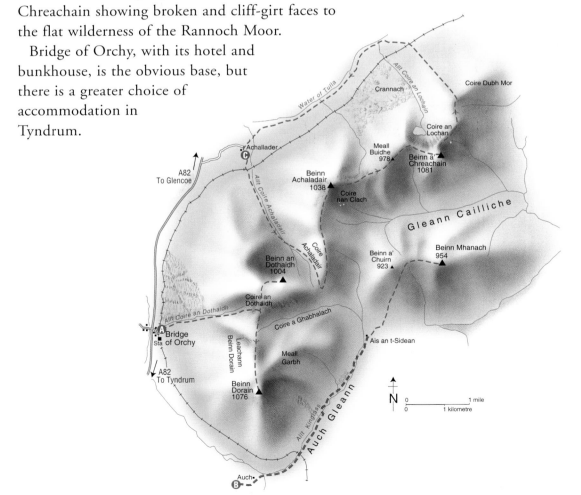

44

Beinn Dorain (64), 1076m/3530ft,
Beinn an Dothaidh (129), 1004m/3294ft

Forming part of the Great Wall of Rannoch, these two hills, along with Beinn Achaladair and Beinn a' Chreachain, form the boundary between the old Pictish Kingdom of Alba to the east and the Dalriadic Kingdom of the Scots in the west and while all four hills can be climbed in a long day of some 25km and 1800m of climbing they are probably more conveniently broken down into two days.

Bridge of Orchy railway station offers the best starting point, with plenty of car parking. You may, of course, wish to arrive by train, timing your descent to catch a later train home. From the underpass beneath the railway line a gate gives access to the open moorland. A well-used path runs up alongside the Allt Coire an Dothaidh to the obvious bealach between the two hills. The last few hundred metres to the bealach steepen considerably, although there are no real difficulties.

From the cairn on the bealach another path weaves its southerly way up a fairly easy angled ridge, avoiding the worst of the outcrops and rocky slabs. This soon gives way to grassy slopes, with a big drop to your right and some wonderful views across to Glen Orchy. Pass a boulder-covered summit, and a large cairn, which fools many into believing this is the summit and continue a couple of hundred metres further south across a shallow dip in the ridge to the true summit. The views from here are a bit disappointing, although you can gaze down into the Auch Glen below, a place long associated with Rob Roy and the MacGregors. They used to walk through from Glen Lyon to bury their dead here – a long way for a wake!

Retrace your steps to the bealach, taking care not to wander too far west into steep and rocky ground, and take a steeper north-north-east line up the grassy flank of Beinn an Dothaidh to the first of three summit tops. The middle one is the true summit. Take care as you descend to the bealach for steep crags, offering some excellent winter climbing, guard the hill on its western and northern flanks.

Route Summary: Leave the railway station (Route A) and make for the obvious bealach on the skyline between the two hills. Once there climb due S following an obvious path up an easy angled ridge then along the edge of a rocky escarpment. Continue up broad grassy slopes to a bouldery summit. The real summit of Beinn Dorain lies about 200m further S. Return to the col and climb a diagonal line NNE to the summit of Beinn an Dothaidh. The highest top is the central one

Map: OS Sheet 50: GR326378, GR332408

Access Point: Bridge of Orchy Station, GR301394

Distance: 13km, 1100m ascent

Approx Time: 5-7 hours

Translation: hill of the otter or small stream; hill of the scorching

Pronunciation: doa-ran; daw-ee

Beinn Mhanach (211), 954m/3130ft

Route Summary: Leave cars by the A82. Walk down the road past Auch (Route B), under the viaduct and up the Auch Glen track which crosses the burn several times to the watershed where the long, steep, grassy slopes lead to Beinn a' Chuirn, 920m. A broad and flat ridge runs E to the summit of Beinn Mhanach

Map: OS Sheet 50

Access Point: A82 near Auch, GR317353

Distance: 19km, 850m ascent

Approx Time: 5-8 hours

Translation: monk hill

Pronunciation: vanach

This hill is awkwardly placed in the grasp of its four near neighbours and it's difficult to connect it to ascents of the other hills. It's a double-topped hill with the lower of the two tops, Beinn a' Chuirn (923m), closer to the hills of the Wall of Rannoch. On one memorable excursion a friend and I skied in from Bridge of Orchy over the bealach between Beinn Dorain and Beinn an Dothaidh. Deep snow gave us good running down to the very head of the Auch Gleann from where we cut round into the head of Gleann Cailliche. A long rising traverse took us to the shallow col between the two tops and from there it was an easy glide to the summit of Beinn Mhanach. The return was even better in first-class snow conditions and I recall a long, easy schuss from the pass between Gleann Cailliche and the Auch Gleann before we had to climb back to the Beinn an Dothaidh bealach and a descent in fast diminishing light back to Bridge of Orchy.

While it's possible to follow this route on foot, rather than on skis, a more interesting route follows the Auch Gleann past Ais-an t-Sidhean, once the home of the eighteenth-century Gaelic bard Duncan Ban MacIntyre. It's ironic that the ruin is now used as a sheep fank – MacIntyre hated the sheep which caused so many people to be cleared from their homes, a hatred which is explained in one of his poems, 'Oran Nam Balgairean', the Song of the Foxes: 'My blessing be upon the foxes, because that they hunt the sheep, The sheep with the brockit faces that have made confusion in all the world.'

About a kilometre beyond the ruin leave the track and climb the steep grassy slopes to the summit of Beinn a' Chuirn. From there it's an easy stroll to the summit of the Munro.

Beinn Achaladair (94), 1038m/3405ft, Beinn a' Chreachain (61), 1081m/3547ft

Route Summary: From the farm head S along a track (Route C), over the railway and up Coire Achaladair. Climb to the col at the head of the corrie then turn N along the grassy ridge to the S top of Beinn Achaladair. Follow the ridge to the summit. Descend E along the corrie rim to the col. Follow the broad ridge over the flat top of Meall Buidhe and then up the stony

Achallader Farm has an interesting history. It was on this spot that Black Duncan of Cowal, Campbell of Glenorchy, built one of his seven castles – the remains can still be seen next to the farmhouse. And it was here that Robert Campbell of Glenlyon rested as he made his way north to Glen Coe before the infamous massacre.

Nowadays it's a working farm and the farmer has kindly built a large car park – it's good manners to ask permission to leave your car though!

Beinn Dorain and the Bridge of Orchy Hills

These two hills show their best faces northwards over the great blanket of Rannoch Moor and you can enjoy the anticipation as you head south from the farm along a track which crosses the railway line and continues up into Coire Achaladair. You can either climb directly to the col at the head of the corrie, or climb south-east between the crags to reach the ridge between Achaladair and its south top.

From the airy perch which heralds the summit of Beinn Achaladair enjoy the high-level promenade eastwards to Meall Buidhe, with the flatness of Rannoch Moor on your left accentuating the height and spaciousness of your situation. A descent to a col above Loch a' Chreachain and then a steeper, stony climb leads to the summit of Beinn a' Chreachain.

Descend the north-east ridge of the hill, a narrow and interesting route, and when the gradient of the grassy slopes begins to lessen turn due north, cross the railway line, drop through the scattered birches and pick up the track which returns you to Achallader Farm.

slopes of Beinn a' Chreachain. Descend by the NE ridge and once the crags are avoided turn N to descend grassy slopes, over the railway, past scattered birches to the track by the Water of Tulla back to the farm

Map: OS Sheet 50

Access Point: Achallader Farm car park

Distance: 15km, 1190m ascent

Approx Time: 6-8 hours

Translation: field of hard water; hill of the clamshell

Pronunciation: byn achalatur; byn a chrech-yin

THE CRUACHAN HILLS

The Munros:
Ben Cruachan   Stob Diamh   Beinn a' Chochuill   Beinn Eunaich

A magnificent group of hills bounded by Loch Etive, Glen Strae and the Pass of Brander, with Cruachan in particular offering an impression that it is almost surrounded by great sea lochs. Such is the hill's proximity to the sea that the coastal views, particularly those across to the Isle of Mull, are superb and that, taken together with spectacular rocky ridges, a series of fine peaks, and some high, imposing corries, makes this one of the finest hills in the Southern Highlands. The most popular route, and one which probably offers the finest impression of the mountain, is the Dalmally Horseshoe which visits half a dozen tops over the 900m contour.

Partially dwarfed by the huge Cruachan massif, Beinn a' Chochuill and Beinn Eunaich are nevertheless fine hills in their own right. The two summits are the high points in a long 12km ridge which rises between Loch Etive and Glen Strae, a fine expedition in itself although most walkers will take the easier option of the route described. The best base is probably Dalmally which is on the Glasgow to Oban railway.

Ben Cruachan (31), 1126m/3694ft, Stob Diamh (143), 998m/3274ft

My first visit to Cruachan was on a Trans-Scotland Oban to Montrose walk and Roger Smith and I had left Oban, walked up the length of Glen Lonan and tackled Cruachan in the afternoon. We followed the tumbling Allt Cruiniche up steep slopes to a boggy bealach between the outlying Meall nan Each and Stob Dearg, Cruachan's western peak, commonly known as the Taynuilt Peak. From Stob Dearg a steepish drop, a long level ridge and a short clamber over boulders took us to the summit where the views took our breath away. Below, the Cruachan reservoir filled the contours of the corrie floor; Loch Awe stretched its long arm south-west and, away beyond, was the island-speckled sea. Eastwards the ridge opened out in a series of bumps, dips and peaks, more like a small range of mountains than one single hill, and beyond rose Ben Laoigh. To the north, the Blackmount and Glencoe tops appeared in a jumble.

Route Summary: Climb steeply up the path beside the Allt Cruachan (Route A) to the Cruachan dam access road. For an E-W round of Cruachan's tops follow the reservoir's E shore before climbing the grassy slopes to Stob Garbh. Continue N, descend slightly then climb to the summit of Stob Diamh. Follow the W ridge over the Drochaid Ghlas (slightly N of the main line of the ridge) then along a narrower bouldery crest to the main summit of Cruachan. The ridge continues to a bealach and the 'Taynuilt Peak', Stob Dearg. Return to the bealach, re-ascend the main peak for some distance to avoid the slabby face of Coire a' Bhachaill, then head due S to Meall Cuanail and the grassy slopes back to the Cruachan dam

Ben Cruachan from the air

Map: OS Sheet 50

Access Point: Falls of Cruachan, GR078268

Distance: 14km, 1490m ascent

Approx Time: 5-8 hours

Translation: stacky hill; peak of the stag

Pronunciation: kroo-achan; stop dyv

From the summit the ridge flows east and then slightly north-east over Drochaid Ghlas, 1000m above sea level. This is a narrow and rocky top and in mist or cloud it would be all too easy to carry on down the steep, narrow north ridge into Glen Noe. The ridge to Stob Diamh is best reached by dropping down about 20m short of Drochaid Ghlas, and on to the north-east ridge which descends, levels out and then climbs again to Cruachan's second Munro. We descended Stob Diamh's north ridge into a high corrie where we camped for the night – Beinn a' Chochuill and Beinn Eunaich beckoned across Glen Noe for the morrow.

Most walkers tackle these two Munros via the Cruachan Horseshoe, a high-level circuit which follows the skyline above the Cruachan Reservoir. From the Power Station beside the A85, follow an access road up to the reservoir. Easy slopes lead to the Lairig Torran where you can reach the south ridge of Stob Garbh. Continue to this top then follow steeper slopes to Stob Diamh. From Cruachan's summit descend via Meall Cuanail back to the reservoir.

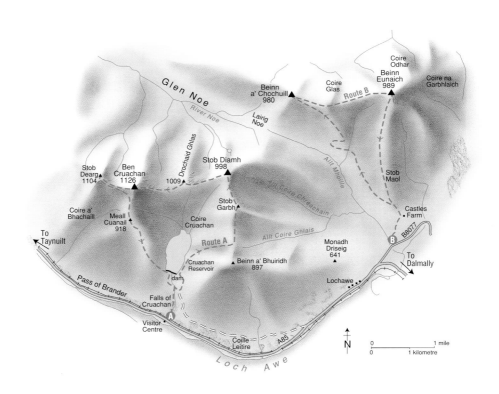

Ben Cruachan and Beinn a' Chochuill from Beinn Eunaich

Beinn a' Chochuill (172), 980m/3215ft, Beinn Eunaich (156), 989m/3245ft

From the Allt Mhoille bridge, a hydro track climbs high into Glen Noe, on the south side of the hills, and gives easy access to a prominent grassy rib that connects with the main Chochuill/Eunaich ridge about 800m east of Beinn a' Chochuill's summit. A long bow-shaped ridge links the two Munros, dropping down to a high bealach from where Beinn Eunaich can be climbed directly to its summit cairn.

The summit of Beinn a' Chochuill offers tantalizing views to the west, with the long arm of Loch Etive running out to sea by the Falls of Lora, the hills of Morven shimmering in the distance and the even bigger hills of Mull forming the western horizon. To the north Ben Nevis stands clear, beyond the jumble of Glen Coe peaks, and to the east lie the Bridge of Orchy hills, Ben Laoigh (looking curiously un-Ben Laoigh-like from this angle), Ben More and Stob Binnein, the Crianlarich hills and the Loch Lomond hills. Best of all though is the view across Glen Noe to Cruachan's less familiar northern slopes.

Route Summary: N of bridge over the Allt Mhoille on the B8077 (Route B) take private road W of Castles Farm to a Hydro road up to the head of Glen Noe. At 360m contour bear right on another track for 100m then leave it to climb up the SE rib of Beinn a' Chocuill to the summit. Return to E end of ridge, it drops to a high bealach, cross this to the shoulder of Beinn Eunaich. Climb to the summit. Broad slopes lead back to the start over Stob Maol

Map: OS Sheet 50

Access Point: B8077, GR 137288

Distance: 13km, 1190m ascent

Approx Time: 5-8 hours

Translation: hill of the hood; fowling hill

Pronunciation: byn a' cho-chil; byn ayneech

THE GLEN ETIVE HILLS

The Munros:

Ben Starav   Glas Bheinn Mhor   Beinn nan Aighenan
Stob Coir' an Albannaich   Meall nan Eun   Stob Ghabhar
Stob a' Choire Odhair   Creise   Meall a'Bhuiridh
Beinn Sgulaird   Beinn Fhionnlaidh

One of the most popular hillwalking areas of the Highlands, a plethora of fine peaks are joined by high and complex ridge systems to offer many multi-peak extravaganzas. These Etive hills are less craggy than their Glencoe neighbours, but nevertheless make up a number of fine high-level excursions. The traverse from Inveroran to Kingshouse, over Stob Ghabhar and Creise, has become known as something of a classic.

Sgulaird and Fhionnlaidh are both big brutes of hills, and since both dip their toes in the waters of Loch Creran hillwalkers have to fully earn their height gain from sea level – Fhionnlaidh in particular is shy and retiring and lies well back from the starting point at Elleric.

Ben Starav (63), 1078m/3537ft, Glas Bheinn Mhor (145), 997m/3271ft, Beinn nan Aighenan (196), 960m/3150ft

Starav and Glas Bheinn Mhor are impressive looking hills when viewed from Glen Etive, Starav looking particularly imposing as its huge north ridge sweeps majestically up from sea level all the way to the summit. There is some uncertainty as to the translation of the name – some suggest it means big and well built, others believe it could come from starabhan, meaning a rustling noise or even starra, a block of rock.

Big and well built it certainly is and probably the best starting point is at Coileitir where a bridge crosses some big deep pools in the river. A rough path crosses the moorland, then another bridge and once past a fine pine-clad gorge brings you nose to nose with the start of the north ridge. It is, undeniably, a brutal ascent, over 1060m of climbing, but be assured it improves as you gain height with rapidly expanding views and a narrowing, interesting ridge as you come closer to the summit.

A fine summit crest then billows out eastwards and down to a col where you can drop down to another, lower col to make the ascent of the outlying Beinn nan Aighenan. Return to the col and it's a

Route Summary: From Glen Coileitir Farm follow a path to a bridge on the Allt Mheuran and a path on its W bank (Route A). After 400m take to the N ridge of Ben Starav. Follow this ridge to the Trig pillar near the summit. The cairn sits a short distance to the SE. From the cairn follow the ridge SE and E to the top of Stob Coire Dheirg and then follow another twist in the ridge to where it turns ESE and drops to an obvious bealach W of Glas Bheinn Mhor. From here head SSE to the broad ridge leading to Beinn nan Aighenan. Retrace your steps to the bealach, turn E and cross the subsidiary top and finish on a rockier ridge to the summit. Return to Glen Etive by Glas Bheinn Mhor's E ridge, then N into the corrie at the head of the Allt Mheuran

Map: OS Sheet 50

Access Point: Glen Etive, GR136467

Distance: 20km, 1710m ascent

Approx Time: 5-8hours

The River Ba and the hills of Black Mount

Translation: unknown; big green/grey hill; hill of the hinds

Pronunciation: byn sta-rav; glas vyn voar; byn yan yanan

Route Summary: Leave Glen Etive but before reaching Coileitir Farm head SE uphill through open woodland (Route B). At the broad NW shoulder of Stob Coir' an Albannaich, follow this ridge to the summit. The continuation to Meall nan Eun involves an awkward switchback ridge and crosses the subsidiary summit of Meall Tarsuinn. The route is obvious in clear conditions but requires careful navigation in bad visibility. From the summit of Meall nan Eun go NW across the plateau and descend in a NW direction towards the waters of the Allt Ceitlein

Map: OS Sheet 50

straightforward ascent of Glas Bheinn Mhor with a twisting descent down to the col beyond from where you can drop down to the head of the Allt Mheuran which is then followed back to Glen Etive by the path on its north-east side.

Stob Coir' an Albannaich (90), 1044m/3425ft, Meall nan Eun (254), 928m/3045ft

Beinn Chaorach, a westerly outlier of Stob Coir' an Albannaich, presents a rather blunt face to Glen Etive, its lower slopes birch clad while higher up it becomes rocky and craggy. Once you've crossed the River Etive you'll reach a junction in the track, and rather than follow it to Coileitir turn left instead until you reach a gate in the adjoining deer fence. Climb over and start the long, steep climb up to Beinn Chaorach.

Once the shoulder is reached things improve dramatically. Much of the walking is now across great boiler-plate slabs of granite which can ice up and become very slippery in winter! Pass the rim of the rather impressive Coire Glas and climb steadily south-eastwards, first of all on a broad grassy ridge which soon narrows appreciably as you approach the summit cairn of Stob Coir' an Albannaich. The Scotsman's corrie lies immediately below you and the next problem, a rather intricate one, is to reach the connecting col to Meall Tarsuinn and Meall nan Eun without tackling the steep crags of the corrie itself.

On a recent New Year trip some friends and I went down Glen Etive to climb Meall nan Eun and Stob Coir' an Albannaich and started the day in dullish, but not unpleasant weather. It wasn't until we broke from the cover of Albannaich's north ridge that the battering fury of the

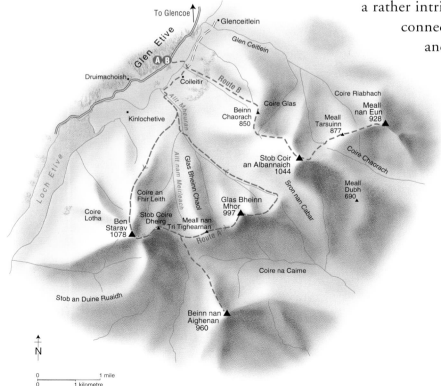

Stob Coir' an Albannaich

wind hit us. From then it was a struggle against the gusts, avoiding the icy granite slabs and navigating through cloud and spindrift.

The usual exit from Stob Coir' an Albannaich's summit ridge was an awkward one and much of the ridge was corniced. The difficulty of the situation was exacerbated by the low visibility and it was only after some trial and error that we managed to locate a section of the ridge where we could descend. It was a long, hard and testing day which again emphasised the caution with which one should approach the Scottish hills in winter.

The best advice is to descend eastwards for almost a kilometre to where the ridge levels off for a short distance, about the 880m contour. A small cairn indicates the best point but of course won't be seen in snow and remember that much of this ridge cornices in winter conditions. At this point the ground is less steep and rocky and it is possible to descend steeply through rock outcrops in a north-north-east line to reach the lochan-dotted bealach.

The bump of Meall Tarsuinn has to be crossed, or bypassed on its south side and then a long pull up fairly gentle slopes leads to the great dome of Meall nan Eun. Typically, the cairn lies some distance off in the wrong direction – at the far point of the extensive summit plateau.

The descent from Meall nan Eun is an interesting one, down enormous granite pavements to the headwaters of the Allt Ceitlin where a footpath on the north bank of the river takes you back to Glen Etive.

Access Point: As for Ben Starav
Distance: 15km, 1300m ascent
Approx Time: 5-8hours
Translation: peak of the corrie of the Scotsman; hill of the birds
Pronunciation: stop kor an ala-paneech; myowl nan ayn

To Glencoe

Kings House
Hotel

A82

Glen Etive

Route B

Blackrock
Cottage

B

To Bridge
of Orchy

Sron na
Creise

Creag Dhubh

Stob a'
Ghlais Choire
996 ▲

P

White Corries
Ski Centre

Carn Ghleann

Allt nan Giubhas

Creise
1100 ▲

Coire Pollach

Meall a'
Bhuiridh
1108 ▲

Mam
Coire
Easein ▲

Coire Odhar

Clach
Leathad
1099 ▲

Sron nam Forsair

Creag an
Fhirich
705 ▲

West Highland Way

Aonach Mor

Meall
Tionall
582 ▲

Coireach a' Ba

River Ba

BLACK MOUNT

Sron na Giubhas

Coirein
Lochain

Stob a'
Choire Odhair
943 ▲

Stob
Ghabhar
1090 ▲

Beinn Toaig
834

Aonach Eagach

Coire Toaig

Coire
Ghabhar

Coire na Muic

Route A

West Highland Way

Allt Toaig

Forest
Lodge

Loch Tulla

↑
N

Abhainn Shira

A

Victoria Bridge

0   1 mile

0   1 kilometre

Inveroran
Hotel

To Bridge
of Orchy

Stob a' Choire Odhair (226), 945m/3100ft,
Stob Ghabhar (55) 1090m/3576ft

The Clachlet Traverse is a classic high-level route from Inveroran to Kingshouse and takes in the Munros of Stob a' Choire Odhair, Stob Ghabhar, Meall a' Bhuiridh and Creise over a distance of about 25km. Height ascended is about 1700m. This is fine if you can arrange transport, with a car to collect you at Kingshouse and return you to your own car at Forest Lodge near Inveroran, but most walkers break this ridge down into two distinct outings, Stob Ghabhar and Stob a' Choire Odhair as one round, and Creise and Meall a' Bhuiridh as the other.

For Stob a' Choire Odhair and Stob Ghabhar take the track by Forest Lodge near Loch Tulla. Walk west along the track beside the Abhainn Shira to the Glasgow University Climbing Club hut at Clashgour. Leave the bulldozed track here and take the footpath northwards beside the Allt Toaig. At GR 252446, the path crosses another burn and west of it a broad ridge rises up to Beinn Toaig and the broad plateau-like ridge which is crowned by the summit of Stob a' Choire Odhair.

Descend west to a wide, knolly bealach, continue west uphill for a few hundred metres then turn south-west and up steep slopes to reach a ridge called the Aonach Eagach.

Several years ago I skied round these two Munros and I recalled a wonderful little arête at the top of this ridge, a thin spine of rock with big drops on either side. On that day it was protected by a double cornice, and I remember tip-toeing very tentatively across it, skis lashed on the pack. Even more recently, at this very spot, I realised the truth behind a statement I saw recently that there is no such thing as winter hillwalking in Scotland – it is mountaineering. From where the Aonach Eagach abuts on to Stob Ghabhar's south-east ridge it's only a short pull to the summit. Descend the south-east ridge back to the Allt Toaig.

Route Summary: From Forest Lodge (Route A) follow the track which leads W along the N bank of the Abhainn Shira. Reach a small corrugated iron hut after about 600m and take the path which runs N from it beside the Allt Toaig. At GR252446, the path crosses another burn and W of it a broad ridge lifts up to Beinn Toaig and the wide plateau-like ridge which is crowned by the summit of Stob a' Choire Odhair. Descend W to a wide knolly bealach, continue W uphill, then turn SW, up steep slopes to reach a ridge called the Aonach Eagach. Follow this ridge, which is narrow and exposed in places, to where it meets the broad SE ridge of Stob Ghabhar. Follow this to the summit. Return by way of the SE ridge

Map: OS Sheet 50: GR258461, GR230455

Access Point: Forest Lodge, GR271423

Distance: 20km, 1380m ascent

Approx Time: 6-8 hours

Translation: peak of the goat; peak of the dun-coloured corrie

Pronunciation: stob a kora ooer; stop gower

Creise (50), 1100m/3609ft, Meall a' Bhuiridh (45), 1108m/3635ft

Gaze across at these hills from the Black Corries on the edge of the Rannoch Moor, and together with the deep defile of Glen Etive and the familiar triangular shape of the Buachaille Etive Mor you have one of the finest mountain panoramas in Scotland. Creise itself is a steep-sided hill which offers some superlative scrambling up the steep north nose of Sron na Creise. The rocky ribs which spill down eastwards into the Cam Gleann provide an easier way to the top, although there is still good scrambling to be found here too.

Route Summary: From the mouth of the Cam Ghleann gain the rocky slopes of Sron na Creise (Route B). Contour W to avoid rocky difficulties and ascend steep slabs to Stob a' Ghlais Choire, the start of the main ridge which runs to Stob Ghabhar. Follow the corrie rim round to a curved crest which rises to Creise. Follow the ridge towards the flat top of Mam Coire Easain. A ridge runs E

Creise (right) and Meall a' Bhuiridh from the north

towards a bealach at the foot of Meall a' Bhuiridh. Navigation can be tricky in poor conditions and cornices can pose problems in winter. Climb to summit of Meall a' Bhuiridh then go back to Blackrock Cottage by way of the ski paraphernalia

Map: OS Sheet 41

Access Point: Blackrock Cottage, GR268531.

Distance: 13km, 970m ascent

Approx Time: 4-6 hours

Translation: unknown; hill of the rutting stags

Pronunciation: kraysh, mowl a vooree

Route Summary: From Elleric take the track past the house to a bridge on the River Ure near Glenure House (Route A). Beyond the house take the steeply rising ground SSE as the most direct ascent to the summit ridge.

Map: OS Sheet 50

Access Point: Elleric, GR035489

Distance: 6km, 930m ascent

Approx Time: 3-5 hours

Translation: unknown

Pronunciation: byn skoolard

Start at Blackrock Cottage, the Scottish Ladies Climbing Club hut on the road which leads to the White Corries ski grounds. Cross the heather moorland around the top of Creag Dhubh to the mouth of the Cam Ghleann to gain the rocky slopes of Sron na Creise. Contour west to avoid rocky difficulties and ascend steep grass and scree slopes to Stob a' Ghlais Choire, the start of the main ridge which eventually terminates at Stob Ghabhar in the south. Follow the corrie rim round to a curved crest which rises to Creise. Follow the ridge towards the flat top of Mam Coire Easain. An interesting stony rib offers a way of escape from the ridge towards a bealach which leads to Meall a' Bhuiridh. Take care in poor conditions as navigation can be tricky and cornices can pose problems hereabouts. Climb to the summit of Meall a' Bhuiridh and then descend to Blackrock Cottage by way of the ski grounds.

Beinn Sgulaird (237), 937m/3074ft

Rising from sea level at the head of Loch Creran, Beinn Sgulaird is a fine vantage point for gazing out towards the hills of Mull. It's a big hill, a long ridge of almost three kilometres in length, much of it over the 800-metre mark. Many walkers simply walk up steep slopes from Elleric, bag the summit and return but this does the hill a great injustice for while the ridge certainly doesn't offer the thrill or exposure of an Aonach Eagach it is nevertheless a fine high-level promenade with extensive views.

I would recommend a north to south traverse, simply because the best views are to the west. From Glenure cross the bridge and climb the long and steep slopes to the summit – the higher you climb the rockier is the terrain. A more interesting alternative is to follow the River Ure, on its south bank, above its fine wooded gorge to where it is joined by the Allt Bealach na h-Innsig. Leave the river now, head south through some woods and climb to the small bealach between Sgulaird and its outlier, Stob Goibhre.

The summit itself lies at the north end of the ridge, and the long gently curving ridge is full of little ups and downs and rocky outcrops. Descend the west ridge and just before the little knoll at 480m turn north and make for the farm at Taravocan. From here a footpath runs back to Glenure via Loch Baile Mhic Chailein.

Beinn Fhionnlaidh (198), 959m/3146ft

Another of those hills described as shy and retiring, Beinn Fhionnlaidh is positively misanthropic! Midway between the head of Glen Creran and Glen Etive, it is defended on its Glen Etive approaches by massive forestry plantations and I must confess that directions which include plodding up forestry fire-breaks leave me cold. The Glen Creran side offers a more benevolent approach, but a long one up Fhionnlaidh's six-kilometre ridge – a ridge of multiple false summits. On the positive side the schistose rock is interlaced in places by great bands of limestone which provide the basis for some magnificent Alpine plants. Much of the ridge itself is rocky and is strewn with erratics, and as you climb the view northwards towards Glencoe gradually opens up to provide a rich panorama of the old area of Appin.

Leave Glenure and take the footpath past the woodland and on to the open hill at the foot of the Leac Bharainn. From there it's simply a case of following the narrowing ridge to the summit.

Route Summary: Start at Glenure (see access for Beinn Sgulaird), and take the lower grassy slopes in a NE direction towards Leac Bharainn (Route B). Above this the obvious W ridge rises gradually to the summit of Beinn Fhionnlaidh. Descend the same way. An ascent from Glen Etive, once the popular route to the summit, cannot now be recommended because of Forestry Commission activities

Map: OS Sheet 41

Access Point: Elleric, GR035489

Distance: 15km, 950m ascent

Approx Time: 5-7 hours

Translation: Finlay's Hill

Pronunciation: byn yoonly

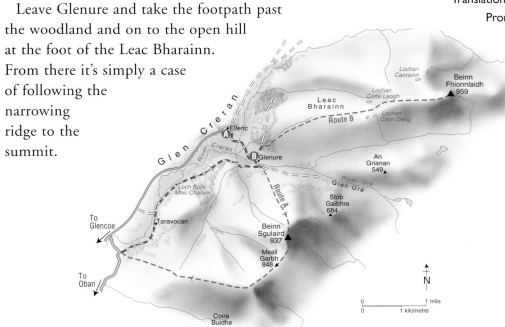

GLENCOE

The Munros:

Sgor na h-Ulaidh   Buachaille Etive Mor (Stob Dearg, Stob na Broige)
Buachaille Etive Beag (Stob Dubh, Stob Coire Raineach)   Bidean nam Bian
Stob Coire Sgreamhach   Aonach Eagach (Meall Dearg, Sgor nam
Fiannaidh)   Beinn a' Bheithir (Sgorr Dhearg, Sgorr Dhonuill)

The Glencoe peaks are well known and loved and it's wise to disregard the description of this as the Glen of Weeping, usually given for tourists' benefit. The Massacre of Glencoe was a dreadful betrayal of hospitality, but was no worse than many others which took place throughout Highland history. Despite the tourism it's a wonderful place, introduced by the majestic Buachaille Etive Mor, and dominated by the high Bidean massif in the south and the spectacular wall of the Aonach Eagach ridge to the north. For many, including myself, this is the spiritual home of Scottish mountaineering.

Sgor na h-Ulaidh (149), 994m/3261ft

The Lost Mountain of Glencoe, Sgor na h-Ulaidh hides its not inconsiderable charms behind the Bidean massif and its long protective ridge, Aonach Dubh a' Ghlinne. The usual way of ascent is to follow the Land Rover track all the way to Gleann-leac-na-muidhe and then follow the Allt na Muidhe halfway up its glen before climbing the west slopes of Aonach Dubh a' Ghlinne to Stob an Fhurain and then the Munro.

A more interesting approach climbs the prominent prow of Aonach Dubh a' Ghlinne, seen clearly from the A82 at Achnacon. It's a steep climb, no doubt about that, but after the initial exertion you can wander happily along the ridge and pour scorn on those climbing the long slopes from the glen below you.

From Stob an Fhurain, a steep descent drops to a high and rocky col, from where very rocky ground leads to the summit of Sgor na h-Ulaidh.

Great care is required in the descent of this hill. Don't try and escape northwards until you have descended west to Corr na Beinne where steep ground takes you to a col from which you can easily walk down to the headwaters of the Allt na Muidhe. If you feel particularly energetic, the Corbett of Meall Ligiche can be

Route Summary: Follow the Land Rover track which follows the W bank of the Allt na Muidhe (Route A). Not far before the cottage of Gleann-leac-na-muidhe leave the track and take to the steep prow of Aonach Dubh a' Ghlinne, a fierce ascent which threads through several rocky outcrops. Continue S on the ridge to the top of Stob an Fhuarain. Descend SW to the bealach and follow the remains of an ancient wall and fence along the crest of the ridge up increasingly rocky ground to the summit. From the summit continue W to the spur of Corr na Beinne and carefully descend its steep N slopes to a col. From here easy slopes to the NE take you to the headwaters of the Allt na Muidhe

Map: OS Sheet 41

Access Point: Achnacon, GR118565

Distance: 13km, 1100m ascent

Approx Time: 4-6 hours

The Glencoe mountains from the air, looking north-east from above Beinn Maol Chaluim

Buachaille Etive Mor from the east

Translation: peak of the treasure
Pronunciation: skor na hoolya

easily linked to this Munro to make a particularly fine high-level horseshoe round Gleann na Muidhe.

Route Summary: Follow a track to the bridge over the River Coupall (Route B) and pass the white-washed climbers' hut called Lagangarbh. Take the right fork in the path and continue into Coire na Tulaich following the path on the W bank of the burn. Follow the path up the corrie to its head where scree slopes offer difficult access to a flat bealach. Turn E and cross red and pink boulders and scree trending E then NE along a ridge which narrows appreciably towards the summit. The complete traverse of the Buachaille Etive Mor ridge is a rewarding walk, from Stob Dearg to Stob na Broige,

Buachaille Etive Mor (Stob Dearg (110), 1021m/3350ft; Stob na Broige (207), 956m/3136ft)

In the few polls that have been taken to determine the most popular mountains in Scotland, the Buachaille Etive Mor has never failed to reach the top five. This impressive cornerstone between Glen Etive and Glen Coe rises in a resplendent squat pyramid, the epitome of mountain grandeur which throws down its gauntlet to every passer-by. Its great walls, ridges and gullies present an air of impregnability, offering few lines of weakness, although there is one, used mainly by climbers, which is an impressive route for the walker who doesn't mind exposure and is happy to use his or her hands. A curved ridge sneaks its way up from near the base of the mountain following the crest of a broad, solid ridge. It is a scrambling route, but the holds are big, generous and plentiful.

GLENCOE

The walker's breach in the Buachaille's defences is Coire na Tulaich, directly behind the SMC's hut at Langangarbh. A track crosses the River Coupall by a footbridge and makes its steep way up into the depths of the corrie. Beetling crags rise above as the track begins to zigzag onto steep scree slopes and care is required on the final 100m or so of the ridge.

As you top-out on the ridge you'll see the other tops of Buachaille Etive Mor which is in essence a long ridge containing four tops. Stob Dearg lies to the left, up a rough boulder-strewn path. As you approach the summit cairn the ridge begins to narrow in a rather satisfying way and after one or two false summits you'll reach the large cairn which appears to sit on the very edge of nothing. From Stob Dearg, continue in a SW direction along the ridge, over Stob na Doire and Stob Coire Altruim to the Buachaille's other Munro, Stob na Broige. Return over Stob Coire Altruim and descend into the Lairig Gartain from the bealach between Altruim and Stob na Doire, and by way of the footpath back to Altnafeadh.

returning to Altnafeadh by the Lairig Gartain pass to the NNW

Map: OS Sheet 41

Access Point: Altnafeadh, GR221563

Distance: 11km, 1001m ascent

Approx Time: 6-8 hours

Translation: big herdsman of Etive; red peak; lively peak

Pronunciation: booachil etiv moar; stop jerrack; stop na broo-ka

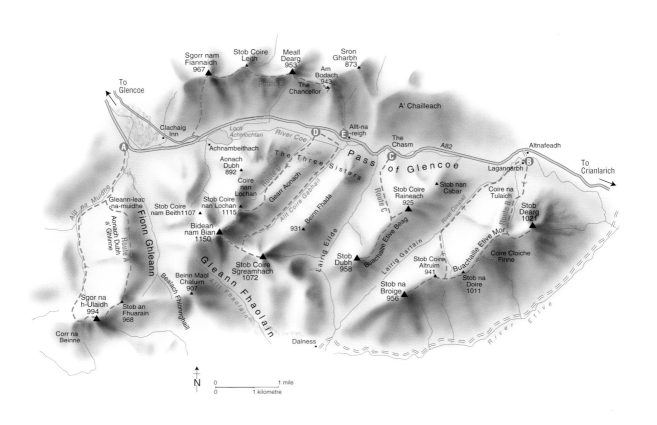

Route Summary: Follow the signpost which indicates the right of way from Lairig Eilde to Glen Etive (Route C). Take the path for about 400m before leaving it for the open hillside in a S direction. Head for the bealach to the SW of Stob Coire Raineach, and then climb this Munro. Follow the obvious ridge onwards to Stob Dubh at the end of the Buachaille Etive Beag ridge. An alternative route climbs Stob Dubh from Dalness in Glen Etive and takes the hill's SSW ridge

Map: OS Sheet 41

Access Point: A82 road, GR188563

Distance: 10km, 840m ascent

Approx Time: 4-6 hours

Translation: small herdsman of Etive; peak of the corrie of ferns; black peak

Pronunciation: booachil etiv bek; stop kora ran-ach; stop doo

Buachaille Etive Beag (Stob Coire Raineach (263), 925m/3035ft; Stob Dubh (201), 958m/3143ft)

The big herdsman's little brother, Buachaille Etive Beag does share a family resemblance but generally lacks all the great features of the bigger hill. Only when viewed from lower Glen Etive do the two hills resemble twins.

Unlike the summit of Buachaille Etive Mor, Stob Dearg, which looks down on the A82 road across the Rannoch Moor, the wee Buachaille reserves its highest point, Stob Dubh, as far from the road as possible, at the end of its 4-km ridge, although the promotion of Stob Coire Raineach to Munro status now gives Buachaille Etive Beag two Munros, one at either end of its ridge. The trade route to the hill runs from the north, from the A82 Glencoe road, but an alternative, shorter route, begins at Dalness in Glen Etive and climbs Stob Dubh directly, and steeply, by its south-west ridge.

Most folk go in from the Chasm, that narrow part of the A82 which has been gouged from the bare rock. Follow the sign into the Lairig Eilde and take the muddy footpath for about half a kilometre before taking to the hill in a rough southerly direction. Climb steepening slopes to the bealach immediately south-west of Stob Coire Raineach and follow the rocky slopes to the summit. Return to the bealeach and follow the ridge in a south-west direction over a minor top and along the now narrowing ridge to Stob Dubh.

Route Summary: Take the path leading into Coire nan Lochan and follow it as it climbs to the Lochans at the head of the Coire. Climb the E ridge of Stob Coire nan Lochan to the summit, descend the SW ridge and climb directly to the summit of Bidean nam Bian. Follow the obvious ridge SE to Stob Coire Sgreamhach. Descend via Coire Gabhail.

Map: OS Sheet 41

Access Point: A82 road GR171568

Distance: 12km, 1090m ascent

Approx Time: 4-7 hours

Translation: peak of the mountains; peak of the fearful corrie

Pronunciation: beetyan nam beeoan; stop korra skree-yach

Bidean nam Bian (23), 1150m/3773ft
Stob Coire Sgreamhach (65), 1072m/3517ft

Bidean nam Bian is the highest hill in the old county of Argyll and retires rather shyly behind its outliers. This Peak of the Mountains is well named for its summit is thrown up by four great ridges which give way to no less than nine separate summits and cradle three deep and distinctive corries. A number of alternative routes ascend Bidean nam Bian but one or two have been over-promoted and have suffered accordingly.

My favourite route is by Coire nan Lochan below the great crags of the east face of Aonach Dubh. A good path runs all the way to the head of the corrie where three lochans reflect the steep crags above which lead to Stob Coire nan Lochan. A path follows the east ridge to the summit and from there a steep descent followed by another steep and rocky climb leads directly to Bidean nam Bian.

Follow the ridge south-east as far as the bealach above Coire Gabhail. From here steep, rocky slopes lead to the sharp summit of Stob Coire Sgreamhach. To descend, retrace your steps back to the bealach above Coire Gabhail. Descend steeply (much erosion) into the corrie and follow the footpath all the way down its length. Descend through the trees and a great jumble of glaciated boulders to where the path crosses the river. Another path drops you down to the footbridge over the River Coe and then back to the layby beside the A82.

Bidean nam Bian and Loch Achtriochtan

Aonach Eagach Ridge: Meall Dearg (212) 953m/3127ft, Sgorr nam Fiannaidh (188), 967m/3173ft

The huge, broken and gully-riven wall that forms the northern barrier of Glen Coe is well named the Notched Ridge. More than three kilometres long and with two Munros it also offers several heart-stopping moments if you're not used to exposure.

A sign-posted path climbs quickly up behind the house at Allt-na-reigh and takes you all the way to the main ridge at the saddle north-east of the Am Bodach summit. From here you get your first view of the sinuous, rocky ridge – a daunting sight. It's a

Route Summary: Follow the path behind the house of Allt-na-reigh up the grassy slopes of Am Bodach (Route E). There are a few rocky outcrops but these can be avoided on the E. To reach the crest of the Aonach Eagach ridge follow the edge of the crags to the left of Am Bodach's cairn in a WNW direction. A sudden drop with a 15m scramble on good but polished holds starts the ridge traverse proper. Follow the crest of the

Aonach Eagach Ridge from the east

ridge to the grassy hump of Meall Dearg. From Meall Dearg follow the line of fence posts along the crest and then traverse the Crazy Pinnacles. This involves some exposed scrambling on the most sensational section of the ridge. After the Pinnacles more fence posts accompany you on the long pull to Stob Coire Leith, before the ridge levels out towards the second Munro, Sgorr nam Fiannaidh. It is advised to descend due S of this summit, picking a route with care through rocky outcrops and grassy slopes. The alternative descent is further W of the summit and follows a very eroded path on the W side of Clachaig Gully

Map: OS Sheet 41

Access Point: Allt-na-reigh, GR176566

Distance: 6km, 914m ascent

Approx Time: 3-5 hours

Translation: notched ridge; red hill; peak of the fair haired warriors.

Pronunciation: oenoch egoch; myowl d-yerrack; sgor nam feeanee

switchbacked fin of rock and grass, steep-sided and exposed, with occasional pinnacles posing as obstacles at points along the way. Wonderful! Sadly you've little time to ease yourself gently into the difficulties – a sudden drop appears, with about 15m of scrambling on fairly polished rock, but it looks worse than it is. Face inwards, and look for the holds – they're there all right, and soon you'll be traversing on good holds on to the crest of the ridge where an easy gradient takes you on to a top beyond which lie the slopes to the first Munro, Meall Dearg.

The next section, the Crazy Pinnacles, is best. Follow the obvious path and the crampon marks on the rock and enjoy the easy scrambling. The final two pinnacles offer the most exposed scrambles, before a dip in the ridge immediately before Stob Coire Leith indicates the end of the difficulties. It's now an easy walk on a broad ridge to the second of the Munros, Sgorr nam Fiannaidh. Descend due south of this summit, picking your way with care through some rocky outcrops and down for a well-earned pint in the Clachaig Inn.

The path, on the west side of Clachaig Gully has a lot of loose stones and rock on it and there is a danger of knocking scree into the gully, putting other climbers at risk. There is also the danger of actually falling into the gully; there have been several fatalities at this point in recent years.

Beinn a' Bheithir (Sgorr Dhearg (107), 1024m/3360ft, Sgorr Dhonuill (137), 1001m/3284ft)

This dramatically named Hill of the Thunderbolt rises gracefully above the narrows of Loch Leven at Ballachulish, a fine mountain in every sense, made up of two peaks on a long, curving ridge forming magnificent north-facing corries.

Forestation has caused considerable access problems to these peaks and you're as well to use the forest tracks to their best advantage. A forest road rises steadily into the Gleann a' Chaolais and after a kilometre or so it begins to zigzag up some steeper ground. Just past an old quarry you'll reach a crossroads – cross over until you reach a concrete bridge over a burn and just east of the stream you'll find a small cairn which marks the start of a boggy path through the trees.

Eventually you'll break clear of the conifers and the path continues up to the high col between the two peaks. Take your choice of which peak to go for first, both offer a good rocky climb and you'll have to return to the col from both of them.

A good alternative descent is to climb Sgorr Dhonuill first, return to the col and climb Sgorr Dhearg, continue round the head of the corrie to descend down Dhearg's north ridge. A good footpath eventually twists its way down the blunt nose of the ridge and deposits you in the forest above the old manse and church east of the Ballachulish Bridge.

Route Summary: Leave the road about 800m W of the Ballachulish Bridge on a minor road which leads you to some houses at the foot of Gleann a' Chaolais. Cars can be left here. Follow Forestry Commission road S and after a while it zigzags up steeper ground, passes an old quarry and comes to a crossroads. Go straight across, round another bend, over a bridge and cross a burn at GR 047569. A cairn by the track indicates the path which climbs SE through the forest and on to the open hillside above the trees. Climb S to the obvious bealach between the two peaks of Beinn a' Bheithir, Sgorr Dhonuill on your right and Sgorr Dhearg on your left. Both peaks are easily reached from the bealach

Map: OS Sheet 41

Access Point: A828, GR044595

Distance: 16km, 1210m ascent

Approx Time: 5-8 hours

Translation: hill of the thunderbolt; red peak; Donald's peak

Pronunciation: byn vair; sgor d-yerrack; sgor ghawil

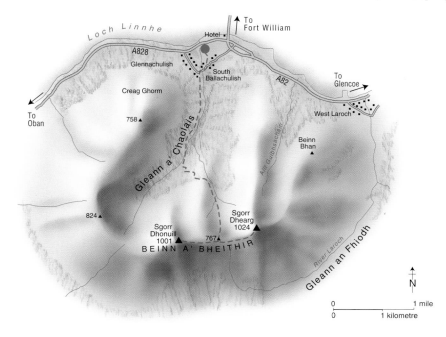

THE MAMORES

The Munros:

Sgurr Eilde Mor   Binnein Beag   Binnein Mor   Na Gruagaichean
An Gearanach   Stob Coire a' Chairn   Am Bodach
Sgurr a' Mhaim   Stob Ban   Mullach nan Coirean

Stretching on for fully 15km, the ridge of the Mamores creates a high, corrie-bitten wall between Glen Nevis in the north and Loch Leven in the south. As a complete traverse it is a long and airy walk along a narrow and curving ridge with very few difficulties to hold up progress. The only real scramble in the entire ridge is the dramatically named Devil's Ridge between the tops of Sgor an Iubhair and Stob Choire a' Mhail, and even that poses little problem in good conditions. In winter snows it demands a little more respect!

Most hillwalkers will satisfy their hunger with bite-sized Mamore chunks and the formation of the ridge breaks down nicely into three superb outings of different character. Another fine characteristic of the Mamores is that they are well served by a fine network of stalkers' paths which can be used to access the main ridge. To make the best use of these, base yourself at Kinlochleven. Alternatively, the big car park at Polldubh in Glen Nevis gives access through the Nevis Gorge to Steall and upper Glen Nevis, north of the Mamore ridge.

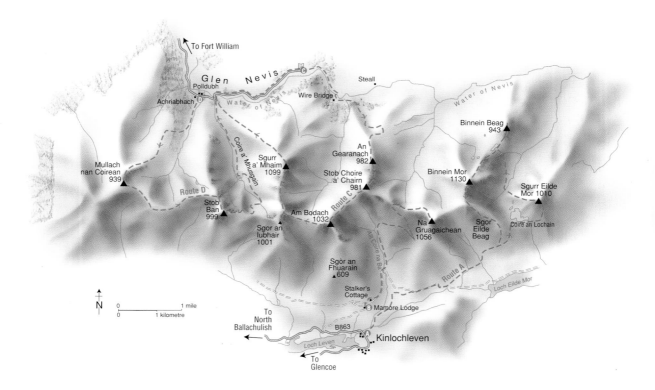

The Mamores – looking west from Na Gruagaichean, north top

Sgurr Eilde Mor (123), 1010m/3314ft, Binnein Beag (230), 943m/3094ft, Binnein Mor (27), 1130m/3707ft

Sgurr Eilde Mor is the most easterly Munro of the Mamores and, of the ten Munros that make up the long Mamores ridge, Sgurr Eilde Mor and its near neighbour, Binnein Beag, are probably the most awkwardly placed for the Munro-bagger intent on climbing a handful or more in one outing.

A good path leaves the village of Kinlochleven past St Paul's Episcopal church and climbs the wooded hillside to the track that runs between Mamore Lodge and Luibelt. Just west of Loch Eilde Mor a stalkers' path leaves the main track, an old and well-used path. As it traverses the south slopes of Sgor Eilde Beag, it tightens up considerably before zigzagging into another traverse that drops you into the atmospheric hollow that cradles Coire an Lochain. Sgurr Eilde Mor is easily climbed from here by its south ridge. Descend by the steep and rocky west ridge to Coire an Lochain and the stalkers' path on the west side of the loch, which descends slightly from Loch Eilde Mor before climbing onto the broad bealach that separates the two Binneins. Binnein Beag is a straightforward climb from here. Return, by the same route, to the bealach before traversing the north-east slopes of Binnein Mor to reach its north ridge, a long, narrow highway that climbs to an impressively narrow summit with barely enough room on it for the cairn. From the un-named summit a broader ridge takes you down Sgor Eilde Beag from where a wonderfully engineered stalkers' path will drop you back to the outward path from Kinlochleven.

Route Summary: Pass E of church (Route A). Turn left and follow paths through a gate, to a bridge over the burn. The path deteriorates as it climbs through woodland onto the open moor. When the path joins the main Loch Eilde Mor track turn right onto it and follow it round a hairpin bend. A path leaves the track NE and rises above the loch, crossing S slopes of Sgor Eilde Beag before descending into Coire an Lochain. Climb Sgurr Eilde Mor by its S ridge, then back to Coire an Lochain by the W ridge. The path descends NW, then crosses the slopes of Binnein Mor to a wide col below Binnein Beag. Leave path and climb rocky slopes to the summit. Descend to the col, then climb slopes to Binnein Mor's N ridge, follow it to the summit. Continue S along ridge to S top then SE to Sgor Eilde Beag. Descend S to a stalkers' path down to the outward path

Map: OS Sheet 41

Access Point: Car park beside St Paul's church, Kinlochleven

Distance: 20km, 1620m ascent

Approx Time: 8-9 hours

Translation: big peak of the hind; small peak; big peak

Pronunciation: skoor alta moar; beenyan beck; beenyan moar

Na Gruagaichean (74), 1056m/3465ft

Route Summary: From car park, follow track around the stalker's cottage (Route B). Follow main track for 1km to a junction at a bridge over the Allt Coire na Ba. Go left and follow the path up the corrie. It swings to the right before traversing N to the main Mamores ridge. Follow ridge SE onto the NW top of Na Gruagaichean, follow summit ridge S and into a deep gap before climbing to the main summit. Retrace route over NW top down to the low point of the ridge, returning by the outward route

Map: OS Sheet 41

Access Point: Car park of the Mamore Lodge Hotel (£3 parking fee payable at the bar)

Distance: 9km, 1050m ascent

Approx Time: 4-6 hours

Translation: the maidens

Pronunciation: na grooakeechan

The twin tops of Na Gruagaichean make up one of the most imposing peaks on the Mamores ridge. A stalkers' path climbs up to the Mamores ridge less than 1.6km north-west of Na Gruagaichean's summit, and starts, very conveniently, about 800m north-east of the Mamore Lodge Hotel above Kinlochleven. The main track, just north of the hotel, runs for 1km to a path junction at a bridge over the Allt Coire na Ba. A footpath leaves the track here and runs past some sheep pens all the way up the corrie, swinging away to the right before traversing north again to reach the main Mamores ridge. From here it's a straightforward climb onto the NW top of Na Gruagaichean. Follow the summit ridge south, down into a deep gap before climbing steeply to the main summit. Return to the north-west top and down to the low point of the ridge before following the path back down Coire na Ba to Mamore Lodge.

The summit of Stob Coire a' Chairn is easily reached along the main ridge and a good horseshoe route could easily include Na Gruagaichean, Stob Coire a' Chairn and Am Bodach.

An Gearanach (166), 982m/3222ft, Stob Choire a' Chairn (171), 981m/3218ft, Am Bodach (99), 1032m/3386ft, Sgurr a' Mhaim (51), 1099m/3606ft

Route Summary: Follow path to Steall (Route C). Cross wire bridge over Water of Nevis, go E past the hut, past the waterfall and a wooded buttress, then S up a small glen. The path zigzags on to NNE spur of An Gearanach (unmarked on OS map). Go S from summit to An Garbhanach, then SW to Stob Choire a' Chairn. The ridge links SW to Am Bodach, then WNW to Sgor an Iubhair. To the N, the Devil's Ridge links with Stob Choire a' Mhail, then open slopes to summit slopes of Sgurr a' Mhaim and a long descent to Glen Nevis

Map: OS Sheet 41

Access Point: Glen Nevis, Polldubh car park

Distance: 14km, 1220m ascent

Approx Time: 7-8 hours

Translation: the complainer; peak of the corrie of the cairn; the old man; peak of the large rounded hill

Pronunciation: an gyeranach; stob corrie a cairn; am podach; skor a vaim

Collectively known as the Ring of Steall, these Munros form a great horseshoe around Coire a' Mhail. Seven tops over 914m (3000ft) make up this superb round, all linked by high, narrow ridges.

From the car park at Polldubh a track weaves through the trees above the deep and noisy Nevis Gorge, a place that WH Murray once described as the 'best half mile in Scotland'. It is truly splendid, made even more impressive by your sudden arrival at Steall meadows. In a total contrast to the confines of the gorge, the green grass of Steall opens out in a wide plain, backed by the 90m white slash of the Grey Mare's Tail above the old cottage.

Many suggest that the Ring of Steall is best walked in an anti-clockwise direction but I would disagree. Far better to cross the wire bridge at Steall and follow the river east to where it is joined by the Allt Coire na Gabhalach. Follow the path up the glen to reach the An Gearanach ridge. From here you start a long, high-level promenade with some fabulous views of the Ben, the Aonachs and the Grey Corries and south across Loch Leven to the Glen Coe hills and beyond.

Fine narrow ridges connect with Stob Choire a' Chairn, Am Bodach, Sgor an Iubhair, the tight and exposed Devil's Ridge (no great difficulties in good conditions, it can be tricky in winter) to Stob Coire a' Mhail and then the wide quartzite-covered slopes of Sgurr a' Mhaim and the long descent back to Polldubh by the north-north-east slopes.

Stob Ban (140), 999m/3277ft, Mullach nan Coirean (236), 939m/3081ft

These two Munros are rich in contrast – one is craggy and rugged, the other whalebacked and smooth topped. A good footpath carries you high above Achriabhach and into the tight confines of Coire a' Mhusgain. Higher up the corrie opens out and you begin to feel the presence of Stob Ban. Towering from its gradual northern ridge it begins to dominate the scene, great scree runnels splitting the steep slopes into a complete system of buttresses and crags, the topmost ones sparkling white in the sun – not the effect of snow but of quartzite.

Stob Ban and Mullach nan Coirean from the air

Soon the path begins to zigzag up the western slopes of Sgurr a' Mhaim and into the head of Coire a' Mhusgain, a wonderful spot complete with a lochan. The footpath crosses the stream well below the lochan and joins up with a stalkers' path that soon dwindles out on the southern slopes of Stob Ban. Continue up the north-east ridge to where a short walk takes you to the summit.

As you descend from the summit of Stob Ban you'll notice the white quartz is replaced by red granite. Follow the rim of the north-facing corries, cross a subsidiary top and then climb the final few metres to the flat-topped Mullach. When you descend check that you take the east ridge – many walkers head directly down the north ridge to reach impenetrable forest far down Glen Nevis. The east ridge eventually swings north and you can either drop down the steep eastern slopes of this ridge to the Allt a' Choire Dheirg and back to Achriabhach, or follow the ridge down to the edge of the forest where a small cairn indicates a route through the trees to a forest drive.

Route Summary: From Achriabhach (Route D), take path through trees which later joins the forestry road. Reach NNE ridge of Mullach, follow to the summit. Descend along ridge SE then S to the SE top. The ridge drops E to the col between the two mountains. Climb E then S up boulders and screes to the summit of Stob Ban. Take E ridge to the head of Coire a' Mhusgain and the stalkers' path N back to Achriabhach

Map: OS Sheet 41

Access Point: Achriabhach

Distance: 14km, 1220m ascent

Approx Time: 5-7 hours

Translation: light-coloured peak; summit of the corries

Pronunciation: stob baan; mullach nan kooran

BEN NEVIS, THE AONACHS AND THE GREY CORRIES

The Munros:

Ben Nevis   Carn Mor Dearg   Aonach Beag
Aonach Mor   Stob Ban   Stob Choire Claurigh
Stob Coire an Laoigh   Sgurr Choinnich Mor

Together with the Mamores, these hills make up the Round of Glen Nevis, one of the great challenges for marathon walkers, but most people will be more than happy to break them down into three or even four outings.

Ben Nevis, Britain's highest hill, can be one of two things: a long, dull plod up the tourist route which in itself is more of a facility than an amenity, or an exciting expedition via Carn Mor Dearg and its superb scythe-like arête, taking the walker high above the Allt a' Mhuillin to gaze upon the incredible north-east faces of this majestic mountain. Really, there's no comparison.

The two Aonachs have been tamed a little by the creation of the Aonach Mor ski development but it's easy to enjoy a day on these hills without coming into contact with any of the paraphernalia at all, and the Grey Corries, like the Mamores, form a long switchbacked ridge of remote and classic proportions.

Fort William makes the best base for these hills, although Spean Bridge or Roy Bridge are best for the Grey Corries.

Ben Nevis (1), 1344m/4409ft, Carn Mor Dearg (9), 1220m/4003ft

There are several routes to the summit of Ben Nevis and all of them are infinitely preferable to the Tourist Route via the Half-Way Lochan. Sadly, the vast majority of folk who climb Ben Nevis never see the real guts of the mountain, but perhaps they wouldn't want to. The north-east crags, buttresses and spires reflect a totally different impression of the mountain, an aspect that is mean and demanding, a gaunt face of, to quote one writer, 'loveless loveliness'.

I can empathise with that quote – there is a sometimes fatal attraction in such places – it is a cold, mean and bare mountain face and all the more attractive for it. Here man realises his own stature, his own insignificance, his mortality – he may come and climb the long buttresses, the big ridges, the steep faces, but he is

Route Summary: Leave Achintee and follow the obvious Ben Nevis track (Route A) as far as Lochan Meall an t-Suidhe. The track to Ben Nevis continues on a series of broad zigzags above but to reach Carn Mor Dearg continue past the loch around the flanks of Carn Dearg to drop down into the valley of the Allt a' Mhuilin. Cross the river near point GR154739 and climb E up rough bouldery slopes to Carn Beag Dearg. Continue SSE on ridge over Carn Dearg Meadhonach to Carn Mor Dearg. To continue to Ben Nevis follow the ridge S and cross the Carn Mor Dearg Arête. Where the arête abuts

Ben Nevis from the air, looking south-west from above Aonach Mor

on to the bulk of Ben Nevis, climb W over blocks and boulders to the summit. Take care in this area in conditions of snow cover: many walkers have slipped from this point into Coire Leis below

Map: OS Sheet 41

Access Point: Achintee

Distance: 20.8km, 1769m ascent

Approx Time: 7-10 hours :

Translation: possibly venomous mountain; big red hill

Pronunciation: byn nevis; caarn more jerrack

never the conqueror. Not on Ben Nevis.

To climb the Ben without experiencing even a hint of what the north-east face is like, is like going to the beach and never seeing the sea. To far too many walkers Ben Nevis is the sum experience of a long trudge up a stony, artificial track in the company of hundreds of others. For too many the summit means piles of human graffiti in the shape of cairns, ruins, a rusting shelter and a misplaced memento of war.

Far better to leave the tourist track at the Half-Way Lochan, Lochan Meall an t-Suidhe, and continue due north into the glen of the Allt a' Mhuillin. Already you'll be aware of the great cliffs to your right. Don't follow the footpath to the right, up the glen, but instead drop down rough heathery slopes, cross the burn and clamber steeply up the red granite slopes of Carn Beag Dearg. Carn Mor Dearg is another 800m or so along the ridge, which also crosses Carn Dearg Meadhonach.

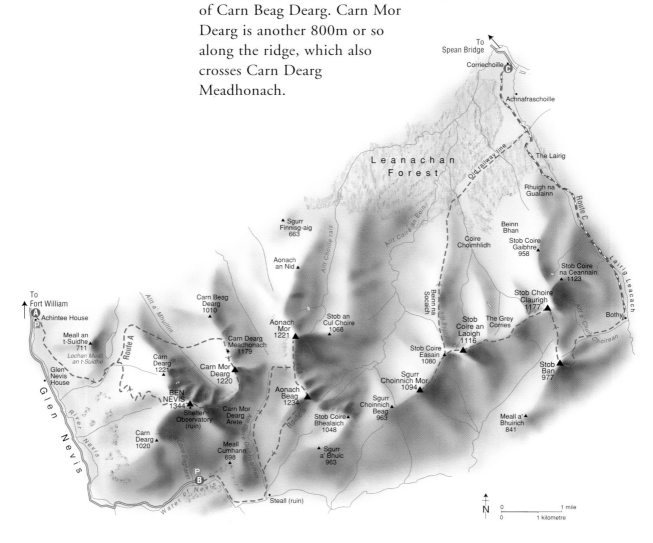

Ben Nevis and the Carn Mor Dearg arête

This crest provides a wonderful high-level walk with superb views across Coire Leis to the frowning crags of the Ben's north-east face.

From Carn Mor Dearg descend south on a rough path to the start of the arête, a high-level exposed ridge which connects the summit with the north-east ridge of Ben Nevis. The great feature of the ridge is its beautifully curved sweep, perfect in its balance and symmetry.

Where the arête eventually merges with the north-east ridge of the Ben a faint track picks its way upwards through a maze of giant boulders to the summit plateau. Pass the huge cairn, the rescue shelter and the ruins of the old weather observatory and make your way carefully across the plateau, especially in wintry weather. Many climbers have mistakenly marched across the plateau and fallen through the cornice into Five Fingers Gully. It's wise to remember that this so-called plateau is really just a wide ridge – accurate navigation is crucial to find the top of the tourist track, back down to Lochan Meall an t-Suidhe and the start at Achintee.

Aonach Beag and An Cul Choire from Stob an Cul Choire

Route Summary: Take the
footpath which runs through
the Nevis Gorge (Route B) to
Steall. Pass the wire bridge and
continue to the bridge and ruin
by the Allt Coire Giubhsachan.
Follow the stream N to the
obvious bealach E of Carn Mor
Dearg. Climb a steep slope E to
the bealach between Aonach
Mor and Aonach Beag. From
the bealach continue N for 1km
over a broad and featureless
ridge to the summit of Aonach
Mor. Return the way you came
to the bealach below Aonach
Beag and climb rocky slopes SE
to the summit. Descend to the
Allt Coire Giubhsachan by the
SW ridge and return to Steall

Map: OS Sheet 41

Access Point: Polldubh car park,
Glen Nevis. GR167691

Aonach Beag (7), 1234m/4049ft, Aonach Mor (8), 1221m/4006ft

The Little Ridge is higher (in terms of height) than the Big Ridge but these names only go to prove that the people who named these hills did so by describing their bulk, not their height. Aonach Beag, as though to confirm its standing as the higher of the two, is also the more interesting mountain.

You can reach these hills by gondola to the Snow Goose gully on the north side of Aonach Mor, from where it is only a short walk to the summit, but I wouldn't recommend it, although the ski uplift is fine in winter, when easy access allows you time to explore, on skis, the great plateau of Aonach Mor, or enjoy an easy trip to Aonach Beag.

Another route to these hills leaves Torlundy on the A82, follows the old British Aluminium Company railway eastwards for about 5km and then takes to the hill to Tom na Sroine, Stob Coire an Fhir Dhuibh, Stob an Cul Choire and a final steepish rib to Aonach Mor itself.

Probably one of the most popular routes starts at Polldubh, follows the wonderful Steall path to the old ruins at the Allt Coire

Giubhsachan, and then follows the burn all the way to the 822m bealach between Carn Mor Dearg and the great wall formed by the western slopes of Aonach Mor. From the bealach a steep climb south-eastwards, then due east, brings you out on the col between the two Aonachs from where it's an easy walk to Aonach Mor. Return to the col, climb Aonach Beag and return to Glen Nevis via the south-west ridge.

Distance: 22.4km, 1488m ascent

Approx Time: 7-10 hours

Translation: little ridge; big (broad) ridge

Pronunciation: oenach bayk; oenach more

Stob Ban (178), 977m/3205ft, Stob Choire Claurigh (15), 1177m/3862ft, Stob Coire an Laoigh (38), 1116m/3661ft, Sgurr Choinnich Mor (52), 1094m/3589ft

These hills, the Grey Corries, make up part of the superb panorama that holds the eye as you drive along the road from Spean Bridge to Roy Bridge in Nether Lochaber, the quartzite summits appearing like the new snows of autumn.

The walk into the Lairig Leacach is an enjoyable one, leaving the forest for the narrow pass with the steep slopes of Stob Coire na Ceannain on one side and the twin Corbetts, Cruach Innse and Sgurr Innse, on the other. Stop for a brew at the bothy and consider the route ahead, a long but easy climb up beside the Allt a' Chuil Choirean into a magnificent upper corrie and the short east-north-east ridge of Stob Ban, a 977m Munro, but dwarfed by its neighbouring Grey Corries.

The descent from Stob Ban to the bealach below Stob Choire Claurigh is very awkward, on moving screes and very loose rock. However it's not a long descent and soon you'll be striding over granite slabs, past a small lochan and on up the rocky slopes of Claurigh.

From here the ridge stretches ahead towards the unmistakable bulk of Ben Nevis, a narrow switchbacked ridge, the whiteness of its quartz illuminating the gloom on dark days. Nowhere is the ridge difficult, there is very little scrambling involved, and it rarely drops below the 1000m contour. Probably the narrowest point is above the Castle, An Caisteil, between Stob Coire Cath na Sine and Stob Coire an Laoigh.

Stob Coire Easain is your departure point from the ridge, but you'll probably want to climb the ridge leading out to Sgurr Choinnich Mor. Unfortunately it's a big drop in height and you have to retrace your steps to Stob Coire Easain, thereby doubling the ascent. Descend by Easain's north ridge, down to the forest and the old railway line which leads you all the way back to Coirechoille.

Route Summary: Take the track past Corriechoille farm and through the forest to the Lairig Leacach (Route C). Follow the track to the hut beside the Allt a' Chuil Choirean. Strike uphill in a SW direction up the ENE ridge of Stob Ban. Follow this ridge to the summit. Take care on the descent to the bealach between Stob Ban and Stob Choire Claurigh as the N slopes are precipitous and very loose. Descend slightly to the W. Above the bealach, there is a sharp pull up to Claurigh on loose scree and blocks. From the summit follow the broad crest W to Stob a' Choire Leith and Stob Coire Cath na Sine, where the ridge narrows considerably, over Caisteil to Stob Coire an Laoigh. The next top on the ridge is Stob Coire Easain, the N ridge of which takes you back to Coirechoille, but first continue on the Grey Corries ridge to Sgurr Choinnich Mor. Return to Easain and follow its N ridge over Beinn na Sachaich and back to Coirechoille

Map: OS Sheet 41

Access Point: Corriechoille, GR252807

Distance: 32km, 2012m ascent

Approx Time: 10-12 hours

Translation: light coloured peak; peak of the corrie of clamouring; peak of the corrie of the calf; big peak of the moss

Pronunciation: stop baan; stop corrie clowree; stop corrie an looee; skoor choanyeech more

LOCH TREIG AND LOCH OSSIAN

The Munros:

Stob a' Choire Mheadhoin   Stob Coire Easain
Stob Coire Sgriodain   Chno Dearg   Beinn na Lap
Sgor Gaibhre   Carn Dearg

These hills border the edges of one of the true wilderness areas of Scotland, the ochreous acres of the vast Rannoch Moor. Loch Treig bites deep into the area, like a long fjord, with the Stob a' Choire Mheadhoin and Stob Coire Easain pair on one side and Stob Coire Sgriodain forming a huge wall on the other. These hills, along with the big rounded hump of Chno Dearg and the vast corrie it shares with Sgriodain, can be easily seen from the Laggan/Spean Bridge road at Tulloch.

More retiring are Beinn na Lap, Sgor Gaibhre and Carn Dearg, true hills of the Rannoch Moor. These can be reached by the marvellous West Highland Railway line, leaving the train at Rannoch or Corrour. The ascent of these hills can make the subject of a marvellous weekend away, in beautiful, remote country with bunkhouse accommodation at Corrour (Morgan's Den), or the Scottish Youth Hostel Association hostel at lovely Loch Ossian. An area for the Munro connoisseur.

Stob a' Choire Mheadhoin (46), 1105m/3625ft,
Stob Coire Easain (39), 1115m/3658ft

Hamish Brown, in his marvellous book Hamish's Mountain Walk, nicknamed these hills 'This Yin' and 'That Yin'. There's an Oriental ring to that and perhaps it is no surprise that these two Munros, lying like Siamese twins to the immediate west of Loch Treig, are joined at the hip by a high bealach.

The minor road from the Laggan/Spean Bridge road at Tulloch to Fersit is a delight, passing the old house where Rudolf Hess was held captive during the war, and the little lochan nearby which always seems to be rippling with rising trout. Near the head of the loch leave the easy walking of the Land Rover track and take to the hill, following easy contours towards the long prominent north-east ridge of Stob a' Choire Mheadhoin. This long ridge rises very sharply in a couple of steep steps, the first over Meall Cian Dearg requiring a bit of easy scrambling. Continue south-south-west to the stony summit of Mheadhoin. Descend south-west down rocky slopes to the bealach and then ascend a rough and rocky ridge west-south-west to Stob Coire Easain. From the

Route Summary: From the dam at the head of Loch Treig climb steep slopes in a SW direction (Route A) to the 760m contour and the open ridge. Climb two small rises and continue SSW to Stob a' Choire Mheadhoin. Descend SW down rocky slopes to the bealach and climb a rock-strewn ridge SSW to Stob Coire Easain. Descend the NW ridge to the open moorland of Coire Laire. Follow the river to the old British Aluminium Company railway track which leads back to Fersit

Map: OS Sheet 41

Access Point: Fersit, GR350782. Tulloch Station is on the Glasgow/Fort William Railway

Distance: 15km, 1006m ascent

Approx Time: 5-7 hours

Stob Coire Easain from above Glen Spean

Translation: peak of the middle corrie; peak of the corrie of the little waterfall

Pronunciation: stop kora vane; stop kora esan

summit cairn follow the steep north-west ridge which drops down to the open moors of Coire Laire. Follow the Allt Laire until you reach another bulldozed track. This leads through a forest plantation and at the far side drop down easy slopes to pick up the old British Aluminium Company railway track which leads leisurely back to your starting point.

Stob Coire Sgriodain (174), 979m/3212ft, Chno Dearg (86), 1046m/3432ft

Route Summary: Take the forestry track E from Fersit (Route B) then take rough ground via various sheep fanks to the S. Climb open slopes then craggy ridge to Sron na

The circuit of these two Munros makes a marvellous ski touring outing, with the big, open corrie between them usually offering great downhill running until well into the spring. From the summit of Chno Dearg there is a run of some 5km with about 750m of descent and even if the snow cover is incomplete, many of the stream beds hold snow well, so by linking these together you can still ski most of the way down.

For the walker, the circuit of the two hills makes a fairly easy day out. Many Munro-baggers are happy to lengthen it by adding Beinn na Lap, although that adds a big descent from the subsidiary top of Meall Garbh southwards and a climb of some 450m to the summit of Beinn na Lap before turning round and having to repeat it to regain the original Chno Dearg route. Alternatively, drop

Stob Coire Easain from the western slopes of Stob a' Choire Mheadhoin

down to Corrour Station from Beinn na Lap and return to Tulloch Station by train.

From the end of the Fersit road follow a forestry road east for about 500m then take rough ground to the south. Climb the rough, open slopes to beyond a small craggy top where the ridge begins to narrow appreciably. Beyond Sron na Garbh-bheinne the ridge flattens and then narrows again before rising to the summit of Stob Coire Sgriodain, with its superb views of Loch Treig and the steep east faces of Stob a' Choire Mheadhoin and Stob Coire Easain. From the summit cairn descend south to an obvious bealach and then south-east to the south top of Sgriodain. Cross bumps and knolls in an east-south-east direction, over a double top and down to another wide bealach with scattered lochans. This all sounds rather confusing but on a clear day the route is quite obvious. In mist it isn't so easy and care should be taken. From the wide bealach easy slopes lead to the subsidiary top of Meall Garbh and from there follow the ridge north-east to the big hump of Chno Dearg. Descend back to Fersit by the obvious north-north-west slopes.

Garbh-bheinne. Follow ridge to Stob Coire Sgriodain. Descend S to bealach and then SE to S top of Sgriodain. Cross more open ground in an ESE direction over a double top and down to another bealach. Climb Meall Garbh. Follow ridge NE to Chno Dearg. Descend easy slopes NNW to Fersit track

Map: OS Sheet 41

Access Point: Fersit, GR350782

Distance: 12km, 914m ascent

Approx Time: 3-5 hours

Translation: peak of the scree corrie; red nut or red hill

Pronunciation: stop kora sgreeadan; knaw jerrack

Beinn na Lap (241), 935m/3068ft

You can make this hill as easy or as difficult as you like – easy by taking the train to Corrour Station and following the track east from the station to Loch Ossian from where you should take the left fork of the track where it splits at the loch and follow it along the north shore. At almost any point before you reach the forestry leave the track and climb the hill's easy angled slopes to the summit ridge.

For a longer, and much more interesting, day take a mountain bike from Fersit and follow the various forestry tracks through the Loch Laggan Forest to reach Strath Ossian above Loch Ghuilbinn. Leave your bike at the bridge over the Allt Feith Thuill and climb the Sron na Cloiche Sgoilte and then head south-west to the summit of Beinn na Lap.

Sgor Gaibhre (208), 955m/3133ft, Carn Dearg (231), 941m/3087ft

These two Munros can be climbed from either Corrour Station on the West Highland Line, or from Rannoch Station further to the south. The advantage of Rannoch is that you're not solely dependent on train times – you can drive there. Park to the north of Loch Eigheach and take the Road to the Isles footpath to the footbridge over the Allt Eigheach. Half a kilometre from here, at a bifurcation in the footpath, take to the lower slopes of Sron Leachd a' Chaorainn which gradually steepen and become narrower until you reach the start of a 3km ridge which leads to the summit of Carn Dearg. All the way along this ridge you can enjoy great views to the west, across the great expanse of the Rannoch Moor towards the distant hills of the Blackmount Deer Forest, or eastwards into Coire Eigheach, the great corrie around which this route forms a great horseshoe.

From the summit take the north-east ridge which drops in a series of steps to the Mam Ban, the White Pass. Continue in an east-north-east direction up easy slopes to Sgor Gaibhre.

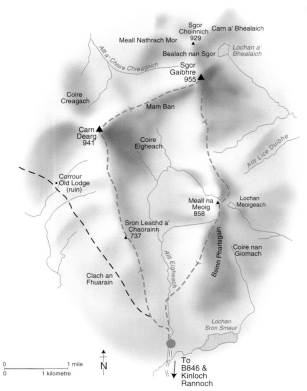

Sgor Gaibhre from Sgor Choinnich

A number of years ago I enjoyed a longer trip following this route to Sgor Gaibhre but instead of completing the horseshoe back to Rannoch I continued north to enjoy the long high-level ridge which leads to Meall a' Bhealaich and Beinn a' Chumhainn. The views from here to the Aonach Beag group in the north and down into the jaws of the Bealach Dubh were magnificent. The parish boundary can then be followed down into the lower reaches of the Bealach Cumhainn and on to Ben Alder Cottage on the shore of Loch Ericht. Next day I made my way back to Rannoch by a series of stalker's paths and rough slopes.

But back to the original horseshoe route. From Sgor Gaibhre follow its south ridge to the Corbett of Meall na Meoig of Beinn Pharlagain, then follow the twisting, undulating ridge to the footbridge over the Allt Eigheach and back to the road.

The route from Corrour takes about 6-8 hours so if you think you can squeeze it in between train times have a go, but in my opinion it's not as fine a route as the one just described. From Corrour, head along the south shore of Loch Ossian to the cottages at the end of the loch. Follow the Uisge Labhair for a short distance before turning south to climb the long, rough slopes of Meall Nathrach Mor. From its summit cross the shallow bealach and climb Sgor Choinnich. Sgor Gaibhre can be easily reached now from the bealach immediately south. Descend west-south-west across the Mam Ban, continue to Carn Dearg and then descend virtually due west to pick up the Road to the Isles footpath back to Corrour.

Dearg. Follow NE ridge to the Mam Ban and climb to Sgor Gaibhre. Follow S ridge over Meall na Meoig of Beinn Pharlagain and continue to the Allt Eigheach

Map: OS Sheet 42

Translation: goat's peak; red hill

Pronunciation: skor gyra; kaarn jarrack

Access Point: Loch Eigheach on the B846 Rannoch Station road

Distance: 25km, 1100m ascent

Approx Time: 7-9 hours

LOCH ERICHT TO LOCH LAGGAN

The Munros:

Carn Dearg   Geal-Charn   Aonach Beag   Beinn Eibhinn
Ben Alder   Beinn Bheoil   Beinn a' Chlachair
Geal Charn   Creag Pitridh

These are amongst the remotest mountains in the Central Highlands and, with the exception of Beinn a' Chlachair, Geal Charn and Creag Pitridh, are best tackled from Loch Pattack/Culra, a good 16km by Land Rover track from Dalwhinnie. Ben Alder and Beinn Bheoil can be climbed from either Culra or from Benalder Cottage in the east.

These hills form the high points in a great tract of land between Loch Laggan and Loch Ericht and although much of it is heavily forested there are no roads and few tracks. Access can be gained by the reinvigorated West Highland Railway, from the station at Corrour, and there is a Youth Hostel at Loch Ossian. This can be the start of a fabulous multi-day expedition taking in the Aonach Beag ridge, the Beinn a' Chlachair trio and Ben Alder and Beinn Bheoil, walking out to Dalwhinnie to return home by train. However you tackle them, you are assured of fine hills making the most of their central position to offer majestic views in all directions.

Carn Dearg (98), 1034m/3392ft, Geal-Charn (26), 1132m/3714ft, Aonach Beag (37), 1116m/3661ft, Beinn Eibhinn (48), 1102m/3615ft

These are remote mountains which come together to provide a worthy ridge walk, full of interest and variety. Many kilometres from the nearest public road these are indeed hills for the connoisseur of isolation and are a good advertisement for the concept of 'the long walk-in'.

When George Oswald was keeper of the Ben Alder estate he would happily allow walkers to drive down Loch Ericht-side as far as Loch Pattack, although he did warn drivers that his white garrons which grazed on the Loch Pattack flats had a liking for chewing wing mirrors. I personally hope that the track down Loch Ericht-side is never open to the public for the 'long walk-in' has a lot going for it. Too many of our hills are being made easy of access, with the

Route Summary: From Culra Bothy climb W and NW on the S flanks of Carn Dearg (Route A) to the summit. Another cairn, slightly S, leads to a ridge which drops to a flat bealach and then rises to Diollaid a' Chairn. Beyond, the ridge narrows and leads to a steep and terraced slope which fronts the plateau of Geal-Charn. Choose a route through the terraces to the plateau and the summit cairn. Beyond, a long slope leads WSW to a grassy bealach. Descend to the bealach and climb to Aonach Beag. At the cairn, turn SW to descend to a narrow bealach above Lochan a' Charra Mhoir. The ascent of Beinn Eibhinn involves a steep

Ben Alder from the air

Beinn Bheoil and Ben Alder from Carn Dearg

pull to the curve of a broad ridge, which in turn rises to the cairn. To return to Culra descend S and E to the Bealach Dubh path and follow it through the Bealach back to the bothy

Map: OS Sheets 41 and 42

Access Point: Culra Bothy, NN523762

Distance: 23km, 1370m ascent

Approx Time: 7-9 hours

Translation: red hill; white hill; small ridge; delightful hill

Pronunciation: caarn jerrack; gyal chaarn; oenach byek; byn ayveen

resulting loss of remoteness and wilderness flavour. What's wrong with riding a mountain bike down the long kilometres?

Using Culra Bothy, 16km from Dalwhinnie, as an access point is the best of many choices. From there climb west and then north-west on the southern flanks of Carn Dearg to the summit. Another cairn, slightly south, leads to the ridge which drops to a flat bealach and then rises to Diollaid a' Chairn. Beyond here the ridge narrows and leads to a steep and terraced buttress-like slope which fronts the plateau of Geal-Charn. Pick a route through the grassy terraces and on to the extensive summit plateau. You may well experience some difficulty locating the summit cairn, even in clear weather. Beyond the cairn a long slope leads west-south-west down to a grassy bealach. Descend to the bealach and climb a short sharp rise to Aonach Beag. At the cairn, turn sharply south-west to descend rough terraces to a narrow bealach above Lochan a' Charra Mhoir. The ascent of Beinn Eibhinn involves a steep pull to the curve of a broad ridge, which in turn rises to the cairn. To return to Culra descend south and east to the Bealach Dubh path and follow it through the Bealach back to the bothy.

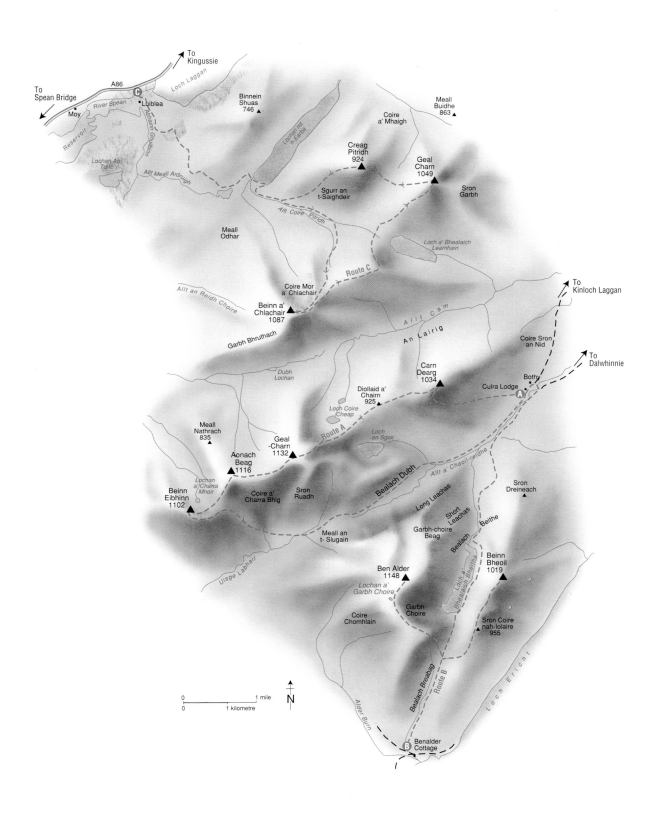

Route Summary: Follow the path on the E bank of the stream behind Benalder Cottage to the Bealach Breabag (Route B). Just short of the summit of the bealach climb the broken and craggy slopes W to a ridge high above the Garbh Choire of Ben Alder. After 800m cross the wide plateau to a high-level lochan and the summit cairn. Return to the Bealach Breabag and climb the short and easy slope to Sron Coire na h-Iolaire. This is a short spur with cairns at either end. To the N of the W cairn a ridge drops to a stony bealach which then rises to the slabby summit slopes of Beinn Bheoil. Return to the Bealach Breabag then via the outward route back to Benalder Cottage

Map: OS Sheet 42

Access Point: Benalder Cottage, GR499680

Distance: 14km, 1070m ascent

Approx Time: 4-6 hours

Translation: hill of the rock water; hill of the mouth

Pronunciation: byn awlder; byn vyawl

Ben Alder (25), 1148m/3766ft, Beinn Bheoil (112), 1019m/3343ft

Ben Alder is a remote mountain, a big bastion of a hill that demands a long walk-in, and I reckon it's all the better for that – it turns an ordinary hill-walk into an expedition and gives the mountain a distinct air of gravitas. A friend of mine was badly frostbitten on Ben Alder a few winters ago and two others severely underestimated the remoteness of the hill and had to be helicoptered out. It's unwise to underestimate Ben Alder.

Ben Alder and Beinn Bheoil form two of the high points in a great tract of land between Loch Laggan and Loch Ericht. No roads and few tracks pierce this wilderness but you can access it by the Glasgow to Fort William West Highland Railway, from the station at Corrour. This is the start of a long 43km traverse of Ben Alder and Beinn Bheoil, eventually walking out to Dalwhinnie to return home by train, a fabulous weekend expedition. Ben Alder and Beinn Bheoil can also be climbed from Culra Bothy via the Lochan a' Bhealaich Beithe, or from Benalder Cottage in the south, a remote bothy on Loch Ericht. It can be reached by a long walk-in from Corrour via Loch Ossian, the Uisge Labhair and the Bealach Cumhain.

From Benalder Cottage the, follow the burn up to the Bealach Breabag. Just short of its summit climb the broken ground to the left to reach the prominent ridge, the rim of the impressive Garbh Coire. Follow the ridge to the Lochan a' Garbh Choire. Now leave the corrie edge and cross the huge, flat plateau to Ben Alder's summit cairn and trig point. In misty weather accurate navigation is essential. North of the summit two slim ridges offer a choice of descent – the Short Leachas drops down just north of Loch a' Bhealaich Bheithe, the Long Leachas, forms the southern boundary of the Bealach Dubh. The Short Leachas is steeper and involves some good scrambling while the Long Leachas is technically easier.

To climb Beinn Bheoil, return to the Bealach Breabag and from a point south of the summit turn north-east and climb slopes to the summit of Sron Coire na h-Iolaire, a fine airy perch high above Loch Ericht. Northwards the ridge stretches out and after a short descent climbs steadily to the summit of Beinn Bheoil. Return to the Bealach Breabaig and the outward route back to Benalder Cottage.

If continuing to Dalwhinnie, an excellent footpath runs downhill from the Lochan a' Bhealaich Bheithe to Culra bothy where another path runs past Loch Pattack to the new Ben Alder Lodge and the track alongside Loch Ericht.

Geal Charn from the east

Beinn a' Chlachair (56), 1087m/3566ft, Geal Charn (81), 1049m/3442ft, Creag Pitridh (264), 924m/3031ft

Not as remote as their neighbours, these hills lack the grandeur and ruggedness of Ben Alder and the Aonach Beag ridge. Beinn a' Chlachair is probably the finest of the three with its big north-facing corrie holding snow well into the spring. It's been suggested to me more than once that it would be ideal for ski development – God forbid!

From the head of Lochan na h-Earba a rough footpath climbs up to a high bealach beside the Allt Coire Pitridh. This pass gives access across to Loch Pattack, provided you can cross the Allt Cam – in times of spate the ford marked on the OS map becomes a raging torrent. Just north of the summit of the pass, the footpath turns south east. Follow it for a short distance and then take to the broad north-east flank of Beinn a' Chlachair. Follow this to the summit. Return to the footpath and pick up another stalkers' path which runs northwards to reach the shallow col between Geal Charn and Creag Pitridh. Don't follow the path as far as the bealach but almost immediately climb easy slopes to the flat summit of Geal Charn. Return to the bealach west of Geal Charn and climb the easy slopes to Craig Pitridh. From the summit descend SW to regain the stalkers' path alongside the Allt Coire Pitridh.

Route Summary: Take the bull-dozed road beside the Amhainn Ghuilbinn for about 1km (Route C). Turn left, follow track for 500m, then right along another track to Lochan na h-Earba. From the SW of the loch take a stalkers' path up beside the Allt Coire Pitridh. After 1.5km bear S on open hillside to NE flank of Beinn a' Chlachair. Climb to the summit. Return ENE along a broad ridge which stops above a large crag. Descend N to a stalkers' path with another path a few metres lower. Follow second path on to the W flank of Geal Charn. Go E, climb easy slopes to the flat summit. Return to the bealach W of Geal Charn and climb Craig Pitridh. Descend SW to the stalkers' path beside the Allt Coire Pitridh

Map: OS Sheet 42

Access Point: Luiblea, GR432830

Distance: 25km, 1220m ascent

Approx Time: 7-9 hours

Translation: stonemason's hill; white hill; possibly Petrie's hill

Pronunciation: byn a' claachar; gyal chaarn; craig peetrie

THE DRUMOCHTER HILLS

The Munros:

A' Bhuidheanach Bheag   Carn na Caim   Meall Chuaich   Geal Charn
A' Mharconaich   Beinn Udlamain   Sgairneach Mhor

In the past few years I sometimes feel that I've set myself up as a lone defender of these rounded Grampians, a voice speaking in a wilderness of sharp Sgurrs and pointed Stobs and Stucs. But the most wonderful aspect of hillwalking in Scotland is the variety that is on offer and these rounded hills are a definite contrast to the craggier peaks of the west and herald their own fine characteristics in a way that is neither overpowering nor lacking in inspiration.

Geal Charn, A' Mharconaich, Beinn Udlamain and Sgairneach Mhor make up a fine round, especially on skis, and from a starting point of over 450m! Carn na Caim and A' Bhuidheanach Bheag are also ski tourers' hills, but in summer offer an experience of these high Grampians with their wide, sweeping skies and gentle curving slopes which can be dominated by plover and skylark song. Meall Chuaich makes an ideal afternoon or evening stroll in summer conditions and offers wide views of Badenoch and Strathspey. Kingussie, Newtonmore and Laggan make the best bases and there is a railway station at Dalwhinnie.

A' Bhuidheanach Bheag (240), 936m/3071ft,
Carn na Caim (232), 941m/3087ft

I'm always surprised to see so many hillwalkers coming down from the hills which form the east side of the Drumochter Pass. I would guess that the majority of them are counting Munros, for Carn na Caim and A' Bhuidheaneach Bheag, the two Munros in the area, have, in the eyes of most walkers, little going for them other than their height above sea level.

In several books I've read these hills are described as dull, but a hill is only dull when seen through dull eyes. Having said that, I too would probably have avoided them if I hadn't been trying to get round the Munros for a second time. My first visit, a good 12-15 years ago, was on a grey misty day and I skied over both hills on wet, slushy snow. I was concentrating so much on my skis that I singularly failed to take in anything about the hills, other than the fact that the descent back down to the A9 was promising in better snow conditions.

A track leads up the hill from the A9 to an old quarry which is gouged out of the hillside and as I made my way uphill I recalled

Route Summary: Leave the A9 S of Balsporran (Route A) and climb steep heathery slopes raked with shallow gullies to Meall a' Chaorainn. Continue E and follow a fence to the summit of A' Bhuidheanach Bheag. N of the summit the fence crosses an area of peat at the head of Coire Chuirn. Follow the fence to Carn na Caim, two rounded tops on either side of a shallow depression. Follow open and obvious slopes SW back to the A9 in Drumochter Pass.

Map: OS Sheet 42

Access Point: Balsporran Cottages

Distance: 12.8km, 610m ascent

Approx Time: 4-6 hours

A' Mharconaich from the north-east

Translation: the little yellow place; cairn of the curve

Pronunciation: a vooanach vek; caarn a kym

some comments of a friend of mine, comments that were made as we walked on the Glencoe peaks a week earlier. He had suggested that the Cairngorms and the hills of the Eastern Highlands had little to offer, and the real thrills were to be found on the sharper peaks of the West.

As I reached the high rounded ridge which joins A' Bhuidheanach Bheag and Carn na Caim the views around me put a perspective on my thoughts. While I love the peaks and pinnacles of the west I also appreciate these big, rounded hills which seem to roll on forever in all directions. Here the skies are huge and dominant, and at virtually 950m, it's good to be able to walk freely for long distances without losing height and having to regain it.

Up here you become aware of the shapes around you, not so much the shape of the hills themselves, but the smooth flowing contours of the corries which bite their way into these high uplands. Here are curves which are sensuous in form, smooth, gradual and majestic, the gracefulness of the high Grampians. There is nothing sharp, or jagged, or jarring to the eye, nothing scabrous nor irregular.

In summer the song of skylarks, with the possible exception of the spring song of the cock snow bunting, the finest of all mountain melodies, fills the air, and watch for snipe darting out from below a peat hag. Now and again you might pick out the plaintive whistle of the golden plover, a melancholy sound which is nevertheless appealing, the sound of these high, rounded places, the song of the Grampians.

The eastern Drumochter Hills from the air

Meall Chuaich (214), 951m/3120 ft

Rising high above the loch of the same name, Meall Chuaich is an isolated top which, because of its position in the clench of Glen Truim and Strathspey offers superb views of Badenoch towards the high Cairngorms and along the length of Loch Ericht towards the Ben Alder group. It's a straightforward ascent and makes a great afternoon jaunt on a winter's day.

A private road leads from the A9 to Loch Cuaich and just to the south of it a footpath runs past a bothy and crosses the Allt Coire Chuaich which runs down from the big, rounded hills of Gaick. On the north side of the stream a path has been worn through the heather straight up the hill's south-west ridge to a flatter, stony area by Stac Meall Chuaich. From there it's a straightforward walk up the stony ridge to the big summit cairn.

Route Summary: Leave the A9 just S of the Cuaich cottages (Route B) and follow a private road through a locked gate. In a short distance reach a track beside an aqueduct and follow it to the Loch Cuaich dam. Open heather slopes lead to the summit of the hill

Map: OS Sheet 42

Access Point: Cuaich, GR654876

Distance: 11.2km 610m ascent

Approx Time: 3-5 hours

Translation: hill of the quaich

Pronunciation: myowl chooeech

Looking north from the summit of A' Mharconaich

Route Summary: Leave
Balsporran Cottages, cross the
railway and follow the track up
Coire Fhar. A sketchy path
leaves the track and runs up the
hillside to the NE ridge of Geal
Charn. Pass the cairns at 840m
and continue W to the rocky
summit. Continue S on a broad
ridge to a height of 970m
where a ridge appears to run
off NE. The summit of A' Mharconaich lies 800m along this
ridge. Return to the 970m
point, cross a wide bealach to
the SW and continue SW on a
broad ridge, over an unnamed
top and across a featureless
plateau to the summit of Beinn
Udlamain. Descend S to a
boggy bealach. On the far side
take an E bearing to locate the
summit cairn on the most W
top of the hill. Descend to

Geal Charn (279), 917m/3008ft, A' Mharconaich (179), 975m/3199ft, Beinn Udlamain (119), 1011m/3317ft, Sgairneach Mhor (155), 991m/3251ft

The Pass of Drumochter separates the rounded hills of Carn na
Caim and A' Bhuidheanach Bheag from these more distinctive
mountains, an area once known as the Druim Uachdair, the ridge
of the upper ground. Gathered nicely together in one corner of this
old area these four Munros make a good expedition and offer some
of the best views possible of the Ben Alder hills across the long
trench of Loch Ericht, particularly from Geal Charn.

  This hill can be reached easily from Balsporran Cottages on the
A9 by a footpath through the deep heather and on up to the
north-east ridge. Higher up the ridge there were once a series of
high, slender cairns which looked like a row of marching men
when seen from below. For some reason someone has knocked
them down but they seem to be growing again. It seems that few
hillwalkers can resist putting stones on cairns – any cairns!

From the summit of Geal Charn, with its long views down the length of Loch Ericht, drop down the very rocky slopes to a col and then climb south-east up grassy slopes to reach A' Mharconaich's long, broad ridge – the summit cairn is at the north-east end, perched high above a big corrie. A long and twisting ridge leads to the next Munro, Beinn Udlamain, the Gloomy Hill, and a line of fence posts marking the boundary between Perthshire and Inverness-shire makes a useful navigational aid. You can follow them all the way on to the wide and fairly featureless plateau and the summit itself.

Continue past the big summit cairn in a southerly direction, still keeping company with the fence posts until they suddenly vanish westwards in a tight right-angle. At this point, marked on the map as Carn 'Ic Loumhaidh, drop down over very rocky ground to the bealach which is in fact the head of Coire Dhomhain, take an easterly bearing and climb grassy slopes to reach the south-west ridge of Sgairneach Mhor which can then be followed to the broad summit and the trig point. Leave the summit in an easterly direction to gain a ridge which gradually swings round to north east. Take care hereabouts in winter for the lip of Coire Creagach cornices quite severely. A friend of mine once skied over the cornice in misty conditions – fortunately he missed the steep, rocky part and eventually managed to stop himself on very steep snow with his ski poles.

Once you reach the footpath in Coire Dhomhain it's an easy walk back to the A9 and a road walk back to Balsporran.

Coire Dhomhain via the E spur, then follow the footpath to the railway and the A9 about 4km S of Balsporran

Map: OS Sheet 42

Access Point: Balsporran Cottages, GR628792

Distance: 25km, 1143m ascent

Approx Time: 6-8 hours

Translation: white hill; the horse place; gloomy mountain; big stony hillside

Pronunciation: gyal chaarn; a varkaneech; byn ootlaman; skaarnyatch vore

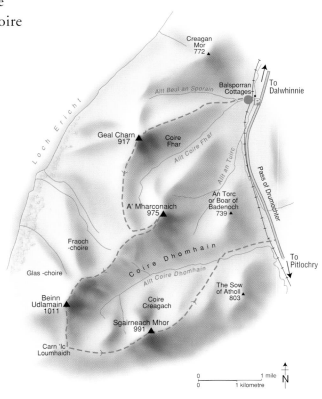

95

THE TARF AND TILT HILLS

The Munros:

Beinn a' Ghlo (Carn Liath, Braigh Coire Chruinn-bhalgain, Carn nan Gabhar)
Beinn Dearg Carn a' Chlamain Carn an Fhidleir An Sgarsoch

Between Glen Bruar and the Cairnwell lies a great wilderness of high tops and deep glens, split right through the middle by the long, deep cleft of Glen Tilt. The high peaty area to the west of Tilt is dominated by Beinn Dearg, Carn a' Chlamain, An Sgarsoch and Carn an Fhidleir, a quartet known as the Ring of Tarf, a long and arduous expedition involving many kilometres of tough, remote walking. To the east of Tilt, the Beinn a' Ghlo massif rises to its four tops, the highest of which is Carn nan Gabhar.

Adam Watson, the ecologist and author has described Beinn a' Ghlo as 'one of the most beautiful and mysterious hills of Scotland', an odd description for a scientist to offer. Perhaps he is referring to the old legend which suggests that the hill has 19 corries, in any of which a rifle could be fired without being heard in another.

Route Summary: Leave the parking place in Glen Fender (Route A, p.99), go through a gate and follow the track for about 2km to a couple of small huts. Note: these are not bothies as suggested in some guidebooks. Cross a boggy area and climb in a NE direction to the summit of Carn Liath. Follow the twisting ridge initially N over Beinn Mhaol and down to the narrow col. A well-worn path continues NE, then N to reach the summit of Braigh Coire Chruinn-bhalgain. Continue NE for 1km before dropping down grassy slopes to cross the Bealach na Fhiodha. Climb roughly E to reach the high col between Airgiod Bheinn and Carn nan Gabhar. Climb the latter, retrace your steps to the col and climb Airgiod Bheinn, descending its steep SW ridge to find a rough path which takes you across the heathery moors to reach

Beinn a' Ghlo (Carn Liath (181), 975m/3199ft, Braigh Coire Chruinn-bhalgain (66), 1070m/3510ft, Carn nan Gabhar (32), 1121m/3678ft)

In clear weather the walk over Beinn a' Ghlo is straightforward, a delightful high-level stravaig over some of the best ridges in the Grampians, but when the cloud is down and visibility is reduced navigation becomes complex. There are some 19 different corries on Beinn a' Ghlo and the summits are formed by the apexes of an elaborate system of ridges and interlinking shoulders.

Most hillwalkers climb the Beinn a' Ghlo trio of summits from Loch Moraig, among the low hills of Glen Fender above Blair Atholl. A track leads to the marshy skirts of Carn Liath, the first of the three Munros that make up the massif of Beinn a' Ghlo, the chief feature of the ancient ducal Forest of Atholl. A worn and eroded path runs directly up the south-west ridge to the summit where the complexity of Beinn a' Ghlo's corries and ridges becomes evident.

A broad ridge falls away to the north before narrowing appreciably and swinging east to end abruptly on what appears to be the blunt nose of Beinn Mhaol, an intermediary top. What you can't see from Carn Liath is the ridge twisting north again beyond Beinn Mhaol before dropping down to a high, pinched col below

Carn Liath from the west

the south-west ridge of Braigh Coire Chruinn-bhalgain. The route climbs steeply from here, joining the hill's south ridge, before rising gently to the rounded summit.

At first glance, Carn nan Gabhar looks isolated from the other tops by a deep, steep-walled glen, but less than 1km from the summit of Braigh Coire Chruinn-bhalgain a high bealach, like a mighty drawbridge between the mountains, gives easy access to the col between Carn nan Gabhar and Airgiod Bheinn. From the col it's an easy walk to the first of three cairns. The highest is, inevitably, the furthest away, beyond the OS trig point. Return down the steep south-west nose of Airgiod Bheinn and follow the footpath back to the Loch Moraig track.

Another route climbs Carn Liath from Balaneasie Cottage in Glen Tilt, returning to the glen north of Forest Lodge via Carn nan Ghabhar's north ridge. This includes part of Glen Tilt, a wonderfully varied glen that's always worth a visit. You can't take a car up Glen Tilt – a parking place has been provided by the estate at the foot of the glen, but a mountain bike would ease the distance considerably!

a track between Glen Girnaig and Loch Moraig

Map: OS Sheet 43

Access Point: Road end at Loch Moraig in Glen Fender GR 905671

Distance: 22km, 1250m ascent

Approx Time: 6-8 hours

Translation: hill of mist; grey hill; upland of the corrie of round blisters; hill of the goats

Pronunciation: byn a gloe; kaarn lee-a; bray corrie kroon vaalakan; kaarn nan gower

Beinn Dearg from the south-west across Glen Garry

Beinn Dearg (124), 1008m/3307ft

Beinn Dearg is one of the highest points in a great wedge of high, broken countryside that lies between the Pass of Drumochter in the west and the line of Glen Tilt, Glen Geldie, and Glen Feshie in the east, and is most conveniently accessed from Glen Bruar. A bulldozed track runs all the way from Calvine, on the A9, to Bruar Lodge, at the foot of Beinn Dearg, allowing you to use a mountain bike, but a much more interesting route follows the course of the ancient Minigaig road from Blair Castle in Blair Atholl.

Beyond the castle, Diana's Grove, a dark wood of conifers, marks the way to Old Blair, where a track strikes off in a north-west direction beside the Banvie Burn. This track climbs gently through dense woods of birch, larch and pine, keeping in sight of the chuckling burn that passes through a series of cascades, pools and deep-set ravines, all darkly shaded in bottle green. After a short time, past the Rumbling Bridge, the Minigaig marches forward through a gate into the Whim Plantation before splitting at another gate at the end of the woods. The Minigaig drops down to the burn side where it crosses the Quarry Bridge and begins to incline as it pulls away from Glen Banvie up the glen of the Allt na Moine Baine towards a tall pile of stones, the Lady March Cairn. Beyond here the road crosses the Allt na Moine Baine and skirts around the long open slopes of Carn Dearg Beag to drop into the shallow valley of the Allt an t-Seapail, the stream of the chapel.

Pass another cairn, the Carn Mhic Shimidh, a memorial to a battle between the Murrays of Atholl and a raiding party of Frasers led by

Simon Lovat, then descend to the bothy beside the Allt Sheicheachain.

The burn beyond the bothy is easily forded and the footpath now straggles around the foot of the Druim Dubh and into Glen Bruar. Beyond the rather dilapidated looking Lodge, another hill track climbs the lower slopes of Beinn Losgarnaich to a broad, boggy bealach where, immediately to the east, the red-scree covered slopes of Beinn Dearg rise to the triple-topped summit ridge.

The southern top is the highest and the views are extensive. Ridge over ridge, horizon over horizon, rolling moors and shadow-stained glens, clear-cut land and glistening water – there are few more remote regions in Scotland. The broad south ridge allows you to stay comparatively high for a while before another path suddenly descends sharply from Meall Dubh nan Dearcag. In no time at all you're back at the bothy, ready for a brew before the big hike back to Blair.

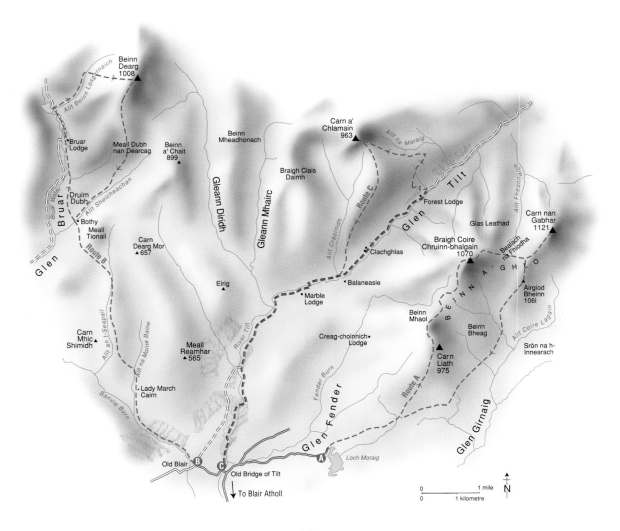

Carn a' Chlamain from the south ridge

Route Summary: Follow the road up Glen Tilt, past Marble Lodge to Forest Lodge (Route C). Just beyond Forest Lodge a zigzag stalkers' path makes its way up the steep hillside. It then crosses easier open slopes running parallel for a distance with the Allt na Maraig before climbing on to the summit of Carn a' Chlamain. Descend the hill's SW ridge back to Glen Tilt and return by the road to Forest Lodge

Map: OS Sheet 43

Access Point: Car park at Old Bridge of Tilt

Distance: 30km, 830m ascent

Approx Time: 8-10 hours

Translation: hill of the kite or buzzard

Pronunciation: kaarn a klaavan

Carn a' Chlamain (192), 963m/3159ft

It was once possible to drive up Glen Tilt to Forest Lodge from where Carn a' Chlamain made a good afternoon's walk. Today you have to leave your car at the estate car park just beyond the Old Bridge of Tilt. It's a long walk up Glen Tilt, past Marble Lodge to Forest Lodge, but mountain bikes are allowed.

Follow the Glen Tilt track past Forest Lodge and through the woodland until you reach a gate. Don't go through the gate but turn left, climb up through the trees and onto the open hillside where you'll find an old stalkers' path which eventually zigzags its way up the steep heather-covered hillside and onto the plateau.

From here the views north and north-east are extensive towards the Cairngorms and the Glenshee hills and westwards towards the hills of Perthshire. The path continues over the undulating plateau and eventually passes close to the summit cairn. To make a circuit of the walk, descend the hill's long curving south-west ridge back down to Glen Tilt then down the long road to Old Bridge of Tilt.

Carn an Fhidhleir (148), 994m/3261ft, An Sgarsoch (126), 1006m/3301ft

These may be big heather-covered domes, lacking the visual features of the western hills, but situated as they are close to the headwaters of the Geldie, the Feshie and the Tarf there is an air of remoteness which challenges most walkers.

It's a long route from Linn of Dee, some 40km for the return trip, so a mountain bike makes good sense if you want to climb these hills in one day. An alternative, of course, is to backpack round the four Munros of the Ring of Tarf.

From Linn of Dee follow the north bank of the River Dee as far as White Bridge, cross it and continue on the bulldozed track beside the forest plantation to where the Geldie turns west. Keep on this track, past the Red House, and continue for another 5km to where the track crosses the river and continues to ruins of Geldie Lodge. Prepare to get your feet wet.

Leave your bike, if you've used one, at Geldie Lodge, and walk up the bulldozed track to its highest point, just above the Allt a' Chaorainn burn. Leave the track now, cross over the burn, and climb the heather-covered slopes of the corrie in a south-west direction to reach the north ridge and the summit of Carn an Fhidhleir. This summit is the meeting place of Perthshire, Inverness-shire and Aberdeenshire and its neighbouring summit, An Sgarsoch, was once a market place, where cattle and horses were bought and sold. The event was known as the Feill Sgarsaich.

To reach the summit, drop down the long, wide and easy slopes of The Fiddler's south-east ridge to an obvious bump in the ridge. From the top of this bump, turn due east and drop down to the col at 710m. From here it's a long pull up heather and moss slopes to the summit of An Sgarsoch. No cattle, horses or merchants here now, just wide open, rolling slopes and even bigger wide open skies. Descend north to Scarsoch Bheag and then north-east to the bulldozed track back to Geldie Lodge.

Route Summary: Follow N bank of the River Dee to White Bridge and then along the Geldie Burn to Geldie Lodge. A mountain bike would be useful. Follow a bulldozed track WSW to its highest point. Continue SW over peat hags and climb the NE slopes of Carn an Fhidhleir to reach the N ridge close to the summit. Drop SSE along a broad ridge and then down the E side of the ridge to reach the bealach at 700m. From there climb NE to the flat summit of An Sgarsoch. Return to Geldie Lodge by following the N ridge and then E of Scarsoch Bheag over peaty ground to reach the bulldozed track again

Map: OS Sheet 43

Access Point: Linn of Dee

Distance: 40km, 910m ascent

Approx Time: 10-12 hours

Translation: hill of the fiddler; the place of sharp rocks

Pronunciation: kaarn an yeelar; an skaarsoch

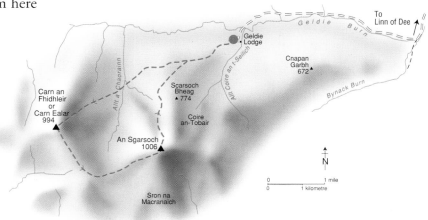

THE CAIRNWELL HILLS

The Munros:

An Socach   Beinn Iutharn Mhor   Carn Bhac   Glas Tulaichean

Carn an Righ   The Cairnwell   Carn a' Gheoidh   Carn Aosda

Bounded by the Dee in the north, the Tilt in the west and the A93 in the east, this large sprawling upland area boasts eight Munros. Unfortunately, two of them represent the most depressing aspect of man's commercial development in the mountains – the Cairnwell ski area. The two Munros, in whose arms much of the development has taken place, The Cairnwell and Carn Aosda, have been hideously scarred. In contrast, the other hills in this area share the same sort of isolation quality of the hills west of Glen Tilt. This is typical rolling Grampian country – heather-covered hills that echo to the guttural call of the red grouse.

An Socach (227), 944m/3097ft, Beinn Iutharn Mhor (88), 1045m/3428ft, Carn Bhac (221), 946m/3104ft

A mountain bike can be used to advantage here by cycling up the 8km from Inverey to Altanour Lodge. South of the lodge ruins An Socach presents its curved ridge and the most direct route is best – due south to climb straight to the summit cairn by the hill's north ridge.

From the summit drop southwards down steep slopes and traverse easy angled slopes to the lonely waters of Loch nan Eun. From the loch climb to the high bealach between Beinn Iutharn Bheag and Mam nan Carn then head south-west up heather-covered slopes to the summit of Mam nan Carn, from where a short descent to the north leads to another high bealach. Stony slopes lead to the rounded summit of Beinn Iutharn Mhor.

It is a long walk over hillocks and across boggy bealachs to reach Carn Bhac, but it is fairly straightforward until you reach the broad and featureless stony plateau where the big problem is deciding which of the cairns is the summit. On the latest maps the summit is correctly shown at the north-east end of Carn Bhac's long and broad summit ridge.

The best route back to Altanour Lodge is by the big open east ridge where easy slopes lead down to the Allt an Odhar and the headwaters of the Ey Burn.

Beinn Iutharn Mhor from above Glen Ey

Route Summary: Walk, or cycle from Inverey to Altanour Lodge (Route A). Head due S and climb N ridge of An Socach. Go past the cairn, descend S, climb easy slopes to Loch nan Eun. Climb to the high bealach between Beinn Iutharn Bheag and Mam nan Carn, then SW to the summit of Mam nan Carn. Descend N, climb Beinn Iutharn Mhor. Follow the summit ridge E then N then leave the ridge NNE to cross to the broad W summit of Carn Bhac. Follow the ridge NE for 1km to the summit cairn. Descend S then SE back to Altanour Lodge

Map: OS Sheet 43

Access Point: Inverey

Distance: 32km, 1120m ascent, This includes the 8km walk-in each way from Inverey to Altanour Lodge

Approx Time: 10-12 hours

Translation: the projecting place; big hill of the edge; hill of peat hags

Pronunciation: an sochkach; byn yooarn vore; kaarn vachk

Glas Tulaichean (79), 1051m/3448ft, Carn an Righ (102), 1029m/3376ft

Route Summary: Take the private road to Dalmunzie Hotel and Glenlochsie Farm (Route B). Beyond the farm follow the track to Glenlochsie Lodge. Beyond it a bulldozed track climbs N to the long, straggling SSW ridge of Glas Tulaichean. Follow it almost all the way to the summit. (To avoid the bulldozed track, climb the ridge on the E side of the Allt Clais Mhor from Glenlochsie Lodge.) From summit cairn descend NW into upper Gleann Mor to a path that runs round the SW nose of Mam nan Carn. From the bealach E of Carn an Righ climb stony slopes W, then N to the summit. Return to the path in Gleann Mor below and follow it E to Loch nan Eun. Descend into Gleann Taitneach, a bulldozed track takes you back down to Dalmunzie and the Spittal of Glenshee

Map: OS Sheet 43: GR135773, GR107767, GR134792

Access Point: Spittal of Glenshee

Distance: 27km, 1090m ascent

Approx Time: 7-9 hours

Translation: green hills; hill of the king

Pronunciation: glas tooleechan; kaarn an rye

Glas Tulaichean and its neighbour, Carn an Righ, are easily reached via Glen Lochsie, past the Dalmunzie Hotel to Glenlochsie Lodge where a long straggling ridge runs south from Glas Tulaichean.

The former Glenlochsie Lodge, 5km up Glen Lochsie from the Spittal of Glenshee, must have been fairly grand at one time. Indeed, the Victorian owners of the estate once operated a light railway to transport deer shooters up the glen! Today a Land Rover track runs up the glen, past the old lodge and up the long south ridge of Glas Tulaichean virtually all the way to the summit.

Descend steeply north from Glas Tulaichean into Gleann Mor then climb up to the path that runs round the south-west nose of Mam nan Carn and from the bealach east of Carn an Righ climb stony slopes west, then north, to the summit.

A well-used and invariably boggy path runs from the bealach between Carn an Righ and its eastern neighbour, Mam nan Carn, all the way to Loch nan Eun before dropping steeply downhill beside the tumbling Allt Easgaidh into the head of Gleann Taitneach. Descend this beautiful glen with the rocky crags of Creag Easgaidh and Creag Dallaig offering a hint of harshness to an otherwise tranquil U-shaped valley. It's a long walk down the glen back to the Spittal of Glenshee but the bubbling river adds company.

The Cairnwell (245), 933m/3061ft, Carn a' Gheoidh (180), 975m/3199ft, Carn Aosda (278), 917m/3008ft

Route Summary: Just S of the ski area climb heather slopes to the summit (Route C). Descend NNW past the top chairlift point and continue on a broad ridge with snow fences. Just before the Cairnwell-Aosda col turn W and drop to another col, the lowest point between The Cairnwell and Carn a' Gheoidh. Continue SW past Carn nan Sac and W over a small plateau to Carn a' Gheoidh. Retrace your route to the Cairnwell-Aosda col, ascend NE then E along a broad ridge to the flat summit of Carn

The Cairnwell and Carn Aosda are probably the most accessible Munros in the country; they are also the most depressing – it's hard to believe that man can cause so much natural damage in such a small area. The visit to Carn a' Gheoidh, beyond Loch Vrotachan, helps add a touch of reality to this outing, but first we must climb The Cairnwell. Leave the road just south of the ski centre buildings, avoiding the worst of the paraphernalia and bulldozed roads. Short, clipped heather and scree offers fairly easy going and there is some consolation in the fact that you don't have to climb far from the road, one of the highest in the country, to reach the summit cairn and ski lift hut. Descend to the north-north-west, first of all past the top chairlift pylon and then along a broad ridge decorated by large snow fences.

After 1km or so, just before the Cairnwell/Aosda col, turn west and descend to the lowest point between The Cairnwell and Carn a' Gheoidh. From here it's a pleasant walk along the lip above the steep and rocky Coire Direach, past Carn nan Sac and across a flat heath to Carn a' Gheoidh. Return to the Cairnwell/Aosda col, follow the bulldozed track north-east and then east, passing the Butchart's ski tow to reach the summit of Carn Aosda. Follow the bulldozed roads south back to the Cairnwell road.

Aosda. Descend S by bulldozed roads to the Cairnwell road

Map: OS Sheet 43

Access Point: Devil's Elbow, GR140780

Distance: 8km, 580m ascent

Approx Time: 3-5 hours

Translation: From Carn Bhalg, hill of bags; hill of the goose; hill of age

Pronunciation: cairnwell; kaarn a yowee; kaarn oesh

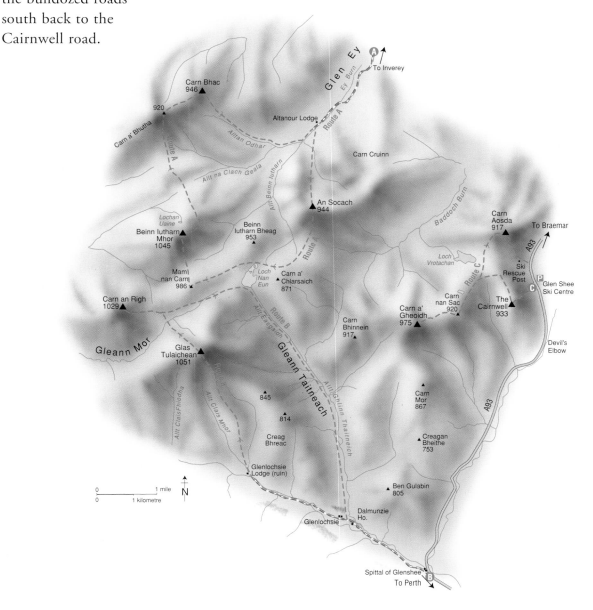

GLENSHEE AND LOCHNAGAR HILLS

The Munros:

Creag Leacach   Glas Maol   Cairn of Claise   Tom Buidhe
Tolmount   Carn an Tuirc   Lochnagar   Carn a' Coire Boidheach
(White Mounth)   Carn an t-Sagairt Mor   Cairn Bannoch
Broad Cairn   Driesh   Mayar   Mount Keen

Bounded by the Cairnwell Pass in the west and Deeside in the north, this corner of the Mounth is epitomised by rounded green hills, vast rolling plateaux and features some wild open glens. At least two of them, Glen Callater and Caenlochan, are glacial trenches with steep-sided corries at their top.

Glen Muick is probably the most dramatic of the glens with its mountain-bound loch and upper glen overlooked by the precipitous Creag an Dubh-Loch. The rock of the area is mainly schist with patches of quartzite but here and there fertile areas of limestone are found – Caenlochan, for example, is rich in uncommon arctic-alpine plants, rivalling Ben Lawers in the south.

The plateau of grass, sedge and moss offers unsurpassed high-level walking and big distances can be covered with a minimum of effort. Sadly, the south side of Loch Muick has been spoiled by the creation of crudely bulldozed tracks, for sporting purposes, but the greater part of the area is still very rewarding for the hillwalker and even more so for the ski tourer.

Because of the nature of the high, rolling terrain, the main chunk of these hills can be easily climbed in a couple of longish expeditions, or broken down into smaller groups. However, apart from Glas Maol and Creag Leacach which can both be climbed from the Cairnwell in a fairly easy afternoon, there is little real advantage in climbing these hills in two or threes. Their relative remoteness requires a big walk-in, from almost any direction, and once you have gained the altitude you are as well to make the most of it and stay high. The judicious use of a mountain bike can also make a huge difference.

Lochnagar is of course the main attraction in the area – the royal mountain ever since Queen Victoria and Prince Albert chose to purchase Balmoral Estate rather than Ardverikie in the west. Celebrated in Byron's 'Lachin y Gair', thousands have come to visit the '...crags that are wild and majestic, the steep frowning glories of dark Lochnagar.'

Lochnagar from the north across Glen Dee

Route Summary: From the Devil's Elbow on the A93 (Route A, p.111) climb the N ridge of Meall Gorm and follow the ridge round to the stony tops of Creag Leacach. Follow the broad ridge N beside a stone wall to the summit of Glas Maol. Continue N and NE on the undulating ridge to Cairn of Claise, then E over the Ca Whims to Tom Buidhe. Return to the Ca Whims, and climb the stony S slopes of the Tolmount. Descend to the W, skirting the head of Glen Callater and Coire Kander to the summit of Carn an Tuirc. Drop down W to the glen and follow the footpath to the old bridge beside the A93

Map: OS Sheets 43, 44

Access Point: A93 at the Devil's Elbow

Distance: 22km, 1017m ascent (5km on the A93 between starting and finishing points.)

Approx Time: 6-8 hours

Translation: slabby rock; green/grey bare hill; hill of the hollow; yellow hill; hill of the valley; hill of the boar

Pronunciation: krayk lyechach; glas moel; kaarn an claes; tom booee; tolmount; kaarn an toork

Creag Leacach (159), 987m/3238ft, Glas Maol (69), 1068m/3504ft, Cairn of Claise (71), 1064m/3491ft, Tom Buidhe (204), 957m/3140ft, Tolmount (202), 958m/3143ft, Carn an Tuirc (113), 1019m/3343ft

Creag Leacach and Glas Maol can easily be climbed in a short day, linking the two by a fine, gently winding ridge, but there are few areas where you can walk over six Munros in such a relatively short distance – about 22km, with only 1017m of climbing. This is possible by using either two cars, or a car and a bicycle.

Drive to where the A93 Cairnwell road crosses over the Allt a' Garbh-choire, just immediately west of Carn an Tuirc. Just south of this point, a footbridge crosses the stream leading to a path which runs up the glen in an eastwards direction. The bridge here stands at the site of An Seann-spideal, the old spital that carried an early military road. Either leave a car, or hide a bicycle in the heather, to be collected at the end of the walk. Now drive southwards over the Cairnwell road to a car park at GR128757, at the Devil's Elbow, drop down heather-covered slopes from the car park, cross the infant Allt a' Ghlinne Bhig and climb the north ridge of Meall Gorm, a fairly steep climb over deep heather. From the summit descend south-eastwards to a wide bealach and continue in much the same direction up the scree-covered slopes of Creag Leacach's south-west top. From there the obvious scree- and boulder-covered ridge swings to the north-east, to the summit of Creag Leacach, and winds its way for about 2.5km to the big dome of Glas Maol. An old wall also runs the entire distance.

With most of the hard work behind you now you can begin to appreciate this high-level promenade. Most of the tops in front of you are mere rises in the mossy plateau and the whole area is typified by rounded smooth slopes, heathery hollows and an air of spaciousness.

Leaving Glas Maol, cross the route of the old Monega Pass which runs from Glen Isla to Glen Clunie, the highest of the rights of way which cross the Mounth, and follow the broad, undulating ridge with the steep hollow of Garbh-choire to your left, to the summit of Cairn of Claise.

It's a pleasant stroll from the summit cairn, across the boggy Ca Whims, towards the unlikely Munro of Tom Buidhe – a mere rise in the centre of a great tableland. It was Sir Hugh Munro himself who said of this area, 'So elevated and flat is the range that a straight line of 10 miles could be drawn from Creag Leacach to the Meikle Pap of Lochnagar.' He went on to suggest that there was some relief for about half a mile, or 1km, on each side of the Tolmount and, indeed, it's from that summit that we get the best view of this particular outing.

Return to Ca Whims and from there it's an easy stroll to the summit of the Tolmount. Perched on the edge of the upper corrie of Glen Callater, the view down the crag-girt glen is a particularly fine one. Descend from the Tolmount around the heads of Glen Callater and Coire Kander and follow the broad grassy ridge between Coire Kander and the Cul Riabhach to the flat stony summit of Carn an Tuirc and views down Glen Clunie. The footpath in the corrie below follows the burn back to your awaiting car or bike, passing the fine rocky gorge of the Allt a' Garbh Choire on the way.

Glas Maol from the north-west

Lochnagar (Cac Carn Beag) (21), 1155m/3789ft, Carn a' Choire Boidheach (White Mount) (42), 1110m/3642ft, Carn an t-Sagairt Mor (83), 1047m/3435ft, Cairn Bannoch (117), 1012m/3320ft, Broad Cairn (142), 998m/3274ft

These hills can also be broken down into shorter expeditions, but a fine horseshoe traverse around the great glaciated trench of Loch Muick and its neighbouring Dubh Loch carries you over all these Munros in one long outing.

There are a number of routes to the summit of Lochnagar, a mountain well appreciated by climbers, walkers, poets and royalty. Contained within the Queen's Balmoral Estate, members of the royal family have enjoyed the mountain since Victoria and Albert bought the estate in the nineteenth century.

Route Summary: Take the path which runs along the edge of the plantation to cross to the other side of the glen at Allt-na-giubhsaich (Route B) and continue along the S bank of the burn through the pinewoods to reach a track. Follow it W for about 3km to the bealach which leads through to Gelder Shiel. At this point take an obvious path WSW across a slight hollow and then more steeply to the Foxes' Well on the left of the path. Soon the slope steepens again before 'The Ladder' and the top of the summit ridge. A short descent across a wide col and another climb leads to the flat summit ridge of Lochnagar. Walk along the rim of the corrie, past Cac Carn Mor and the deep chasm of the Black Spout to the summit cone of Cac Carn Beag where you'll find the trig point. Return to Cac Carn Mor and take another footpath in a SW direction to a shallow col. Leave the path and climb Carn a' Choire Boidheach. Continue over the summit to regain the footpath and where it crosses the Allt an Dubh-loch climb W to the summit of Carn an t-Sagairt Mor. Walk SE from the summit onto a flat plateau and ascend the slight rise to Cairn Bannoch. Continue SE over Cairn of Gowal, ENE to a col and E to the summit of Broad Cairn. From there descend E to pick up a footpath which soon becomes a bulldozed track. Pass a wooden shelter, drop down a footpath into Corrie Chash to the head of Loch Muick and follow the footpath and bulldozed tracks alongside the loch to Spittal of Glenmuick

Map: OS Sheet 44

Access Point: Spittal of Glenmuick car park

Distance: 32km, 1100m ascent

Approx Time: 8-10hours

Translation: named after Lochan na Gaire in Lochnagar's NE Corrie. Little loch of the noisy sound; hill of the beautiful corrie; big hill of the priest; possibly peaked hill; broad cairn

Pronunciation: loch-na-gar; kaarn a corrie vawyach; kaarn an takarsht moar; kaarn bannoch; broad kaarn

Probably the finest approach to Lochnagar is from the Invercauld Bridge through the Ballochbuie Forest, the oldest stand of ancient Caledonian pines in Scotland. Another route from the north is via the estate cottage and adjacent hut at Gelder Shiel, while walkers staying in Braemar frequently take the footpath from Glen Callater via the stalker's path up Carn an t-Sagairt Mor. By far the most popular, and the most eroded, route is from the Spittal of Glenmuick at the end of the public road which runs up Glen Muick from Ballater.

The tracks from Gelder Shiel and the Spittal of Glenmuick meet at the foot of the slopes east of Meikle Pap where a badly eroded footpath runs roughly westwards up towards the col between Meikle Pap and the Cuidhe Crom passing the Foxes' Well, or the Fox Well Cairn to give it its proper name. Just before the col is reached the path starts to zigzag its way leftwards up a steeper slope known as The Ladder, to reach the plateau above. It's well worth a little divergence below The Ladder to catch a glimpse down into the Corrie of Lochnagar, a great cirque of granite cliffs rising sheer from the dark lochan away below.

From the north-west shoulder of Cuidhe Crom above The Ladder, the path makes its way across the plateau, close to the corrie rim. Just before the cairn of Cac Carn Mor, the path splits, with one branch dropping downhill in a south-westwards direction and another continuing northwards. This latter path carries you past the deepset gully of the Black Spout, to the rocky summit, Cac Carn Beag, about 400m away across the plateau, complete with cairn, trig point and view indicator. Return on the same path to the junction below Cac Carn Mor, and follow the south-west path around the head of the cliffs of The Stuic, which rise from Loch nan Eun below. Just as the path begins to ascend again, bear slightly left from the footpath and climb the easy tundra-like slopes to the summit of Carn a' Choire Boidheach, sometimes known as the White Mounth.

Beyond the summit, wide stony slopes lead you back to the footpath which skirts the slopes of Carn an t-Sagairt Beag and crosses the infant Allt an Dubh-loch. Just at this point leave the path again to climb westwards to Carn an-Sagairt Mor where some rocks form a rude cairn around some crashed aircraft debris.

The route between Carn an-Sagairt Mor and Cairn Bannoch is a easy stroll over springy turf, but don't be fooled – in misty weather many walkers pass Cairn Bannoch without realising it. It is an imperceptible rise to Cairn Bannoch, but a couple of kilometres further on, passing the crags of Creag an Dubh Loch on your left, Broad Cairn offers greater character, with its rocky, granite summit. Descend eastwards across fields of broken granite to reach a path which soon becomes a rudely gouged-out track – the work of the uncaring bulldozer. Pass the wooden hut and continue east for a short distance to where another path drops down Corrie Chash to the head of Loch Muick, follows the south shore through some scattered birch woods and meets up with the bulldozed track again at the Black Burn. Follow the track all the way to Spittal of Glenmuick.

Cac Carn Beag 1155
Cac Carn Mor
Meikle Pap 980
Clais Rathadan
Lochnagar Burn
Route B
Allt na giubhsaich
To Ballater
LOCHNAGAR
Loch nan Eun
The Stulc
Fox Well Cairn
Carn an t-Sagairt Beag 1044
Carn an t-Sagairt Mor 1047
Carn a' Choire Boidheach 1110
Coire Boidheach
Cuidhe Crom 1083
Spittal of Glenmuick
Visitor Centre
White Mounth
Glen Callater
Eagles Rock
Dubh Loch
Loch Muick
Cairn Bannoch 1012
Fafernie 1000
Creag an Dubh-loch
Carn Dubh 822
Coire Kander
Knaps of Fafernie
Cairn of Gowal 983
Broad Cairn 998
Corrie Chash
Carn an Tuirc 1019
Loch Kander
Tolmount 958
To Braemar
Sron na Gaoithe 814
Allt a' Garbh-choire
Cairn of Claise 1064
Crow Craggies
Loch Esk
Glenshee Ski Centre
Ca Whims
Tom Buidhe 957
Jock's Road
Garbh-choire
Route A
Caenlochan Glen
Glen Doll
Glendoll Lodge
To Kirriemuir
To Perth
A93
Devil's Elbow
Allt a' Ghlinne Bhig
Glas Maol 1068
Little Glas Maol 973
Monega Hill 908
White Water
Acharn
Meall Gorm 759
Creag Leacach 987
Caenlochan Forest
River Isla
Corrie Fee
Route C
Fee Burn
Glendoll Forest
The Scorrie
Shank of Drumfollow
Winter Corrie
Mayar 928
Driesh 947

0 — 1 mile
0 — 1 kilometre
N

Driesh from the summit of Mayar

Route Summary: Start at the Forestry Commission car park 400m past Braedownie Farm (Route C). A track from Acharn, near the Youth Hostel in Glen Doll, crosses the White Water to a forestry fence which runs up the hill for just under 300m. Where the fence contours off to the W continue directly upwards to the top of The Scorrie, where the slopes ease off. Continue to the summit. From Driesh follow the long and obvious ridge W for about 3km to Mayar. To descend follow grassy slopes NNE to the edge of Corrie Fee. Continue on the SE side of the Fee Burn to a path at the foot of one of the steeper sections. Follow this ENE down the lower corrie, over a stile and into the forest. The path soon becomes a forest road which eventually runs past the Youth Hostel to the car park

Map: OS Sheet 44

Access Point: Braedownie, GR 288757

Distance: 12.8km, 823m ascent

Approx Time: 4-6 hours

Translation: From Gaelic dris, bramble or thorn bush; possibly from m' aighear, my delight, or from magh, a plain

Pronunciation: dreesh; may-yer

Driesh (219), 947m/3107ft, Mayar (253), 928m/3045ft

The lovely Glen Clova and Glen Doll are heavily coniferised which inevitably means that there can often be some confusion over forestry tracks and footpaths. The most popular route to the summit of Driesh climbs for a distance up through the Glendoll Forest, following the old Kilbo hill path. Shortly after leaving the forest at a deer fence the path rises uphill above the deep Shank of Drumfollow to the high col between Driesh and Mayar where Driesh is easily reached in about 1.5km of easy walking. Mayar is reached by returning to the col and following an old fence west over grassy slopes. From the summit, steepening slopes drop away northwards to the head of Corrie Fee, where a steep section to the south east of the burn leads you down past some waterfalls to a footpath which continues to follow the Fee Burn into the forest where the footpath becomes a forestry road leading all the way back to Glen Doll past the Youth Hostel.

An alternative route of ascent, which is steeper but does have the advantage of cutting out a bit of forestry walking, climbs The Scorrie, a bold prow which climbs steeply up the west side of Winter Corrie, known locally as Corrie Winter! Cross the White Water by the bridge at Acharn, just east of the Youth Hostel, follow the forestry fence for a short distance and then climb the obvious steep ridge. At the top of the Scorrie you're well rewarded for your efforts by superb views into the cliffs of Corrie Winter, the redeeming feature of what is otherwise a rather dull hill. From the top of Corrie Winter it's an easy walk to the summit of Driesh.

Mount Keen (235), 939m/3081ft

Glen Tanar is magnificent, Mount Keen less so! The hill's chief claim to fame is that it is the most easterly of all the Munros and the fact that it is also one of the most solitary means that you can't just hinge it on to a round of other Munros. Lying mid-way between Glen Tanar and Glen Esk the summit of Mount Keen lies immediately adjacent to the easternmost of the Mounth roads, the Mounth Keen, so access can be easily gained from the south, in Glen Esk, or Glen Tanar on Deeside in the north.

My own preference is for the Glen Tanar approach, largely because of the lovely walk-in to the mountain through the Glen Tanar pine woods, a fine remnant of the Great Forest of Caledon. Glen Tanar lies south-west of Aboyne where a public road runs to a car park beside Glen Tanar House. From there a track follows the lovely Water of Tanar through the woods and out on to open moorland beyond the Half Way Hut. The track continues in a more southerly direction beyond Etnach to the Shiel of Glentanar which was burned down in 1992. Just before the track sweeps round to the remains of the Shiel, a crude bulldozed track crosses the river and makes its way up the north-west ridge of Mount Keen. Just beyond, above the rocky hollow known as the 'korlach' (the OS call it Corrach for some reason), another path forks to the left, up to Mount Keen's stony granite summit.

The southern route starts from a car park where Glen Esk splits into Glen Lee and Glen Mark. The path then follows the Water of Mark in a north-westerly direction for just over 2km where it passes a monument known as the Queen's Well where, apparently, Queen Victoria stopped for refreshment during one of her excursions in 1861.

From the monument, the track splits and the Mounth road follows the right-hand branch, climbing quite steeply up beside the Ladder Burn to where a series of zigzags climb the southern shoulder of Mount Keen. Higher up the ridge, the track bifurcates again, the left-hand one being the Mounth road, while the right-hand branch takes you directly to the summit.

Route Summary: Start at the end of the public road which runs up Glen Tanar. Walk past a sawmill and through a gate which leads to an estate road. Follow this through pinewoods for about 5km and on up the open glen, crossing the river twice. At the third crossing (GR 407896) ascend the Mounth road S by a bulldozed track through heathery slopes. Diverge SE up the path to Mount Keen's summit

Map: OS Sheet 44

Access Point: Glen Tanar House, GR473957

Distance: 24km, 762m ascent

Approx Time: 6-10 hours

Translation: from monadh caoin, smooth or pleasant hill

Pronunciation: mount keen

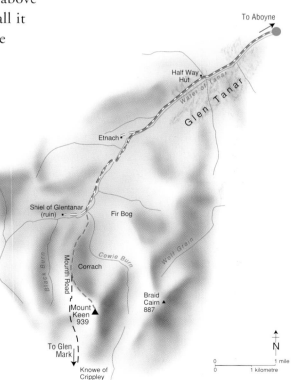

NORTHERN CAIRNGORMS

The Munros:

Mullach Clach a' Bhlair   Sgor Gaoith   Braeriach   Cairn Gorm
Beinn Mheadhoin   Bynack More

The Cairngorms, for practical purposes, can be broken up into two groups of hills – those that are normally climbed from Strathspey in the north, and those climbed from Deeside in the south. Needless to say, many of the hills can be climbed in groupings other than these listed here, for example Braeriach and Cairn Toul can be climbed together and all the hills of the Moine Mhor, Mullach Clach a' Bhlair, Sgor Gaoith, Monadh Mor and Beinn Bhrotain can be climbed in one round.

From Speyside, particularly around Aviemore, the Cairngorms appear almost as a high escarpment rising above the Queen's and Rothiemurchus Forests with the deep defile of the Lairig Ghru separating the main Cairn Gorm massif from the corrie-sculptured dome of Braeriach. From Loch Morlich at the foot of Glen More, Cairn Gorm and its corries form one of the finest views in Scotland.

The Cairngorms are broken into three major massifs. The Ben Avon/Beinn a' Bhuird group is separated from the Cairn Gorm/Macdui group by the long Lairig an Laoigh, while the Braeriach/Cairn Toul group is separated from the central group by the Lairig Ghru. On the fringes lie the hills of the Moine Mhor and Bynack More/A' Choinnich.

It is probably true that the name 'Cairngorms' is a modern misnomer. These hills were once known as Am Monadh Ruadh, the red hills, distinguishing them from Am Monadh Liath, or the grey hills west of the Spey. In the nineteenth century, visitors began referring to the hills collectively as the Cairngorms, using the name of the hill most obviously visible from Strathspey.

Geologically, the Cairngorms are very uniform, rough weathered granite forming high plateaux, the largest tracts of land over 600m, 900m and 1200m in the British Isles. Because of their height and exposure, these hills have the most Arctic-type climate of all the British hills, and the landforms, soils, vegetation, invertebrates and birds all have a greater similarity to those of Arctic Canada, Iceland or Greenland than to the southern European ranges of the Alps, Pyrenees or Caucasus.

The wonders of the Cairngorms can't be experienced by gazing up at the hills from below. They are too big and rounded for that. The Cairngorms demand that you climb to the high summits and vast plateaux and gaze down into the deep trenches and chasms, and the plethora of wind-scoured craggy corries.

These are the most important mountains, ecologically, in Britain, and have been

Carn Eilrig, Lurcher's Crag and Cairn Lochan, Cairngorms National Park

The Cairngorms from the north (Bynack More on the left, Cairn Gorm right of centre)

subjected to a whole host of potentially detrimental developments. The ski development on Cairn Gorm is generally reckoned to have been an ecological mistake, and subsequent proposals to extend the ski-ing facilities into the northern corries and Lurcher's Gully area were the subject of a public enquiry before the Secretary of State for Scotland finally decided against the proposals. Despite considerable opposition from conservationists, a funicular train now runs up the slopes of Cairn Gorm, ostensibly to serve a ski industry that is affected by the unpredictable snowfall.

In the past decade conservation bodies have bought large chunks of the Cairngorms and it is encouraging that the area has now been given National Park status.

Route Summary: Leave Achlean in Glen Feshie by the Fox-hunter's Path which climbs Carn Ban Mor E above the Allt Fhear-nagan. Continue over the shoulder S of Carn Ban Mor until the footpath joins up with a bull-dozed track. Follow this track SW and S over the Moine Mhor and past the head of Coire Garbhlach. Beyond this point another track joins from the W but continue S and where the track begins to bend due E leave it and climb the easy stony slopes of Mullach Clach a' Bhlair. Return to Carn Ban Mor over

Mullach Clach a' Bhlair (114), 1019m/3343ft, Sgor Gaoith (36), 1118m/3668ft

The Moine Mhor, the Great Moss, is a vast expanse of stony ridge, green hollows of turf and moss, with a profusion of sparkling clear streams. A high tableland, it is a favourite feeding place for red deer and a haunt of ptarmigan and dotterel and although it's not much lower in height than the great plateaux of Braeriach and Cairn Gorm it doesn't share the harshness and bite of these lofty areas. Instead it offers a lonely solitude, green rather than grey, tending to the softer end of harsh, a pearl in a crown of diamonds.

In winter, under a mantle of snow, the character of the place changes. The Great Moss is often a desert of driving wind and blinding snow and even when the sun shines from a deep blue, almost black, sky, there is an ominous feel to these vast, white, endless morraines. I have seen it when not a rock, blade of grass, nor clump of heather protuded from the snow – a never-ending blanket of white, offering no relief to sun-strained eyes.

Most walkers approach the Moine Mhor from Glen Feshie where the public road stops at the little farm of Achlean. From behind the farmhouse, the Foxhunter's Path (the name of the path recalls a family of celebrated foxhunters who once lived at Achlean) skirts the Scottish Natural Heritage woods of Baden Mosach and climbs to Carn Ban Mor by way of Coire Fhearnagan. Once over the crest of the broad Carn Ban Mor ridge the vast sweep of the Great Moss becomes apparent.

If you follow the contours due south the great gouge of Coire Garbhlach appears, biting its way into the tableland. This is a long winding corridor housing the Allt Garbhlach and it is possible to gain access to the Moine Mhor via a steep climb up one of the corries' headwalls.

Unfortunately man has blighted the superb feeling of wilderness on the Moine Mhor in the form of bulldozed roads. The track can be put to advantage to reach the most southerly of the Moine Mhor Munros, Mullach Clach a' Bhlair. Despite its 1019m elevation, Mullach is a mere swell in the rolling terrain, although a series of rocky outcrops in the vicinity gives promise of better things.

To the north of Carn Ban Mor, broad slopes lead to a shallow col before rising again to Sgur Gaoith. This, the Peak of the Wind, is one of the finest summits of the Cairngorms. It rises gracefully in a long sweep from Sguran Dubh Mor and ends abruptly at its cairn. Some 600m below shimmer the waters of Loch Einich. Long ridges of granite

the bulldozed track or wander straight across the Moine Mhor on bearings and from there descend NNE to the broad bealach above the Fuaran Dio-tach then climb the easy slopes of Sgor Gaoith. Return to Achlean via Carn Ban Mor

Map: OS Sheet 43

Access Point: Car park just N of Achlean in Glen Feshie

Distance: 26km, 820m ascent

Approx Time: 6-8 hours

Translation: summit of the stone of the plain; peak of the wind

Pronunciation: moolach clach a vaar; skor goo-ee

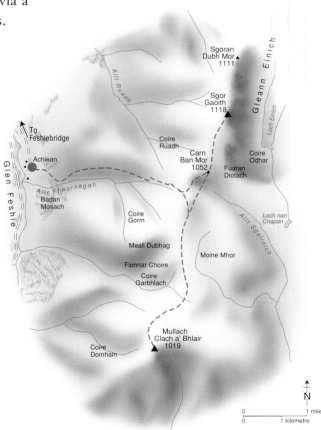

blocks, seemingly thrown together in haphazard fashion, lead down towards the loch, offering some good scrambling routes.

Sgur Gaoith can also be climbed via Sguran Dubh Mor from Rothiemurchus, or indeed can be included in a fine traverse from the Foxhunter's Path to Carn Ban Mor, over Sgur Gaoith, Sguran Dubh Mor and Sguran Dubh Beag and down to Rothiemurchus near Loch Gamhna or Loch an Eilein.

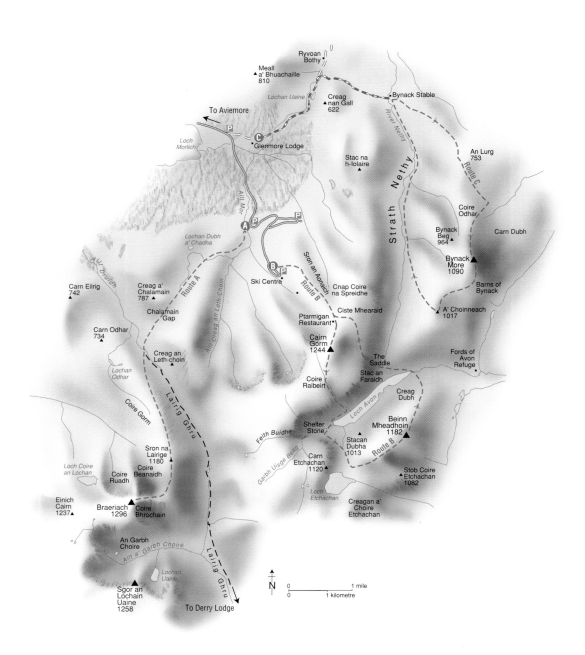

Braeriach (3), 1296m/4252ft

Braeriach is the Brindled Upland and it's an airy place. If you stand by the summit cairn and gaze down the long empty kilometres of Glen Dee, past the bulk of Beinn Macdui and the long arm of Carn a' Mhaim, you'll see great cliffs of red granite thrust up out of the rough corrie below you in pinnacles and buttresses and spires and the snow wreaths which circle the upper corries until late in summer. The summit of Braeriach is actually made up from the apexes of no less than five corries and in the depth of winter it becomes a complex system of snow cornices.

Most folk climb Braeriach from the car park known as the Sugar Bowl. This lies just below the first steep bend on the road from Glenmore up to the Cairn Gorm car park. From there a good footpath runs through the impressively rocky Chalamain Gap and down into the Lairig Ghru (where the Sinclair Memorial Hut stood before its demolition.) From there an obvious path climbs onto the long ridge of Sron na Lairige, over a high col between Coire Beanaidh and Coire Ruadh and up the narrowing eastern ridge of Braeriach to the summit, perched precariously above the pinnacles and buttresses of Coire Bhrochain.

A much longer expedition follows this route to Braeriach, and then proceeds to Sgor an Lochain Uaine and Cairn Toul around the rim of the An Garbh Coire, the huge corrie which separates Braeriach from Cairn Toul. This latter Munro can also be climbed along with Braeriach from the Moine Mhor via Loch nan Stuirteag, returning via Einich Cairn.

Braeriach, on its own, can also be climbed from the Moine Mhor, arguably a route of greater variety than the others. From the top of the Foxhunter's Path from Achlean the route to Braeriach takes an uncompromising line across the high plateau following the Allt Sgairnich to Loch nan Cnapan. From here a north-easterly line follows the broad south-west shoulder of Einch Cairn to its flat, gravelly plateau, with views to your left down into the great trench of Gleann Einich. The loch lies deep in this glen gaurded by the steep ribs and buttresses of the Sgorans and Sgor Gaoith on one side and the great scoop of Coire Dhondail on the other. It's an easy walk across the plateau from Einich Cairn to Braeriach but you'll have to navigate fairly precisely in misty weather. In winter conditions this is a long and demanding route.

Route Summary: Leave the Sugar Bowl car park, cross the ski road and follow the footpath over the Allt Mor bridge (Route A). Continue on this path to the Chalamain Gap. Go through the gap and descend to the Lairig Ghru. Climb the hillside opposite by way of the obvious footpath and reach the Sron na Lairige ridge which is then followed S to the edge of Coire Ruadh. Here the ridge swings to the right to meet the E ridge of Braeriach. Follow this ridge to the edge of Coire Bhrochain and then follow the corrie lip to the summit

Map: OS Sheets 36 and 43

Access Point: Sugar Bowl car park on the Glenmore to Cairn Gorm ski road

Distance: 21km, 840m ascent

Approx Time: 8-10 hours

Translation: brindled upland

Pronunciation: brae-reeach

Map: OS Sheet 36

Access Point: Coire Cas car park

Distance: 18km, 1680m ascent

Approx Time: 6-10 hours

Translation: blue hill; middle hill

Pronunciation: cairngorom; byn vee-an

Cairn Gorm (6), 1244m/4081ft, Beinn Mheadhoin (13), 1182m/3878ft

Cairn Gorm is, of course, home to Scotland's major ski development where two of its corries, Coire na Ciste and Coire Cas, have largely been developed into pistes. A system of ski tows operates in both corries and a funicular train now runs up the slopes of Coire Cas.

A long route to the summit of Cairn Gorm, which largely avoids the ski paraphernalia, runs from Ryvoan Pass just south of An Lochan Uaine, the Green Lochan. A rough path climbs up onto heather moorland north of Carn Lochan na Beinne and then follows the lovely ridge of Sron a' Cha-no high above the steep slopes which drop down into Strath Nethy. It then skirts the rocky tor of Cnap Coire na Spreidhe and climbs the final slopes of Cairn Gorm above Ciste Mhearad, Margaret's Coffin.

Another route leaves the ski car park in Coire Cas, climbs steeply north-east to reach the path which follows the Sron an Aonaich between Coire Cas and Coire na Ciste, and then proceeds to the top station of the funicular railway. The summit lies about 1km to the south via a cairned tourist path.

From the summit of Cairn Gorm, leave the grossly enlarged cairn and weather station behind you and drop down rocky slopes in a southerly direction into the flushes of Coire Raibeirt. Even here, a few minutes from the crowds, you can begin to feel something of the splendour of the Cairngorms. Ahead of you, across the great gulf that contain Loch Avon, the tor-studded whaleback of Beinn Mheadhoin is obvious, rising beside the glittering waters of Loch Etchachan, whose shoreline caresses the 914m (3000 ft) contour. This is big country, an area of deep-cut chasms, high craggy cliffs and great rounded prows.

A well-maintained path follows the burn down Coire Raibeirt to the lovely Loch Avon where another path follows the shoreline to the head of the loch. A great jumble of massive boulders lies below the frowning precipices of the Sticil (sometimes referred to as the Shelter Stone Crag), and Carn Etchachan. The old howff below the Shelter Stone is in the middle of this great boulder field. Continue south-eastwards up the slanting path that soon lifts you high above the loch and into the great glaciated hollow that houses Loch Etchachan, one of the most atmospheric parts of the Cairngorms.

Just before you reach the loch leave the path and climb eastwards up to the first of Beinn Meadhoin's granite tops. Follow the broad crest along the line of tors to the highest which forms the summit.

Loch Etchachan and Cairn Gorm

It can be climbed in a simple scramble from its north side.

You can return to Cairn Gorm either by retracing your footsteps to the Shelter Stone and climbing onto the Cairn Gorm plateau via Coire Dhomhain, completely retracing your steps via Coire Raibeirt, or by dropping down steep slopes north-north-east of the summit of Beinn Mheadhoin, avoiding the crags of Creag Dhubh to your left, to the foot of Loch Avon. Cross the outflow of the loch and follow the footpath onto The Saddle at the head of Strath Nethy. From there, climb steeply in a north-north-west direction to the shallow scoop of Ciste Mhearad and across the Ptarmigan Bowl to Sron an Aonaich. Alternatively, follow Strath Nethy to Bynack Stable where a bulldozed track continues to the Pass of Ryvoan.

Beinn Mheadhoin can also be climbed from the south. From the Linn of Dee take the track to Derry Lodge and through Glen Derry to Coire Etchachan. Follow the path up through the corrie past the Hutchison Memorial Hut to Loch Etchachan. From there climb north-eastwards to reach the first of Beinn Mheadhoin's summits.

Bynack More (54), 1090m/3576ft

Route Summary: Leave parking area just beyond Glenmore Lodge and follow the forestry track into the Pass of Ryvoan (Route C). Continue through the Pass, past Lochan Uaine. About 400m beyond the lochan take another path E to the River Nethy. Cross the river and follow the footpath SE over the lower shoulder of Bynack More. Follow this path to its highest point then leave it to bear S up the N ridge to the summit. Return the same way or by Strath Nethy

Map: OS Sheet 36

Access Point: Glenmore Lodge, GR992097

Distance: 20km, 760m ascent

Approx Time: 5-8 hours

Translation: big cap

Pronunciation: bie-nack moar

Rising from the flattish hills to the north-east of the main Cairn Gorm group, Bynack More is a peak of some individuality and character and shows its finest aspect to the north above the Forest of Abernethy. From here it forms a fine conical peak, unusual in the rounded Cairngorms, although it must be said that it is dominated by the massive shoulders of Cairn Gorm.

The Lairig an Laoigh path from Glenmore to Braemar skirts Bynack More's northern and eastern slopes and offers a good approach to the hill, but first, enjoy the delights of Ryvoan.

Just beyond Glenmore Lodge the National Mountaineering Centre, there is a small parking area. From there a Forestry track enters the Scottish Wildlife Trust Reserve of Ryvoan, a beautiful stretch of Caledonian Pine, juniper and birch. A little further on, An Lochan Uaine, or the Green Lochan, lies in a hollow below the scree-girt slopes of Creag nan Gall, the Crag of the Stranger. The waters of the lochan are an unusual translucent greenish-blue colour, the local legend claiming that the tint comes from the fairies washing their green clothes in it!

Sadly, the bank leading down to An Lochan Uaine has been severely eroded which has led to the building of a fence round the loch and wooden steps being built down to the shore.

About 500m beyond the lochan another path leads off to the right and crosses the heather moorland to the River Nethy. The river is crossed by a footbridge and the path continues up the long, broad north ridge of Bynack More. This footpath, the Lairig an Laoigh path, climbs gradually onto a high plateau north of Bynack Mor and swings gently to the left of the mountain. As it begins to drop down into Coire Odhar, leave the path and head for the prominent north nose of Bynack Mor where another path climbs up the rocky ridge to the summit. Further on, on the south east slopes of the mountain, the amazing granite tors of the Barns of Bynack are well worth a visit.

Return to Glenmore by the outward route or for an alternative continue from the summit south westwards to the flat-topped A' Choinnich with its fine views up Loch Avon to the Sticil and Carn Etchachan, returning to Glenmore by Strath Nethy.

The Cairngorm plateau from the north in winter

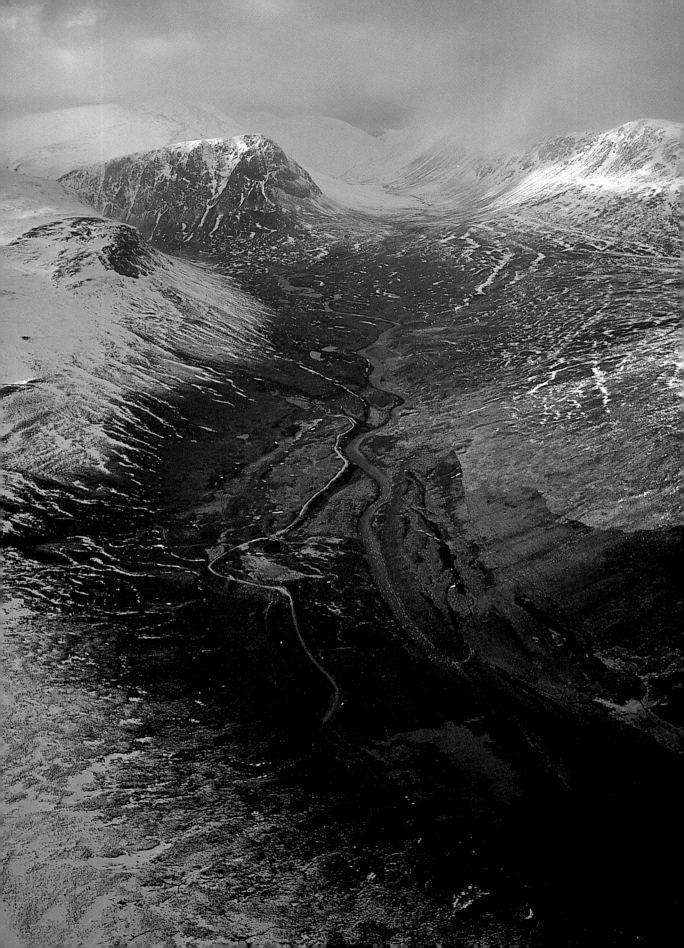

SOUTHERN CAIRNGORMS

The Munros:

Devil's Point   Cairn Toul   Sgor an Lochain Uaine
Monadh Mor   Beinn Bhrotain   Carn a' Mhaim   Ben Macdui
Derry Cairngorm   Beinn Bhreac   Beinn a' Chaorainn
Beinn a' Bhuird   Ben Avon (Leabaidh an Daimh Bhuidhe)

In 1995 the National Trust for Scotland, with the help of National Lottery money, bought the Mar Lodge Estate in the Cairngorms, an estate which contains the vast majority of the Munros in this section. The importance of that purchase highlights the significance of this area, arguably the most important mountain landscape in Britain. The plethora of corries and the high Arctic-like plateaux are the two most important landscape features of the Cairngorms and the associated flora, fauna and birds of these high wind-scoured quarters unite to make the Cairngorms unique.

In the first edition of the Scottish Mountaineering Club's *District Guide to the Cairngorms* (1928), Sir Henry Alexander suggested that for many, first acquaintance with these hills was occasionally accompanied by a sense of disappointment. But, he goes on to say, 'as one explores them and wanders among them, the magnitude of everything begins to reveal itself, and one realises the immensity of the scale upon which the scene is set, and the greatness and dignity and calm of the Cairngorms cast their spell over the spirit.'

The Devil's Point (Bod an Deamhain) (130), 1004m/3294ft, Cairn Toul (4), 1291m/4236ft, Sgor an Lochain Uaine (5), 1258m/4127ft

There is an apocryphal story which suggests that Queen Victoria once asked her ghillie John Brown the name of a rather fine mountain just south of Cairn Toul. Knowing that if he told her the Gaelic name she would immediately ask for a translation he thought it best to offer her a euphemistic translation. The literal translation of Bod an Deamhain (pronounced pot-in-john), the penis of the demon, could have caused some embarrassment. Sadly the translation he offered, The Devil's Point, has stuck and now we even have an Angel's Peak (Sgor an Lochain Uaine) one of the latest Munro additions, above An Garbh Choire to help balance out the religious analogy.

Route Summary: Take the private road from Linn of Dee to Derry Lodge (Route A, p.127). Follow the track up Glen Luibeg to the Lairig Ghru. Follow the path which skirts the southern slopes of Carn a' Mhaim and drops to Glen Dee. Cross the river to Corrour Bothy. A worn path leads W behind the bothy up steep zigzags above the Allt a' Choire Odhair. From the col at the head of the corrie head S then bear E to the summit of the Devil's Point. Return to the col. Follow the broad grassy ridge which rises N to Stob Coire an t-Saighdeir and then to

The Devil's Point and Glen Dee from the air

Cairn Toul and Sgor an Lochain Uaine from the south

Cairn Toul. Follow the ridge WNW to a bealach and climb Sgor an Lochain Uaine. Return to the bealach, drop down by the Allt Glais an t-Sabhail to the head of Glen Geusachan. Follow faint path ESE to An Diolland, then take the stalkers' path to Corrour

Map: OS Sheets 36 and 43

Access Point: Linn of Dee

Distance: 40km, 1140m ascent

Approx Time: 8-12 hours

Translation: from the Gaelic Bod an Deamhain, penis of the devil; from Carn an t-Sabhail, hill of the barn; peak of the small green loch.

Pronunciation: pot-in-john; kaarn towel; skoor an lochan oo-anya

I'd love to see a campaign mounted which encouraged the Ordnance Survey to revert to the original name – surely there should be no place in these Highland mountains for such woolly translations, even if it does come from a good story.

Cairn Toul comes from Carn an t-Sabhail, the hill of the barn, a name which seems unlikely when the hill is viewed from the east. This aspect presents a shapely and attractive form, a wedge of a summit formed by the apex of three great scalloped corries. But from the west, particularly from the Moine Mhor, it does appear square shaped and uninspiring, and probably deserving of the name.

Cairn Toul and Sgor an Lochain Uaine are often climbed with Braeriach in a traverse around the rim of An Garbh Choire, one of the finest corries in the Highlands. This expedition, most often attempted from the north, is a big day out and should only be tackled in the long days of summer. However, the Devil's Point, Cairn Toul, and Sgor an Lochain Uaine can all be climbed quite comfortably in a day from Linn of Dee, especially if you use a bike as far as Glen Luibeg.

The Lairig Ghru path from Glen Luibeg meets another path from White Bridge just opposite Corrour Bothy which is named after the corrie which lies behind it, Coire Odhar, or Dun Corrie. This great scoop stretches from the black glistening slabs of The

Devil's Point all the way round to the containing ridge of Coire an t-Saighdeir of Cairn Toul and a stalkers' path climbs its steep slopes from behind the bothy.

The final zigzags of this path thrust you on to one of the most delightful spots in the Cairngorms, An Diolland, the mossy saddle. Head north along the edge of the precipitous Coire an t-Saighdeir, the soldier's corrie, to a small dip in the ridge. A final climb over angular blocks brings you to the narrow summit of Cairn Toul. Follow the rocky ridge west-north-west to a bealach then climb to the summit of Sgor an Lochain Uaine. Return to the bealach and drop down by the Allt Glais an t-Sabhail all the way to the head of Glen Geusachan. Follow a faint path in an east-south-east direction to An Diolland and then follow gentle slopes to the summit of the Devil's Point. Return to An Diolland and the stalkers' path to Corrour.

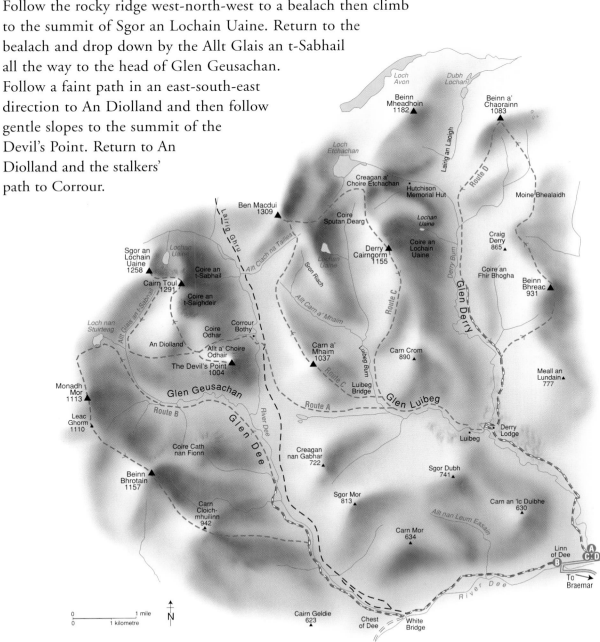

Route Summary: Take the private road W from Linn of Dee to White Bridge (Route B). Continue past the Chest of Dee and along the path to its end. Take to the rough moor and enter Glen Geusachan. Follow the stream up the glen and climb to the outflow from Loch nan Stuirteag. Turn S and climb the obvious ridge of Monadh Mor to the summit. Head S to another top at 1110m and then descend SE above the head of Coire Cath nam Fionn. From the col continue SE to the summit of Beinn Bhrotain. Continue SE over Carn Cloich-mhuilinn and down its E ridge to Glen Dee

Map: OS Sheet 43

Access Point: Linn of Dee

Distance: 37km, 910m ascent

Approx Time: 8-12 hours

Translation: big hill; hill of the mastiff

Pronunciation: monagh moar; byn vrotan

Monadh Mor (40), 1113m/3652ft, Beinn Bhrotain (19), 1157m/3796ft

Loch nan Stuirteag makes a fine destination for a day on the Great Moss, nestling snugly as it does into a fold in the hills between Monadh Mor and the long slopes of Cairn Toul and the Einich Cairn massif. It's a place of desolate beauty, this Loch of the Gulls, the reed-edged waters lapping gently on the tiny sand beaches. To my mind, little gems like this are the real Cairngorms, too remote for day trippers and far removed from the busy trade routes of Cairngorm and Macdui.

You can reach Loch nan Stuirteag from either Glen Geusachan in the east, or Glen Feshie in the west. Although I've described the eastern approach in the Route Summary, the western approach is equally fine, offering an opportunity to wander over the Moine Mhor towards the Loch, high above the head of Loch Einich. Probably the best way of visiting these high hills is to make a camp by Loch nan Stuirteag, explore the hills of the Moine Mhor on one day and then climb Cairn Toul and the Devil's Point the next, allowing yourself to be seduced by the remoteness and scale of this massive massif.

Behind the loch, Monadh Mor lies with its long ridge leading south, a sore temptation for Munro folk. To bag Monadh Mor and then cross the steep bealach and grab Beinn Bhrotain fills a summer evening well from a high camp, but in winter an expedition to these two hills is a major undertaking. It's a long way for the short days of November, but if there is time it's good to sit for a while between these two big hills, just above the screes of Coire Cath nam Fionn, the Corrie of the Battle of the Fingalians.

As the breeze sighs coldly up from Glen Geusachan, let your imagination wander back through the mists of time, back to a time as old as these hills themselves. Who fought in the Battle of the Fingalians? Who won? Only the remaining rocks can tell of the deeds of that once proud race. The distant voice of Ossian, Fingal's bardic son, casts little light on the matter:

'Though the plains of our battles are dark and silent, our fame is in the four grey stones. The voice of Ossian has been heard. The harp has been strung in Selma. Come Ossian, come away, come fly with thy father on clouds. I come, I come, thou king of men.'

Ben Macdui from the north

Carn a' Mhaim (95), 1037m/3402ft, Ben Macdui (2), 1309m/4295ft, Derry Cairngorm (20), 1155m/3789ft

This big horseshoe walk takes you into the very heart of the central massif of the Cairngorms and touches on some of the real splendours of this area – the beauty of Glen Luibeg, the long ridge of Carn a' Mhaim, an unusual feature for the Cairngorms, the wide and spacious tundra of Macdui, the crags and cliffs of Coire Sputain Dearg and the spectacular situation of Loch Etchachan.

Ben Macdui, Britain's second-highest mountain and for many years thought to be the highest (Cairn Gorm enthusiasts from Strathspey were determined to build a huge cairn on the summit when it was discovered that Ben Nevis was just over 30m higher. Thankfully their plans never succeeded.), is most often climbed either from Cairn Gorm, across the plateau via Lochan Bhuidhe, or via the lovely Sron Riach ridge in Glen Luibeg. Carn a' Mhaim is occasionally climbed from the north but it's a long way from Ben Macdui when you have to retrace your steps back over Macdui's stony dome.

Derry Cairngorm can be climbed in another long day from the

Route Summary: Take the private road from Linn of Dee to Derry Lodge. Cross the Derry Burn by the bridge W of Derry Lodge. Follow the track to the SNH deer fences S of Luibeg Bridge and then leave the track to climb the SE ridge of Carn a' Mhaim (Route C, p.127). The NW top is the summit. From here follow the narrowing ridge in a NNW direction to a wide col at 800m. Climb the steep and stony slopes due N to the summit of Ben Macdui. Descend E over wide bouldery and featureless slopes to the edge of Coire Sputan Dearg and follow the ridge NE to a col just W of Creagan a Choire Etchachan. Skirting the SW slopes of Creagan a Choire Etchachan descend S to the bealach N of Derry Cairngorm. Climb bouldery slopes S to the summit.

Return to Derry Lodge by Carn Crom

Map: OS Sheets 36 and 43

Access Point: Linn of Dee

Distance: 30km, 1370m ascent

Approx Time: 8-12 hours

Translation: cairn of the large round hill; hill of the black pig; blue hill of Derry (from doire, a thicket)

Pronunciation: kaarn a vame; byn macdooee; derry cairngorom

north and some even combine it with Beinn Mheadhoin in a big day from Cairn Gorm via the head of Loch Avon. A shorter round can be enjoyed by approaching from Glen Derry, climbing Coire Etchachan to the loch and then heading south over a stony ridge to the summit. The descent is then via the long south ridge before heading south-west over heathery slopes into Glen Luibeg.

Long walk-ins tend to be a feature of the Braemar side of the Cairngorms and regular Cairngormers become very, very familiar with the track from Linn of Dee to Derry Lodge – mountain bikes are now regularly used to speed up access and it is well worth while using a bike on this route as far as the Scottish Natural Heritage enclosures just south of the Luibeg Bridge.

This plethora of deer fencing has undoubtedly spoiled what was once a lovely area and it could be that it will be there for many years until the pine woods recover from the ravages of too many hungry deer. If you can find your way through the fencing stay on the west-bound Lairig Ghru track as it climbs on to the south-east ridge of Carn a' Mhaim. The popularity of the Lairig Ghru is revealed hereabouts by massive erosion and that, if nothing else, is a good excuse to leave the path and take to the heather in a north-west direction, climbing increasingly stony slopes to the 1014m south top of Carn a' Mhaim.

From here it's only a short distance to the summit, then the long bumpy ridge which becomes increasingly narrow towards the Ceann Crionn, or thin end. From the high bealach between Carn a' Mhaim and Macdui it's a long pull over boulders and scree to the summit of Britain's second highest hill, but the views west to The Devil's Point, Cairn Toul and Braeriach are justly rewarding. The line of the Allt Clach nan Taillear, the Tailors' Burn, is a good one to follow and takes you on to the broad stony expanse just east of Macdui's summit – it's an easy walk on a gravelly path to the huge summit cairn and view indicator.

From the summit return to the top of the Tailors' Burn and follow the Loch Etchachan path round the head of Coire Sputain Dearg for about a kilometre. Leave the path and climb to the 1108m top of Creagan a' Choire Etchachan and follow its broad stony ridge southwards to a shallow col at 1014m. From here Derry Cairngorm lifts its head in rocky dominance and it's a straightforward walk to its bouldery summit. Descend south to the col between it and its southern top, Carn Crom and follow the more open, heather-covered slopes in a west-south-west direction towards the Luibeg Burn, where a footpath takes you back to the enclosures in Glen Luibeg.

The Cairngorms from the south (Glen Derry on the left and Glen Quoich on the right)

Beinn Bhreac (249), 931m/3054ft,
Beinn a' Chaorainn (58), 1083m/3553ft

These two hills form the northern and southern limit of a vast upland plateau, the slopes of which pour down from the north top of Beinn a' Bhuird. Forming the eastern boundary to Glen Derry, this huge area, the Moine Bhealaidh, the peat moss of the broom, is a lumpy expanse of peat hags, bog, turf and countless pools of water.

Both Munros can be climbed independently, Beinn Bhreac from Glen Derry and Beinn a Chaorainn from the Fords of Avon Bothy by the River Avon in the north, but a good route combines both summits with a fine walk down the length of Glen Derry making use of the ancient Lairig an Laoigh path. Just past Derry Lodge a bulldozed track forces its ugly way through the trees on the east bank of the river and rises to a high point of about 500m. From here, about 2km from Derry Lodge, leave the track and work your way between the trees and up heathery slopes in a north-east direction to the obvious col between Meall an Lundain and the scree-speckled Beinn Bhreac. From the col it's an easy walk to the summit from where the lochan-splattered Moine Bhealaidh lies at your feet. Beyond it the conical shape of Beinn a' Chaorainn gives way to steep crags which pour down westwards into the defile of the Lairig an Laoigh pass.

You can treat the Moine Bhealaidh two ways – curse it for its boggy, peat hag ridden nature, or enjoy the plover-haunted atmosphere of it. It helps to follow the high ground of it as much as possible and in good weather you'll be delighted by the westward views over Glen Derry to the tops of the central massif.

Route Summary: Take the private road to Derry Lodge. Continue on the bulldozed track on the E side of Glen Derry for 1.6km or so (Route D, p.127) then strike uphill over heathery slopes and through trees to the col between Meall an Lundain and Beinn Bhreac. From here climb NNE to the summit. Continue NW then N across the Moine Bhealaidh to Beinn a' Chaorainn. Return to Derry Lodge by the Lairig an Laoigh

Map: OS Sheets 36 and 43

Access Point: Linn of Dee

Distance: 29km, 820m ascent

Approx Time: 8-10 hours

Translation: speckled hill; hill of the rowan

Pronunciation: byn vrechk; byn a choeran

Beinn a' Bhuird from the slopes of Ben Avon

The closer you come to Beinn a' Chaorainn the easier is the terrain, eventually climbing the mountain's broad south ridge over gravel and scree to the summit.

Descend in a south-west direction then westwards steeply down into the Lairig an Laoigh with direct views up the length of Coire Etchachan towards Ben Macdui. From the summit of the pass walk south into Glen Derry and over the flats to the pines of Derry Lodge.

Beinn a' Bhuird (11), 1197m/3927ft, Ben Avon (Leabaidh an Daimh Bhuidhe) (17), 1171m/3842ft

From Allanaquoich a footpath runs above the Linn of Quoich to a footbridge over the burn. Once across the bridge the track up the west side of Glen Quoich offers an opportunity to enjoy the combination of river and Caledonian pine scenery, an evocation of Cairn Gorm finery. Beyond a path junction a newer footpath has replaced the old bulldozed track that once climbed the An Diollaid shoulder of Beinn a' Bhuird. The old track has been removed by the National Trust for Scotland, who own this Mar Lodge estate. Suffice to say that the old bulldozed track has now gone and what was once an ugly scar on the face of the hill is growing over well. The new path takes a more direct line from the Alltan na Beinne and gradually climbs to the hill above the An Diollaid shoulder.

Below, the slopes drop away into the Dubh Gleann, the dark glen that bites its way into the Arctic plateau of the Moine Bhealaidh, and beyond Beinn Bhreac appear the hills of central Cairngorms – the massive Cairn Gorm/Beinn Macdui massif.

The new path straggles on to the vast summit plateau of Beinn a' Bhuird where enormous cornices often overhang the east-facing Coire nan Clach, Coire an Dubh Lochain and Coire na Ciche. Ahead lies the small pile of rocks that represents the north summit cairn of Beinn a' Bhuird, a mere speck on the vast, gently curving

Route Summary: Take footpath from Allanaquoich above the Linn of Quoich and cross the footbridge over the burn. Follow the track up W side of Glen Quoich. Go past a path junction and climb to An Diollaid. From the ridge the path straggles up onto the bare plateau. From the path end it's a straightforward stroll to the summit, difficult in misty conditions. From here head E to The Sneck, then climb a zigzagging path on to the Beinn Avon plateau. Cross open ground to Leabaidh an Daimh Bhuidhe. The summit of Ben Avon is the top of this granite tor. Return to The Sneck and descend S down grassy slopes to the Clach a' Cleirich. Follow footpath S past a path junction

horizon. From the cairn you can see the massive granite tor, the Leabaidh an Daimh Bhuidhe, that is the highest point on neighbouring Ben Avon.

The great corries of Beinn a' Bhuird look spectacular as you descend to The Sneck, the slim and rocky ridge that connects with Ben Avon. Once across the narrow neck, complete with its own natural standing stones, a zigzagging path lifts you onto the vast Ben Avon plateau. The Leabaidh an Daimh Bhuidhe is only minutes away, although it takes a scramble to reach the highest point of the tor, and the summit of Ben Avon.

Return to The Sneck and down the comparatively sheltered corrie to a huge erratic known as the Clach a' Chleirich, the Stone of the Clergyman. From here, a footpath leads down towards Gleann an t-Slugain to where a minor path breaks away to the right to take you through the pine woods above the upper reaches of the Quoich Water. Enjoy this downhill ramble through the ancient pine forest back to the firm track that runs all the way back to Allanaquoich.

and at the next path junction turn right. Drop down through Glen Quoich, on the N side of the Quoich Water, to the track back to Allanaquoich

Map: OS Sheets 43 and 36
Access Point: Allanaquoich

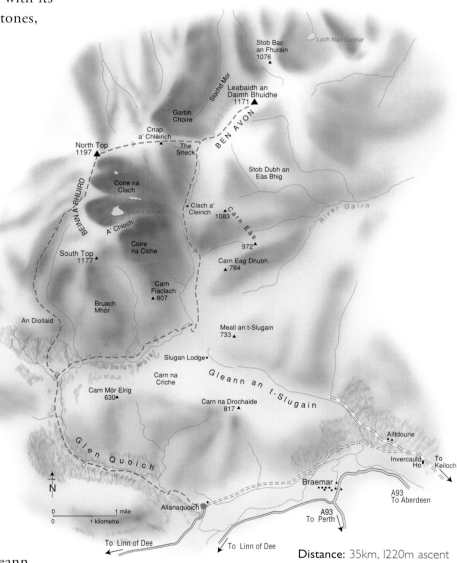

Distance: 35km, 1220m ascent
Approx Time: 10-12 hours
Translation: hill of the table; bed of the yellow stag
Pronunciation: byn a voord; lyepay an dyv vooee

LAGGAN AND THE MONADH LIATH

The Munros:

A' Chailleach   Carn Sgulain   Carn Dearg   Geal Charn
Carn Liath   Stob Poite Coire Ardair   Creag Meagaidh
Beinn a' Chaorainn   Beinn Teallach

The Monadh Liath have suffered a bad press. Several writers on the outdoors have written off these hills as dull and uninspiring but while the summits may be rounded and bald, they nevertheless rise above a clutch of interesting side glens running off the main one, Glen Banchor. Indeed the whole area is rather like the back of a hand, with several long fingers running on from a great central plateau. There may not be any great pinnacles here, rocky spires and sheer rock faces are non-existent, but there are other attributes – a wide open aspect, a feeling of vast skyscapes and spaciousness, and you'll see more wildlife here in a day than you'll see in the Skye Cuillin in a week.

Further west, Creag Meagaidh has gained a little more respect – this is a big mountain with a huge character, a mastiff of a mountain and every winter climbers enjoy the snow- and ice-covered crags of the huge Coire Ardair. In summer these same crags are slippery and vegetated but the scale never changes – it is a fine walk around the summits that enclose the long Coire Ardair.

Beinn Teallach was promoted to Munro status in 1984, after a re-survey by the Ordnance Survey, and while it keeps its best attributes hidden for most of the ascent, it's well worth combining with neighbouring Beinn a' Chaorainn to experience its finer aspects.

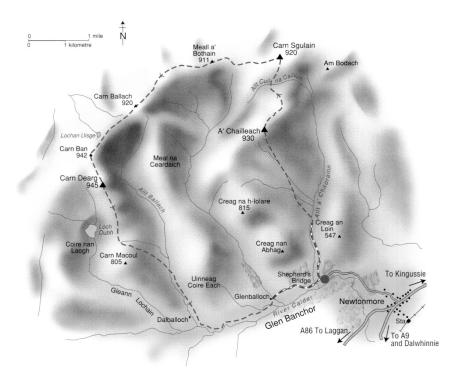

A' Chailleach (251), 930m/3051ft, Carn Sgulain (271), 920m/3018ft, Carn Dearg (225), 945m/3100ft

The Allt a' Chaorainn runs down from Coire a' Chaorainn and into the River Calder in Glen Banchor, a broad and lovely glen to the north of Creag Dhubh. A motorable road runs up to the glen from Newtonmore as far as a parking space above the Shepherd's Bridge. In front of you the flat glen floor gives rise to the birch-covered slopes of Creag Dhubh on the left, while to the right, the north, several long ridges run down from a high plateau. A' Chailleach is the high point of the first of those fingers, while Carn Dearg is several fingers up the glen. Carn Sgulain is the high point of the plateau from which these long fingers run.

A' Chailleach offers its best profile from the footpath which runs north from Shepherd's Bridge. Its north-east facing corrie, which is the hill's finest feature, is hardly spectacular but when snow swathes the steep, rocky flanks of its north-east buttress there's fun, if not a little challenge, to be had by following the line of least resistance up through the rock-bands and steep terraces.

The usual route of ascent is from the end of the footpath which runs north from Shepherd's Bridge. At the turning point in the track drop down to the left to where a footbridge across the stream is partly hidden by some trees. For years I crossed the burn here, usually getting very wet feet, before I noticed there was a bridge!

Long heathery slopes roll down from A' Chailleach's summit ridge in a southerly direction and from the crossing of the Allt a' Chaorainn it's a long relentless pull up these slopes to the summit. Things improve as you climb higher – once over a series of peat hags the going becomes easier over stony ground.

Carn Sgulain lies less than two kilometres north of A' Chailleach, and easy slopes drop down to the narrow defile which contains the Allt Cuil na Caillich. Beyond it, steeper grassy slopes climb to the broad summit of Sgulain, complete with fence posts leading past the summit. These same fence posts make navigation easy almost all the way to Carn Dearg for 8km over a series of minor tops and bumps. The going is not difficult, although it's quite featureless, over grass and heather and a couple of small lochans. The fence posts can be followed as far as Carn Mor just to the south of Lochan Uisge, where you must leave them behind and climb the north-north-east ridge of Carn Dearg. This is probably the finest of the Monadh Liath hills, a long two-and-a-half kilometre ridge with steep craggy slopes dropping to the east. On the other side grassy slopes drop down to secretive Loch Dubh and lonely Coire nan Laogh.

Route Summary: Drive up Glen Banchor to the parking area above Shepherd's Bridge. Follow the footpath N beside the Allt a' Chaorainn till it ends in a turning point. Drop down to the stream and cross by a footbridge which is hidden from the path. Climb heathery slopes NNE to the rounded summit of A' Chailleach. Descend N into a deep glen and then continue N on steep and tussocky grass to the summit of Carn Sgulain. From the summit follow a line of fence posts W then SW over an undulating plateau crossing several minor tops. At Carn Ban, leave the fence posts and go S to a short and steep climb to the summit of Carn Dearg. Continue on the narrow ridge S to a bealach and drop E into Gleann Balloch down broad heathery slopes. A narrow footpath follows the stream back into Glen Banchor from where a track beside the River Calder takes you back to Shepherd's Bridge

Map: OS Sheet 35

Access Point: Glen Banchor, GR693998

Distance: 24.1km, 838m ascent

Approx Time: 6-8 hours

Translation: red hill; the old woman; hill of the basket or of the old man

Pronunciation: a kaalyach; kaarn skoolin; kaarn jerrack

To return to Shepherd's Bridge, follow the ridge south of the summit cairn over a subsidiary top and down to the bealach below Carn Macoul. From the bealach descend eastwards to the Allt Ballach, cross the burn and follow the footpath past Dalballoch into Glen Banchor where a path on the north side of the River Calder takes you back to your starting point.

Geal Charn (260), 926m/3038ft

Route Summary: From the bridge follow the path which runs up the SE side of the Feith Talagain. At the end of the path cross the Allt Coire nan Dearcag and climb the heather-covered SW ridge of Geal Charn direct to the summit. Return by Beinn Sgiath and the SW ridge

Map: OS Sheet 35

Access Point: Garva Bridge

Distance: 14.4km, 610m ascent

Approx Time: 4-6hours

Translation: white hill

Pronunciation: gyal kaarn

The most westerly of the Monadh Liath Munros, Geal Charn rears up its rounded shoulders above lonely Glen Markie north-west of Laggan. Twin spurs emanate from the hill's twin summits and drop down grassy slopes south westwards to Garva Bridge while the north-east of the mountain shows a very different face. A craggy corrie wall is split by a steep-sided col, the result of glaciation, separating Geal Charn from its subsidiary top, Beinn Sgiath. Lochan a' Choire lies in the deep grasp of the corrie.

Two alternatives offer straightforward routes to the summit. A sketchy path follows the east bank of the Feith Talagain from near Garva Bridge, 10km west of Laggan Bridge. At the termination of this path cross the Allt Coire nan Dearcag and climb the heathery south west spur of Geal Charn to the wide grassy summit and finely built cairn. A good descent is by the southern top, Beinn Sgiath and down its spur to Meall an Domhnaich and Garvabeg.

Probably the most popular route is by Glen Markie. A track runs for 3.5km beside the Markie Burn from Spey Dam before turning into a footpath. A short distance beyond this, Piper's Burn runs down the hillside from Geal Charn's north-east corrie. Cross the Markie Burn and follow the Piper's Burn to where it flows out from Lochan a' Choire. Continue climbing easy slopes north of the lochan, avoiding the crags, to crest the summit ridge. Go south west now on to the grassy summit plateau and the cairn.

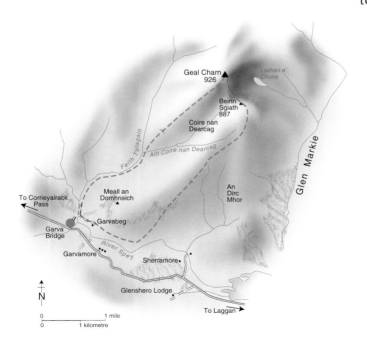

Coire Ardair, Creag Meagaidh

Carn Liath (127), 1006m/3301ft, Stob Poite Coire Ardair (76), 1054m/3458ft, Creag Meagaidh (30), 1128m/3701ft

Lying midway between Fort William and Aviemore, just east of the Lochaber/Badenoch boundary, the great whaleback of Creag Meagaidh has been popular with walkers and climbers for generations. In many ways she's a contrary mountain – straddling the historic Druim Alban, the watershed of Scotland, she can offer delights when others cannot, and conversely, she can be a miserable huddle of cloud and rain when other hills are bathing in sunshine. But when Creah Meagaidh smiles she smiles in a thoroughly hospitable way and shows off her great and cavernous Coire Ardair to best possible advantage.

And it's this great array of vegetated cliffs which makes Creag Meagaidh so special. Laid out for almost two kilometres and in places reaching higher than 450m above the waters of Lochan a' Choire, the cliffs are breached only by a high 'window', a glaciated gap in the curtain which offers access from the corrie floor to the high plateau-like summit.

There is little decent rock climbing in Coire Ardair although the

Route Summary: Behind the Scottish Natural Heritage buildings at Aberarder Farm a good path crosses the lower moorland (Route A, p.139). After 1.5km or so, as the track climbs through birch trees strike uphill NNE on the heather-clad slopes of Carn Liath. From the summit head NW to follow the edge of Coire Ardair over Meall an t-Snaim, Sron Garbh Choire and the E top of Stob Poite Coire Ardair. Continue W to the summit. From the cairn continue W then S as the slopes fall away to 'The Window', a deep col. Climb the steep slopes on to the plateau, past Mad Meg's Cairn to the true summit. Walk E to the edge of the corrie and follow the ridge SE and E over Puist Coire Ardair, and Creag

Mhor. Drop down open slopes to Aberarder.

Map: OS Sheets 34 and 42

Access Point: Aberarder Farm

Distance: 25.6km, 1372m ascent

Approx Time: 8-12 hours

Translation: grey hill; peak of the pot of the high corrie; bog-land rock

Pronunciation: kaarn leea; stop potya kor aardar; crayk meggie

winter climber can have a thoroughly grand time when the cliffs are plastered with snow and ice and the vegetated cliffs freeze up. For mountain walkers, the round of Carn Liath, Stob Poite Coire Ardair and Creag Meagaidh itself makes a marvellous high-level walk.

Carn Liath is reached after a long climb over heather covered slopes from the Coire Ardair footpath and the walker is rewarded for his efforts by a tremendous direct view up into the corrie and its huge headwall. From the stony summit head west and follow the mossy ridge along the edge of Coire Ardair over Meall an t-Snaim to where it narrows above Coire a' Chriochairein. The next steeper rise leads to the crest of Stob Poite Coire Ardair, the highest point of which is at the west end. From the summit continue west than south as the slopes fall away to The Window, a narrow pass which cuts over the ridge from Coire Ardair to the headwaters of the River Roy.

From this narrow pass climb up steep grassy slopes on to the vast summit plateau. Pass Mad Meg's cairn and continue over the plateau beyond it to the true summit cairn which lies at the west end of the plateau. Either descend back to The Window and down into Coire Ardair to return to Aberarder, or cross the plateau eastwards to the corrie rim and continue round the edge of the cliffs. A well defined ridge runs south east then east over Puist Coire Ardair and Creag Mhor from where open slopes can be followed back to Aberarder.

Beinn a' Chaorainn (80), 1049m/3442ft,
Beinn Teallach (282), 915m/3002ft

While these two hills are separated by the long glen containing the Allt a' Chaorainn, the high bealach at its head, at a height of just under 600m, links the two hills quite nicely. Beinn a' Chaorainn's summit ridge runs in a north/south direction over three tops the highest of which is the middle one. It's a ridge on which considerable snow cornices build up in winter and several walkers have fallen through this cornice, so beware!

The western and southern slopes of the hill are steep but not rocky other than one or two small outcrops although dense forestry does skirt the lower southern slopes and can make access difficult.

Beinn Teallach, on the other hand, rises from wide easy angled slopes, although the eastern and northern slopes are much steeper and rockier. Sitting a good 5km back from the Laggan-Spean Bridge road it has a rather shy and retiring air. The old Ordnance Survey one inch to the mile maps gave it a height of 2994ft while the Second

Route Summary: Follow the forestry road NW for 800m to the slopes below Meall Clachaig (Route B). Follow a firebreak N to reach a deer fence and a gate near the road junction. Climb N and then bear NE up easy slopes to the S top and then along the broad ridge to the summit of Beinn a' Chaorainn. Continue on the ridge to the N top and then drop NNW, then W to the col at the head of the Allt a' Chaorainn. Climb the slopes W to reach the NE ridge of Beinn Teallach. Follow the ridge to the summit

Map: OS Sheets 34 and 41 GR337813

Distance: 17.6km, 1143m ascent

Approx Time: 4-7 hours

Series of their 1:50,000 maps confirmed that with 913m/2995ft. However, the later 1:25000 series gave Beinn Teallach a height of 915m, which, at 3002ft, took it over the 3000ft Plimsoll line.

Forestry roads lead into the forest from a lay-by across the road from the cottages at Roughburn. The main track runs in a north-west direction for about 800m before turning sharply right and climbing across the lower slopes of Coire Clachaig. Some distance after this turning a firebreak gives access to the open corrie by the Allt Clachaig. Climb the slopes past Meall Clachaig in Coire Clachaig to reach the broad south-west shoulder of Beinn a' Chaorainn which can be followed to the south summit.

Continue north on the summit ridge, being careful to avoid any cornices, over the main summit and on to the north summit. Long heather slopes now lead down to a cairn at Tom Mor at the top of the Allt a' Chaorainn glen. Climb the rocky slopes immediately to the west of the cairn to reach the north-east ridge which leads to the summit.

Descend the long southern ridge and drop down into the Allt a' Chaorainn glen as soon as possible to cross the burn before it becomes too wide. Follow the footpath back down the glen to the start.

Translation: hill of the rowan; forge hill

Pronunciation: byn a choerin; byn tyellach

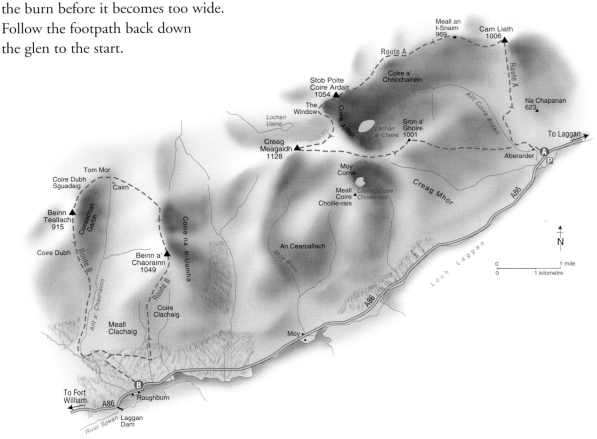

LOCH LOCHY, LOCH ARKAIG AND LOCH EIL

The Munros:

Meall na Teanga   Sron a' Choire Ghairbh   Gulvain
Sgurr Thuilm   Sgurr nan Coireachan

This is Jacobite country, rich in historic association, legend and romance. At the head of Loch Shiel, Charles Edward Stuart raised his Standard at the spot where the clans gathered to begin their long, and subsequently tragic, 1745 campaign – a Rising which gave way to the destruction of a highland way of life, the death of the clan system and a culture which some would suggest led to the Highland clearances and a vastly different land use – sheep instead of people. Months later, after the fateful Battle of Culloden, Charles returned to this area but this time as a fugitive, spending a night out on Sgurr Thuilm itself.

There is a danger in writing a book about the Munros that you ignore the other, smaller hills, and here I would put in a plea for the Corbetts, those mountains between 2500ft (762m) and 2999ft (914m). While your attention may be taken up with Sgurr Thuilm and Sgurr nan Coireachan, south of the A830 Mallaig road lie no fewer than 16 Corbetts some of which, like the Rois-bheinn horseshoe or Sgurr Ghuibhsachain or Garbh-Bheinn of Ardgour, compare favourably with most Munros.

Meall na Teanga (275), 918m/3012ft
Sron a' Choire Ghairbh (239), 937m/3074ft,

Easily seen from the A82 road north of Spean Bridge, these two hills dominate the north-western side of Loch Lochy, rising up on bulging shoulders from their green skirt of forestry plantations. For some years the Forestry Commission has been busy clear-felling in this area and access to these two hills via the connecting Cam Bhealach has been tricky, unless you've been willing to wade through the forestry debris of broken branches and felled trees. I tried it once and swore I'd never do it again. However, the little footpath which runs up from the forest road on the north-west shore of Loch Lochy is clear, once again offering the best approach to these two hills.

From Kilfinnan, just beyond the Laggan Locks, a forest road runs

Route Summary: At the N end of Loch Lochy cross by the Laggan Locks to Kilfinnan. Follow the Forestry Commission track SW above the loch. After about 3.2km follow a track which climbs from the forest track uphill NW then W to the obvious pass between the two hills. From the top of the pass, climb Meall na Teanga first, return to the head of the pass then climb Sron a' Choire Ghairbh. Descend by the latter's long E spur to Kilfinnan.

Map: OS Sheet 34

Access Point: North end of Loch Lochy

Distance: 20.8km, 1295m ascent

Meall na Teanga from the air above Loch Lochy

Approx Time: 6-9 hours

Translation: hill of the tongue; nose of the rough corrie

Pronunciation: myowl na tyenga; srawn a corrie ghirav

in a south-west direction. After 1km the road splits – keep to the higher one for just over another 2km, beside the Allt Glas-Dhoire, which has given its name to a ruin just below on the shore of the loch, Glas-dhoire. There is a small cairn at the side of the road which indicates the start of a footpath which runs north-west and then steeply west between craggy mountain walls to the summit of the Cam Bhealach.

It's best to climb Meall na Teanga first – steeply south up on to the spur of Meall Dubh, across a shallow bealach and onto the north ridge of Teanga. The summit cairn is a few hundred metres to the south. Return to the Cam Bhealach and climb the zigzags of an old stalker's path which leads almost all the way to the south-east ridge of Sron a' Choire Ghairbh. An easy walk along the mossy ridge leads to the summit. You can either return to the Cam Bhealach the way you came or, alternatively, follow the east ridge of Sron a' Choire Ghairbh over Sean Mheall and Meall nan Dearcag and down to the Kilfinnan Burn. Take some time to view the Kilfinnan Falls, a dramatic waterfall which hurtles down into a craggy gorge. It's well worth a visit and makes a great finale to a grand hill day.

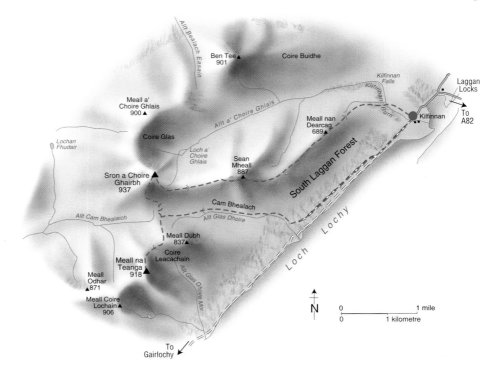

Looking south-west along the summit of Gulvain

Gulvain (161), 987m/3238ft

Gulvain is a shy hill, hiding itself well back from the road and even throwing up a high top between its summit and the route from the south. The ridge between these two tops dips only slightly but gives the hill a remarkable linear feel – it runs in a rough north/south direction between the long trenches of Gleann Fionnlighe and Glen Mallie and when you stand by the summit cairn there is a distinct awareness of remoteness. Long steep slopes drop away on either side and the long ridge you have just climbed reminds you that you have to return along it, together with a steep climb back onto the south top. Gulvain, as much as any other Munro, makes you work for your tick in the book!

A good footpath runs up Gleann Fionnlighe from Drumsallie on the A830 Mallaig road and a bike would be useful to ride along the 5-6km to the footbridge over the Allt a' Choire Reidh. Beyond the bridge the path continues but soon fades out on Gulvain's south-south-east ridge. Some guidebooks describe this ridge as 'relentless', and it is, but underfoot conditions are good and it's just a question of plodding upwards with ever widening views all around you as consolation. Pass a craggy knoll on to the south summit, complete with trig point and continue down steep and rocky slopes to the broad ridge. Once past the low point of the ridge it narrows considerably and is quite entertaining, though widens again just before the summit and large cairn. Return to the start by re-tracing your steps – the west slopes of the hill are steep and craggy.

Route Summary: Start from Drumsallie on the A830 Fort William to Mallaig road and follow the track up the E side of the Fionn Lighe river (Route A, p.145). Continue up the glen for about 6km to the foot of the SSE ridge of Gulvain. Climb the ridge, past a craggy knoll and the S top (trig point) and climb the narrowing ridge to the summit

Map: OS Sheets 40 and 41

Access Point: Drumsallie, GR960794

Distance: 19.2km, 1128m ascent

Approx Time: 6-8 hours .

Translation: from Gaor Bheinn, possibly filthy hill

Pronunciation: goolvan

Sgurr nan Coireachan from Sgurr Thuilm

Sgurr Thuilm (193), 963m/3159 ft,
Sgurr nan Coireachan (206), 956m/3136ft

Route Summary: Follow the private road up the right side of the River Finnan below the railway viaduct (Route B). Just over 3km up the glen pass the Corryhully Bothy and continue on the track until it crosses the stream that drains Coire Thollaidh and Coire a' Bheithe. Cross the stream and head for the obvious spur that leads to Druim Coire a' Bheithe and the summit of Sgurr Thuilm. From the cairn return S for a short distance to join the main ridge which runs W over the ups and downs of Beinn Gharbh and Meall an Tarmachain to the final climb to Sgurr nan Coireachan. From the summit descend SE and then climb to Sgurr a' Choire Riabhaich where the ridge becomes very steep sided and care should be taken. Follow the ridge to the track NE of the Corryhully Bothy

Map: OS Sheet 40

Access Point: Glenfinnan

Distance: 19.2km, 1219m ascent

Approx Time: 6-9 hours

Translation: peak of the round hillock; peak of the corries

Pronunciation: skoor hoolim; skoor nam korachan

The round of these hills, the Glenfinnan Horseshoe, as well as being a superb outing in its own right, gives a taste of the rough conditions found slightly north in the Knoydart area. Leave your car at the small car park on the A830 on the west side of the River Finnan and walk up the private road, below the West Highland Railway viaduct, an impressive feat of engineering which was completed in 1899. It was claimed that during the construction a horse and cart fell into one of the hollow pillars.

After a kilometre or so, a road branches off to the left to service the Glen Finnan Lodge, don't take this but continue past Corryhully Bothy, a rather luxurious doss complete with electric lighting, to where the road ends at the stream which drains Coire Thollaidh and Coire a' Bheithe. Just beyond this point an obvious spur leads to the long ridge called Druim Coire a' Bheithe. This is where the climbing begins. Easy grassy slopes lead to a small subsidiary top and then north to the summit of Sgurr Thuilm. From here the Knoydart hills fill the horizon to the north-west, fronted by the remote Loch Morar. To the north Loch Arkaig gives way to the Loch Quoich hills. In front of you, Sgurr nan Coireachan fills the view, at the end of a broad and knobbly ridge, splattered with tiny lochans and lined by old fence-posts.

From the summit descend south for a short distance before continuing the traverse westwards. Some rocky outcrops offer easy scrambles, and the views are continuously stunning.

Sgurr nan Coireachan is slightly lower than Sgurr Thuilm but is a much better summit – this Peak of the Corries is well named, being thrown up by a number of remote corries, craggy and wild.

The south-east ridge is steep and rocky and abuts on to some steep cliffs which drop into Coire Thollaidh, a craggy and tumbling place of immense character. The ridge continues, in form and interest, across the minor top of Sgurr a' Choire Riabhaich and down towards the River Finnan again. Drop off the ridge in an easterly direction to where a good stalker's path skirts the foot of the crags to link up with the main Land Rover track again. Return past Corryhully Bothy and back to Glenfinnan.

KNOYDART AND LOCH QUOICH

The Munros:

Sgurr nan Coireachan   Garbh Chioch Mhor   Sgurr na Ciche
Sgurr Mor   Gairich   Gleouraich   Spidean Mialach
Luinne Bheinn   Meall Buidhe   Ladhar Bheinn
Beinn Sgritheall   Sgurr a' Mhaoraich

The peninsula of Knoydart, jutting out into the Sound of Sleat with all the character of an island, is generally perceived to be a wilderness. When the MoD wanted to buy it at the end of the 1980s there was a public outcry. 'Scotland's last wilderness,' said the press proclamations. And yet, Knoydart is, and always was, less of a natural wilderness than the Cairngorms, Torridon, the Cuillin, Inverpollaidh, the Fannaichs, the Blackmount and many other mountain areas of Scotland. This is no savage or untamed land.

Just after the 1745 rebellion there were over 1000 young men, the area's fighting force, working the land, paying what was known as 'warrior rent.' Skiary and Barisdale, Doune, Airor and Glenguserain, Sandaig and Inverie were sizeable townships. Even inland, in Glen Dubhlochain and Glen Meadale there were farmlands growing grain and potatoes, and an etching from the nineteenth century clearly shows 40 to 50 trading ships at anchor in Barrisdale Bay.

But thanks to the Clearances, the townships have gone. Today, Inverie is the only remaining village with a pier, a cluster of whitewashed cottages, a pub, a guest house and a couple of hostels. Stretching out west from those rugged mountains which form the romantic sounding Rough Bounds of Knoydart, the peninsula is sequestered from the rest of the mainland by long, winding sea lochs. Common belief suggests that Loch Hourn and Loch Nevis are corruptions of the Gaelic words for Heaven and Hell, placing Knoydart in some sort of montane limbo.

Choice of access is limited – a long walk from Kinlochhourn in the north or from Glen Dessarry via the Mam na Cloich Airde in the south, or ferry from Mallaig or Arnisdale, the latter being the keeper's rowing boat. Perhaps it's no small wonder that people regard Knoydart as being as remote as anywhere on the mainland.

The three Munros of Knoydart itself, Ladhar Bheinn, Luinne Bheinn and Meall Buidhe, are best climbed from Inverie in the south or from Barrisdale – reached by a lovely 8km coastal walk from Kinlochhourn, while the hills that fringe the Loch Quoich area can be climbed from Glen Dessarry in the south or from Loch Quoich-side in the north. Beinn Sgritheall is climbed from the Glenelg/Arnisdale road.

Gleouraich and Spidean Mialach from high in Glen Quoich

The Knoydart hills and Beinn Sgritheall from Sgurr na Ciche

Route Summary: Follow the track from Strathan to Glen Dessarry. Take the path past the house of Upper Glendessarry to reach the Allt Coire nan Uth (Route A) and just beyond the burn climb steep slopes to the summit of Sgurr nan Coireachan. Descend in a WSW direction to the Bealach nan Gall and continue W up increasingly rocky slopes to the ridge which leads to Garbh Chioch Bheag and then Garbh Chioch Mhor. Beyond the summit the ridge narrows considerably on the descent to Feadan na Ciche. From the pass take the obvious grassy ramp which leads to a succession of grassy ledges which lead through the rocky screes and blocks to the summit rib of Sgurr na Ciche. From the summit return to the

Sgurr nan Coireachan (213), 953m/3127ft, Garbh Chioch Mhor (116), 1013m/3323ft, Sgurr na Ciche (92), 1040m/3412ft

Sgurr na Ciche is the highest point in the Rough Bounds of Knoydart, that area of hills and glens which forms a wild barrier between the rest of the Knoydart peninsula and the hinterland. It's a particularly dominant mountain, its prominent peak recognisable from many points distant. If you are staying at the bothy at Sourlies or approaching from the head of Loch Nevis the obvious route of ascent is up the Druim a' Ghoirtein, the long ridge which rises in one steepening swoop all the way from the head of the loch to the summit.

If your approach is from Glen Dessarry then follow the path up the glen for about 2.5km beyond the house at Upper Glendessarry and climb north up a steep and narrowing rocky corrie to the bealach, the Bealach nan Gall, on the west side of Sgurr nan Coireachan. A path weaves its way through a rocky landscape all the way to the summit.

Most walkers nowadays tend to climb Sgurr na Ciche along with its near neighbours, Sgurr nan Coireachan and Garbh Chioch Mhor, a sensible alternative since the three are linked by a long rocky ridge, making a very enjoyable expedition.

Take the path from Strathan into Glen Dessarry, past Glen Dessarry House and continue as far as Upper Glendessarry. It is possible to travel this distance (4km) by mountain bike. Beyond Upper Glendessarry a footpath continues above the forestry and crosses a footbridge over the Allt Coire nan Uth. Beyond the bridge continue on the footpath for 200m and then take to the steep south ridge of Sgurr nan Coireachan and follow its rough and rocky slopes to the summit.

Descend in a west-south-west direction down a steep path to the Bealach nan Gall and then continue westwards over the Garbh Chiochs, a rough and rocky undulating ridge which is crowned by a stone wall. Cross Garbh Chioch Bheag, with the craggy slopes of Coire nan Gall dropping away to the north, and follow the narrowing ridge to Garbh Chioch Mhor. Beyond the summit the wall continues westwards, then north-westwards down into the col of the Feadan na Ciche, the whistle of the peak! The path to Sgurr nan Ciche weaves an intricate route up through the crags but is fairly straightforward – the problems arise when the slope is snow-covered. Descend via the Feadan Gap, down the narrow gully towards Coire na Ciche and where the gully opens out below Garbh Chioch Mhor skirt its south-west slopes to descend steep grassy slopes to the pass at the head of Glen Dessarry where the footpath takes you back to your starting point.

Feadan Gap. From here descend SW down the course of the Allt Coire na Ciche, steep in places to a grassy terrace from which easy slopes drop down to the Mam na Cloich Airde pass. Follow the path back to Glen Dessarry and Strathan

Map: OS Sheets 33 and 40

Access Point: Strathan

Distance: 21km, 914m ascent

Approx Time: 7-9 hours

Translation: peak of the corries; big rough place of the breast; peak of the breast

Pronunciation: skoor nan korachan; garav kee-ach voar; skoor na keesh

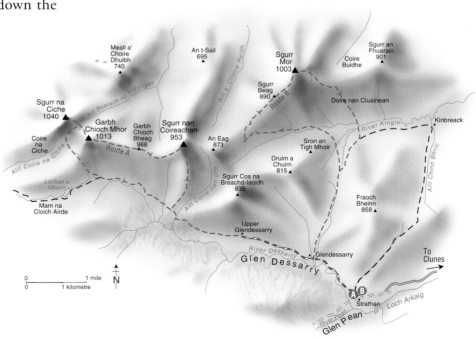

Sgurr Mor (132), 1003m/3291ft

Route Summary: From Strathan take the track to Glendessarry Lodge and just before the building turn N (Route B, p.149) onto a footpath which runs over a bealach between Druim a' Chuirn and Fraoch Bheinn. As you descend the N side of the col leave the path and head NW to cross the River Kingie. Follow the stalkers' path W then N, up steep zigzags to the col between An Eag and Sgurr Beag. Follow the path over Sgurr Beag. Beyond another small dip in the ridge a 180m climb takes you to the summit of Sgurr Mor. Return via the ridge above Coire Buidhe where long, grassy slopes lead S to Glen Kingie and the path back to Glendessary Lodge

Map: OS Sheets 33 and 40

Access Point: Strathan

Distance: 22km/1520m ascent

Approx Time: 8-10 hours

Translation: big peak

Pronunciation: skoor mor

This hill, and its near neighbour Gairich, are awkwardly placed in the upper reaches of Glen Kingie, a long and desolate glen which runs out eastwards into Glen Garry. There is a bothy at Kinbreack which provides a spartan base for climbing both peaks but it is possibly better to climb Sgurr Mor from Strathan at the end of Loch Arkaig, leaving Gairich to be climbed from the Loch Quoich dam.

A footpath runs north from Glendessarry Lodge beside the Feith a' Chicheanais and drops down into the head of Glen Kingie where it sweeps round eastwards towards Kinbreack bothy. Leave the path before it turns and traverse over the rough grassy slopes of Sron an Tigh Mhoir and into the wild upper reaches of Glen Kingie. On the north side of the river a stalker's path heads westwards before suddenly turning to zigzag its way up the col between An Eag and Sgurr Beag. From the col the path continues northwards towards Loch Quoich while another path follows the ridge over Sgurr Beag and up steepening slopes onto Sgurr Mor.

The best way of descent is to continue over the summit and down to the ridge above Coire Buidhe. From here, long grassy slopes lead southwards to the River Kingie and the path back to Glendessarry Lodge.

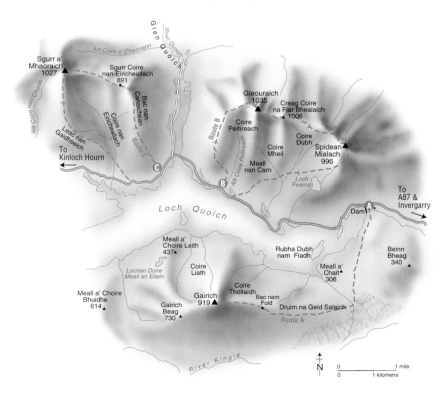

Gairich and Loch Quoich

Gairich (272), 919m/3015ft

I've often driven along the road on the north side of Loch Quoich and thought that the finest way to climb Gairich would be to canoe across the loch and climb the hill by its broad north ridge. You could then canoe back over the loch and climb Sgurr a' Mhaoraich in the afternoon! As it is, most folk climb the two hills in a day, using a car between Loch Quoich dam and the foot of Sgurr a' Mhaoraich.

The normal approach to Gairich is from Loch Quoich dam. From the dam follow a path southwards across the boggy moor to the edge of the forestry plantation in Glen Kingie and then take the stalker's path westwards along the length of the Druim na Geid Salaich. As the ridge widens out on to the Bac nam Foid it becomes increasingly boggy and cut up by peat hags. Continue right up this ridge which is broad at first but which soon steepens as the path begins to climb through rocky outcrops and crags. Various tracks cross the south-east slopes of the hill and it's easy to follow these too far west, but by keeping on a rising traverse as close to the crest as you can it is possible to pick a line through the difficulties to the surprisingly broad summit ridge and massive cairn.

An alternative route to Gairich is from Glen Kingie in the south, using Kinbreack bothy as a base. A good stalkers' path climbs Gairich Beag from the A' Mhaingir pass between Glen Kingie and Loch Quoich from where a rough path follows the ridge east-north-east to the summit.

Route Summary: From the S end of the dam (Route A) a path leads to an old stalkers' path which runs S over boggy moorland to the edge of a forestry plantation. Here, another path runs due W, up the Druim na Geid Salaich. Once the broad ridge crest is reached the path peters out. The going is easy however, and the broad ridge should be followed W to the final steep pull to Gairich. At the foot of this final rise a path reappears, but after a while it runs out on to the S face. Don't be tempted by it but continue climbing on the crest of the ridge to the spacious summit and large cairn

Map: OS Sheet 33

Access Point: Loch Quoich dam

Distance: 15km, 760m ascent

Approx Time: 6-7 hours

Translation: roaring

Pronunciation: gaareech

Looking west towards the Inner Hebrides from Meall Buidhe

Route Summary: A cairn on the W side of the Allt Coire Peitireach indicates the beginning of what becomes a very good stalkers' path (Route B, p.150). Above the 300m contour the path moves on to a grassy spur and then zigzags uphill and continues all the way to the rocky crest of the hill. A wide stony ridge continues E, drops and then rises to Craig Coire na Fiar Bhealaich. Beyond, another stalkers' path zigzags down to the Fiar Bhealaich and then another climb brings you to the summit of Spidean Mialach. Descend easy slopes to the SW, passing Loch Fearna and down the slopes of Coire Mheil to the roadside

Map: OS Sheet 33

Access Point: Loch Quoich, GR029030

Distance: 11km, 1100m ascent

Approx Time: 4-6 hours

Translation: uproar or noise; peak of wild animals

Pronunciation: glyawreech; speet yan meealach

Gleouraich (97), 1035m/3396ft, Spidean Mialach (146), 996m/3268ft

Another fine round which makes the most of excellent stalkers' paths, one of the great features of this entire area. Both Gleouraich and Spidean Mialach have several great corries biting into their steep flanks from the north and the walker, traversing both hills, can admire them from best advantage. Snow cornices lie deep into the early summer and the views north to the Glen Shiel hills are particularly fine.

While the south-facing slopes of both hills are fairly uniform and uninteresting, an amazing stalkers' path leaves the road near the Allt Coire Peitireach. A roadside cairn marks its start. This fantastic example of footpath engineering makes a series of rising traverses onto Gleouraich's south ridge where it continues above the hill's precipitous western slopes. Further on the path follows the ridge to the right and stops at the foot of the final steep rise to Gleouraich's summit.

From the top, the route onwards to Spidean Mialach follows the rim of several huge corries which fall away to the north in spectacular fashion. There is a considerable drop between the two Munro summits, but there is plenty of interest. From the summit of Spidean Mialach continue in a south-east direction for a while before dropping down an obvious spur towards Loch Fearna. From the small saddle above the loch make your way across Coire Mheil to pick up the stalkers' path on the west side of the burn, a path which can then be followed back to the road near the starting point.

Luinne Bheinn (234), 939m/3081ft, Meall Buidhe (222), 946m/3104ft

These two hills, along with Ladhar Bheinn, are the real hills of Knoydart. The first two rise from extremely rough and rocky corries and are separated from their western neighbour by the high pass of the Mam Barrisdale. A path which runs from Inverie to Barrisdale, crosses the pass, the summit of which gives excellent access to the north-west ridge of Luinne Bheinn. Barrisdale is reached by a wonderfully scenic footpath which follows the south shore of Loch Hourn from Kinlochhourn, while Inverie is reached either by ferry from Mallaig, or by a long walk-in from Glen Dessarry to the head of Loch Nevis and then through the Mam Meadail.

From Barrisdale a track runs to the summit of the Mam Barrisdale, and easy slopes climb east on to the Bachd Mhic an Tosaich, from where the ridge to Luinne Bheinn both narrows and steepens in a rough and rocky climb to the summit ridge. A lower, muddier path has evolved in recent years, which follows a line of old fence posts onto Luinne Bheinn's south-west ridge, a path that's better used in descent.

The name Luinne Bheinn has been translated as meaning the hill of anger, or the hill of melody, or even the hill of mirth. Hamish Brown suggested it perhaps should just be the hill of moods! From the summit there is a long-ranging view down Gleann an Dubh-Lochain and out beyond Loch Nevis where, shimmering on a flat sea, lie the contrasting outlines of mountainous Rum and flat-topped Eigg.

At the east end of the summit ridge a steep southern flank drops down to a broad, undulating ridge that forms a back wall to the rugged corries between the two Munros. This ridge eventually borders the remote and desolate north corrie of Meall Buidhe, and leads to the obvious north-east summit ridge. The highest of the two tops is the western one, at 946m.

The best return route involves some more climbing but takes you through the rugged landscape that lies between the two Munros. Descend Meall Buidhe's north ridge and make your way gradually north-east, down long rocky ribs into the heart of this wonderfully rough and rugged mountain bowl. A short climb up grassy slopes leads to a pair of high-evel lochans and from the second one a long easy angled gully leads back to Luinne Bheinn's south-west ridge. It's a short traverse to the path and those old fence posts that lead down to the summit of the pass, then downhill back to Barrisdale.

Route Summary: Take the Inverie-Barrisdale path to the summit of the Mam Barrisdale (Route A, p155). Above the pass, the NW ridge of Luinne Bheinn drops down in a sharp even line. Follow this ridge to the summit. At the E end of Luinne Bheinn a steep S flank drops to a broad knoll-covered ridge that eventually forms Druim Leac a' Shith. Follow this ridge, over its complex bumps and knolls, and climb gradually to the more obviously defined NE ridge of Meall Buidhe, which takes you to the E summit. The true summit is a few hundred metres to the W. Descend via the hill's N ridge, make your way through the rock-covered corrie to a pair of lochans and from the second one follow an easy-angled gully to Luinne Bheinn's SW ridge. A short traverse leads to a muddy path that returns to the Mam Barrisdale

Map: OS Sheets 33 and 40

Access Point: Inverie or Barrisdale

Distance: 20km, 1370m ascent

Approx Time: 7-9 hours

Translation: hill of anger, or hill of melody; yellow hill

Pronunciation: loonya vyn; myowl booee

Ladhar Bheinn from Stob a' Chearcaill

Route Summary: A bridge crosses the river above Barrisdale to a path which in turn crosses the saltings to meet a stalkers' path below Creag Bheithe (Route B, p.155). Follow this path up zigzags, round the nose of Creag Bheithe and through some woodland into Coire Dhorrcail. Cross the Allt Coire Dhorrcail and climb grassy slopes W to the ridge of Druim a' Choire Odhair. Follow this narrowing ridge to the crest of Stob a' Choire Odhair, then on to the summit ridge of Ladhar Bheinn. A cairn at this point is often mistaken for the summit, but the true summit lies a few hundred metres to the west. To complicate matters further an OS trig point lies at the W end of the ridge. The best descent lies SE, over the ridges above Coire Dhorrcail and Coire na Cabaig, over Aonach Sgoilte and down the E ridge to Mam Barrisdale

Map: OS Sheet 33

Access Point: Barrisdale

Distance: 15km, 1070m ascent

Approx Time: 4-6 hours

Translation: hoof or claw hill

Pronunciation: laarven

Ladhar Bheinn (111), 1020m/3346ft

Ladhar Bheinn can be climbed from Folach in Gleann na Guiserein, south-west of the mountain, by Coire a' Phuill from the Mam Barrisdale or by the magnificent Coire Dhorcaill from Barrisdale. The latter route is by far the finest.

While Barrisdale is probably the best approach, walkers who are staying at Inverie may find the Gleann na Guiserein approach quicker, if duller. From the village a road runs through the forest and over the Mam Uidhe pass. About 1km beyond the summit of the pass a footpath leaves the road in a north-east direction and into Gleann na Guiserein. From the ruins at Folach, interminable slopes lead to the summit ridge, but a better route follows a footpath northwards beside the Abhainn Bheag to reach the western ridge of the mountain above the forestry plantations. This ridge can easily be climbed, over An Diollaid to the narrow summit ridge and cairn.

The Coire a' Phuill route climbs grassy slopes and then increasingly rocky ground to the narrow ridge between Stob a' Chearchaill and the top of the Aonach Sgoilte from where the ridge can be followed north-westwards to the summit ridge, high above the craggy walls of Coire Dhorrcail.

Coire Dhorrcail itself is enclosed by the subsidiary peaks of Stob a' Chearcaill and Stob a' Choire Odhair and a circuit of the corrie makes a superb expedition. A zigzagged stalkers' path climbs on to the lower reaches of Creag Bheithe from Barrisdale, before turning south-westwards and through the trees in the lower reaches of Coire Dhorrcail. This side of Ladhar Bheinn is owned by the John Muir Trust, who purchased it a number of years ago. On Ladhar Bheinn the Trust is primarily trying to regenerate the native Caledonian pine woods.

A horseshoe of ridges and peaks encloses the corrie to form this high cirque of riven cliffs and buttresses still rimmed by sparkling snow cornices well into the spring. Our route is by the long, bumpy ridge of the Druim a' Choire Odhair which rises gently in stages, each protuberance offering grander and wider views out over Loch Hourn towards Beinn Sgriol and Skye. The summit is close to where this long ridge abuts onto the main ridge. The cairn itself is on the west-north-west ridge just a short distance from the junction.

Ladhar Bheinn is a magnificent, complex mountain, rising above a series of corries which bite into its steep north-eastern slopes. A good descent to the Mam Barrisdale follows the line of these corries, down to the Bealach Coire Dhorrcail, round the head of another steep corrie before the junction with the long Aonach Sgoilte ridge, and then down to another bealach before Stob a' Chearcaill and the long, wet, slippery slopes which lead down eastwards to the Mam Barrisdale.

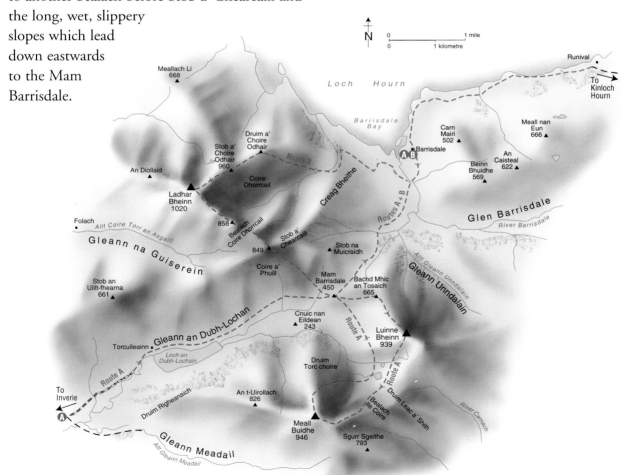

Beinn Sgritheall (183), 974m/3195ft

Route Summary: Follow the old
hill track to Glenelg up through
some scattered woods and
make for an obvious break in
the rocky escarpment above
you. Above the crags turn right
and cross some moorland with
scattered lochans. The W ridge
of Sgritheall is now quite obvious and leads to the summit.
Continue E on the ridge which
soon narrows again. Follow it to
the Bealach Arnasdail; a stream
offers the best guide back to
Arnisdale itself and the Loch
Hourn road

Map: OS Sheet 33

Access Point: Opposite Eilean
Rarsaidh on the Arnisdale road,
GR815120

Distance: 10km, 970m ascent

Approx Time: 5-7 hours

Translation: hill of screes

Pronunciation: byn skreehal

This shapely hill dominates the rough quarter between Loch
Hourn and the glens which run inland from Glenelg. It is, by
association, Gavin Maxwell's hill, for the author's Camusfearna was
near Sandaig on the very western tip of the peninsula. It was here
that he wrote that classic of nature writing, *Ring of Bright Water*.

The south face of the mountain is scree girt and very steep, rising
almost 1000m above the shore of Loch Hourn in only 1.6km.
Despite that, the easiest routes of ascent are on this side of the hill
though they do avoid the worst of the screes.

The most straightforward route leaves the road below the
wooded hillside called Coille Mhialairigh at a point roughly
opposite Eilean Rarsaidh. Clamber uphill through the trees until
a faint path is found, which leads to an old shieling on the hillside
and continues in a north-westerly direction to cross a rough
escarpment on to the west ridge of the mountain, near a tiny
lochan. From there the increasingly steep ridge is climbed to
the summit over rocky terrain.

Another route of ascent goes uphill behind Arnisdale village
to the Bealach Arnasdail then north-west up steep screes to a
subsidiary peak and finally along the connecting ridge to the
summit. This also makes a good descent if you want
to enjoy a complete traverse of the
mountain, although you will
have a 5km walk back
along the road at
the end.

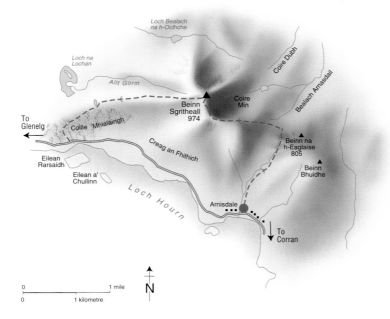

The summit of Beinn Sgritheall from its east top

Sgurr a' Mhaoraich (104), 1027m/3369ft

Often climbed together in one day with Gairich, Sgurr a' Mhaoraich is a big, bluff hill which rises in a series of broad muscle-bound shoulders above Kinlochhourn. Perhaps not surprisingly, very few climb it from the village, preferring to gain some height perhaps by starting from the road that runs along the north shore of Loch Quoich.

Excellent stalkers' paths offer a variety of routes to and from the summit. The normal route of ascent is via the long ridge of Bac nan Canaichean, above the northern arm of Loch Quoich, over Sgurr Coire nan-Eiricheallach and along the rocky ridge to the final scramble to the summit. The climb is enjoyable, with views down to Loch Quoich's northern arm and the empty glens at its head. The zigzagging path continues over Sgurr Coire nan Eiricheallach, down to the ridge that links with Sgurr a' Mhaoraich. From the end of the ridge some scrambling through rocks takes you on to the summit. It's a straightforward descent down the hill's south ridge to the Leac nan Gaidhseich and the Coire nan Eiricheallach path down to the lochside road about 1km west of the starting point.

A route that is rarely climbed is from Glen Quoich, beyond the loch's northern finger. A stalkers' path runs up the length of Coire a' Chaorainn, while another takes the east ridge of An Bathaich in a series of tight zigzags and crosses a narrow ridge to the rocky summit of An Bathaich. A high bealach separates this summit from Sgurr a' Mhaoraich.

Route Summary: Follow a stalkers' path which starts just SW of the bridge (Route C, p.150). Follow the path N up the ridge of Bac nan Canaichean to Sgurr Coire nan Eiricheallach and then across a slight dip to its NW top. From here another ridge leads W to the summit of Sgurr a' Mhaoraich. Descend via the hill's S ridge and the Leac nan Gaidhseich back to the Glen Quoich road

Map: OS Sheet 33

Access Point: Loch Quoich road. GR011035

Distance: 17km, 970m ascent

Approx Time: 6-8 hours

Translation: peak of the shellfish

Pronunciation: skoor a vooreach

GLEN SHIEL HILLS

The Munros:

The Saddle   Sgurr na Sgine   Saileag
Sgurr a' Bhealaich Dheirg   Aonach Meadhoin   Ciste Dhubh
Sisters of Kintail (Sgurr na Ciste Duibhe; Sgurr na Carnach; Sgurr Fhuaran)
The South Glen Shiel Ridge (Creag a' Mhaim; Druim Shionnach; Aonach air
Chrith; Maol Chinn-dearg; Sgurr an Doire Leathain; Sgurr an Lochain;
Creag nan Damh)   A' Chralaig   Mullach Fraoch-choire
Carn Ghluasaid   Sgurr nan Conbhairean   Sail Chaorainn

With no fewer than 21 Munros accessible from the A87 road which runs down its length, it's no wonder that Glen Shiel is popular with hillwalkers. With nine Munros on the south side, seven of them capable of being climbed in one day-long expedition, and 12 on the north side, the area is not only convenient for the car-borne enthusiast but boasts some of the finest hills in the Western Highlands.

The Saddle is generally recognised as being the finest mountain in the area, and its long eastern ridge, known as the Forcan Ridge, is a classic scramble in its own right.

The mountains on the north side of the glen have a much more complex topography than those of the south and break down into several groups, the most famous of them, The Five Sisters of Kintail, also comprising one of the great picture postcard views of Scotland. Unfortunately, only three of the Five Sisters are Munros, but the traverse of the whole ridge makes a very worthwhile expedition.

The Saddle (121), 1010m/3314ft, Sgurr na Sgine (223), 946m/3104ft

The Saddle is a peak of narrow ridges, deep corries and superb views. The best feature of the mountain and one that shouldn't be missed, is the Forcan Ridge, a great scrambling route which follows The Saddle's east ridge. Approach by the stalker's path which leaves Glen Shiel just south-east of Achnangart, and from the end of this path climb south over Meallan Odhar and then continue south west across a grassy col to reach the foot of the rocky Forcan Ridge.

As you gain height the ridge becomes narrower and tighter, and

Route Summary: Start SE of the quarry at Achnangart. A stalker's path leads W to a bealach between Biod an Fhithich and Meallan Odhar (Route A, p.161). From here go S then SW to the bottom of the Saddle's E ridge, known as the Forcan Ridge. Follow this ridge, knife edged and exposed in places, to Sgurr na Forcan. Continue W down a steep rock pitch with good holds and tra-

Looking west towards Sgurr na Ciste Duibhe, Sgurr na Carnach and Sgurr Fhuaran

The Saddle from Sgurr nan Forcan

verse a narrow ridge to the E top of the Saddle and then the summit. The OS trig point is further on and lower than the cairn which marks the summit. Descend to the Bealach Coire Mhalagain down rough bouldery slopes and climb to the NW top of Sgurr na Sgine. Follow a rocky ridge SE to the summit cairn. Descend by way of Faochag and its fine NE ridge

Map: OS Sheet 33

Access Point: Achnangart, GR968142

Distance: 16km, 1430m ascent

Approx Time: 5-7 hours

Translation: the saddle; peak of the knife

Pronunciation: the saddle; skoor na skeena

for good stretches it's very rocky with some great scrambling if you stick with the crest. A rough path avoids the best of the scrambling up the right-hand side of the ridge but this really is an inferior way of climbing the hill. The continuation to The Saddle from the top of the Forcan Ridge, Sgurr nan Forcan, is narrow and steep in places and care should be taken.

Descents can be made down the north ridge over Sgurr na Creige, or west and then north round Coire Uaine but most visitors will want to add Sgurr na Sgine to their day's tally and this Munro, and its outlier, Faochag (The Whelk) are situated about 1.6km south-east of the summit.

Sgurr na Sgine can be easily climbed from the Bealach Coire Mhalagain – up on to the north ridge which is then followed round the head of Coire Toiteil to the summit. Descend northwards again, and then round the corrie rim to Faochag whose steep uniform north-east ridge can be followed back to the A87.

Saileag (205), 956m/3136ft, Sgurr a' Bhealaich Dheirg (96), 1036m/3399ft, Aonach Meadhoin (135), 1001m/3284ft, Ciste Dhubh (173), 979m/3212ft

These hills are generally referred to as the North Glen Shiel Ridge. They have very similar characteristics to their southerly sisters.

It's possible to climb the hills of this group with the Five Sisters, but that's a long, strenuous day. Taken on its own the North Glen Shiel Ridge route offers a straightforward traverse between An Caorann Mor, the pass between Cluanie Inn and Glen Affric, and the Bealach an Lapain.

If tackling the ridge from west to east ascend the grassy wall of Meall a' Charra from Glenlicht House in Glen Lichd (access by track from Morvich near Loch Duich) to Saileag, traverse the ridge, and return westwards by the Glen Affric track. Ciste Dubh is a steep and fairly isolated peak which lies about 5km north of Cluanie Inn and which is easily accessible when approached from An Caorann Mor. Climb to the Bealach a' Choinich and up the south ridge of the peak which becomes very narrow near the summit.

The ridge can then be tackled by returning to the Bealach a' Choinich and following the ridge over the top of Sgurr Fhuarail, Aonach Meadhoin and westwards to Sgurr a' Bhealaich Dheirg and Saileag.

Route Summary: From Glenlicht House climb SE up Meall a' Charra, then up the long grassy spur which leads to Saileag (Route B). Follow the ridge E above the Fraoch-choire to Sgurr a' Bhealaich Dheirg. The summit cairn lies about 50m N of the main ridge. Return to the ridge and continue ESE to Aonach Meadhoin, then to another top on Sgurr an Fhuarail. A wide ridge now runs N and dips to a green bealach. Above this pass a steep and narrow ridge runs north to Ciste Dhubh from where the NW ridge can be descended to the Allt Cam-ban

Map: OS Sheet 33

Access Point: Glenlicht House

Distance: 17.6km, 1676m ascent

Approx Time: 6-8 hours.

Translation: little heel; peak of the red pass; middle hill; black chest

Pronunciation: saalak; skoor a vyaleech yerak; oenach vain; keesta doo

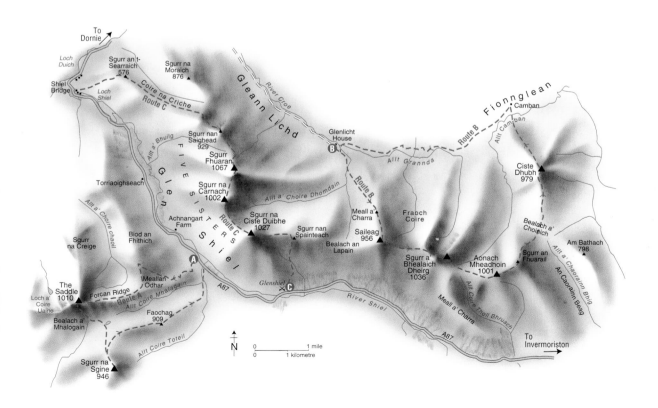

The Five Sisters of Kintail and Loch Duich

Route Summary: From Glenshiel Bridge climb the steep and unrelenting slopes of Sgurr na Ciste Duibhe (Route C, p.161). Make for the ridge W of Sgurr nan Spainteach. From here follow the narrow ridge W to Sgurr na Ciste Duibhe's summit. Avoiding a false ridge which runs N of the peak continue NW and descend to the Bealach na Craoibhe. Turn and climb over Sgurr na Carnach to a V-shaped gap of the Bealach na Carnach. From here a short and steep ascent leads to the summit of Sgurr Fhuaran. A possible descent from here goes by the E ridge to Glenlicht House but most walkers continue N for the full traverse, over Sgurr nan Saighead and down the NW spur to Sgurr an t-Searraich from where steep rough slopes lead to the cottages at Shiel Bridge

Map: OS Sheet 33

Access Point: Glenshiel Bridge

Distance: 16km, 1524m ascent

Approx Time: 6-8 hours

Translation: peak of the black chest; peak of stones; meaning obscure

Pronunciation: skoor na keesta ghoo; skoor na kaa-nach; skoor ooaran

Five Sisters of Kintail (Sgurr na Ciste Duibhe (105), 1027m/3369ft, Sgurr na Carnach (134), 1002m/3287ft, Sgurr Fhuaran (70), 1067m/3501ft)

The mountains which stretch along the north side of Glen Shiel form a barrier some 16km long and the peaks at the north-west end of this long ridge are known as the Five Sisters of Kintail, although only three are Munros. One of the notable features of these hills is the fact that their western flanks rise for over 1000m in one fell swoop from glen floor to the rocky crest. The average angle is about 30°!

The traverse of the Five Sisters of Kintail must be considered as one of the real classic hill walks in the UK. The best direction is from south-east to north-west and the best route is to leave the Glen Shiel road below the Bealach na Lapain. The ascent north-wards to the bealach is a steep one but relatively short, and from the col the ridge, which is grassy and narrow at this point, rises gradually over two minor tops to Sgurr na Ciste Duibhe. Continue north west to Sgurr na Carnach, then north where the ridge begins to broaden out considerably. A steep climb continues to the next Munro, Sgurr Fhuaran, the highest of the Five Sisters. The next top, Sgurr nan Saighead, is tight and exposed and is in many ways the finest of the group, although it's not even of Munro status! Descend to Loch Duich down Coire na Criche or down the west ridge of Sgurr nan Saighead, followed by a steep descent to Loch Shiel where a footbridge carries you over the river.

The South Glen Shiel Ridge: Creag a' Mhaim (218), 947m/3107ft, Druim Shionnach (160), 987m/3238ft, Aonach air Chrith (109), 1021m/3350ft, Maol Chinn-dearg (168), 981m/3218ft, Sgurr an Doire Leathain (122), 1010m/3314ft, Sgurr an Lochain (131), 1004m/3294ft, Creag nan Damh (274), 918m/3012ft

Possibly the best way to begin this traverse is to walk up the old road which goes south-east from the Cluanie Inn towards the eastern end of the ridge. From the high-point of the road a stalkers' path leads to the summit of Creag a' Mhaim. From here the whole of the ridge stretches out before you to end at Creag nan Damh, some 11km away. The main problem of the day is how to get back to your starting point from the far end of the ridge. Ideally you can get a lift, if you can't it's a long walk back to Cluanie – it's mostly uphill too!

While many will want to climb all seven Munros in one outing, others may be happier breaking the route down into two easier sections. The most obvious breakdown is probably to climb Creag a' Mhaim by the route mentioned above, then follow the ridge over Druim Shionnach, Aonach air Chrith, and Maol Chinn-dearg and descend back to the road in Glen Shiel by the north ridge, which is steep at first but eases off lower down where a stalker's path takes you to a point about 4km west of your starting point.

The other section takes in Sgurr an Doire Leathain, Sgurr an Lochain and finally, Creag nan Damh. The ridge is gained by the long spur of the Druim Thollaidh to Sgurr Coire na Feinne then north west along the main ridge to Sgurr an Doire Leathain.

Route Summary: Take the old road from Cluanie Inn to Glen Loyne and climb Creag a' Mhaim by the streams which flow down Coirean an Eich Bhric. Follow the broad ridge NW to Druim Shionnach, descend a short dip then a gradual rise brings you to Aonach air Chrith. Continue on the narrowest section of the ridge towards Maol Chinn-dearg. Continue NW to the minor top of Sgurr Coire na Feinne, then W to the flat topped Sgurr an Doire Leathain. From here the ridge dips again, before rising to Sgurr an Lochain. Another minor top follows, Sgurr Beag, before the last Munro of the ridge, Creag nan Damh. From here a fence leads W to the Bealach Duibh Leac and a stalkers' path to Glen Shiel

Map: OS Sheet 33

Access Point: Cluanie Inn

Distance: 24km, 1829m ascent

Approx Time: 7-11 hours

Translation: rock of the large round hill; ridge of the fox; trembling hill; bald red hill; peak of the broad thicket; peak of the little loch; rock of the stags

Pronunciation: crayk a vaim; drim heeanach; oenach ayr chree; moel chan dyerack; skoor an dira lehan; skoor an lochan; creag nan dav

Route Summary: Leave the A87 near the W end of Loch Cluanie (Route A) where a stalkers' track leaves the road to run through the An Caorann Mor to Glen Affric. Don't follow the track but climb steeply NE up grassy slopes on A' Chralaig. Continue until the angle eases on the S ridge, and follow this ridge to the large summit cairn. Continue N along a grassy ridge and cross the top of Stob Coire na Cralaig. After this the ridge narrows considerably and several pinnacles have to be crossed before reaching the summit of Mullach. Either return to the start the way you came, or alternatively drop down into Coire Odhar (steep at first) and return by the track in An Caorrann Mor

Map: OS Sheet 33 and 34

Access Point: West end of Loch Cluanie

Distance: 12.8km, 1067m ascent

Approx Time: 5-8 hours

Translation: basket or creel; heather-corrie peak

Pronunciation: a chraalik; moolach froech-chora

A' Chralaig (33), 1120m/3674ft, Mullach Fraoch-choire (49), 1102m/3615ft

These two hills are best climbed from the Cluanie Inn, taking a rising traverse over grassy slopes up a wide and open corrie to the stony summit ridge of A' Chralaig. The route continues north to Stob Coire na Cralaig, with deep corries, Coire Odhar and Coire na Cralaig, on either side of the rock-strewn ridge. From Stob Coire na Cralaig the ridge veers suddenly to the north-east and then north again towards Mullach Fraoch-choire. This next section is the finest feature of all these hills, a ridge which is narrow and contains a number of fine rocky pinnacles which give the ridge such character. In snowy conditions this ridge can be extremely tricky, but when clear a footpath is obvious, weaving its way around the major difficulties.

The best route of descent is to follow your footsteps back around the ridge to Stob Coire na Cralaig and then drop down its broad grassy western ridge which leads back down to the footpath in An Caorann Mor and the Cluanie Inn.

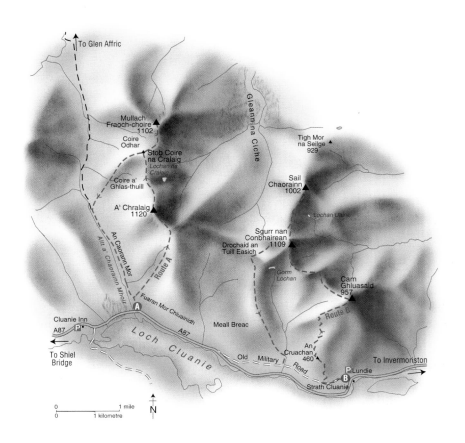

The Glen Shiel Hills from Sgurr nan Conbhairean

Carn Ghluasaid (203), 957m/3140ft, Sgurr nan Conbhairean (44), 1109m/3638ft, Sail Chaorainn (133), 1002m/3287ft

These three mountains form a compact little group on the north side of Loch Cluanie. Viewed from the north and east, from the headwaters of the River Doe you'll see great corries biting into the hillsides, culminating in crag-girt eastern facing cliffs.

From Lundie on Cluanie-side, a footpath, an old military road, runs westwards, parallel to the road for some distance and should be followed for about 500m or so to where a stalker's path climbs northwards all the way on to the flat stony plateau of Carn Ghluasaid. Cross the flat summit to find the cairn which is fairly close to the edge of the north face.

Head westwards then north-west along the broad ridge crossing the rise of Creag a' Chaorainn, across a col and then the final stony slopes to Sgurr nan Conbhairean.

By descending northwards down a distinctly curving ridge you'll reach a shallow col and gently rising slopes which lead northwards to the summit of Sail Chaorainn.

To return, follow the route of ascent but rather than climb back on to the summit of Sgurr nan Conbhairean, follow the rough path across its western slopes to reach the ridge above Gorm Lochan and the summit which is to the north west of the lochan, Drochaid an Tuill Easaich (unnamed by the OS). Turn south from the summit and descend the easy grass slopes down the shoulder of Meall Breac, eventually veering south east to cross the Allt Coire Lair. Follow the old military road back to Lundie.

Route Summary: Leave the A87 at Lundie (Route B) and follow the old military road W for a few hundred metres then take the obvious stalker's path which climbs the S slopes of Carn Ghluasaid. Cross the plateau to the summit. Continue W then NW along the broad ridge, crossing Creag a' Chaorainn then W to cross a col and the final climb to Sgurr nan Conbhairean. From here descend N down an easy ridge to a col and climb Sail Chaorainn. To return follow the ridge back towards Conbhairean but bypass the summit on its W side. Continue SW to a col above Gorm Lochan and continue a short distance to Drochaid an Tuill Easaich. Descend the S ridge to the old military road which will take you back to Lundie

Map: OS Sheet 34

Access Point: Lundie; Loch Cluanie

Distance: 16km, 1067m ascent

Approx Time: 6-8 hours

Translation: hill of movement; peak of the keeper of the hounds; hill (heel) of the rowan

Pronunciation: kaarn ghlooasat; skoor nan konavaran; sale choeran

GLEN AFFRIC AND STRATHFARRAR

The Munros:

Beinn Fhada (Ben Attow)   A' Ghlas-bheinn   An Socach
Sgurr nan Ceathreamhnan   Mullach na Dheiragain   Toll Creagach
Tom a' Choinich   Carn Eige (Eighe)   Beinn Fhionnlaidh
Mam Sodhail (Mam Soul)   Carn nan Gobhar   Sgurr na Lapaich
An Riabhachan   An Socach   Sgurr Fhuar-thuill   Sgurr a' Choire Ghlais
Carn nan Ghobhar   Sgurr na Ruaidhe.

Glen Affric, Glen Cannich and Strathfarrar are the three great inland glens which feed the River Glass, which becomes the River Beauly in its lower reaches. All three glens can be best reached by road from the east, for all lead to the roadless west, although rights of way run through all of them. A remote youth hostel, Alltbeithe, offers access to the Sgurr nan Ceathreamhnan hills, while a side glen, the Gleann nam Fiadh, gives access to the Carn Eighe hills. The Sgurr na Lapaich group can be reached from Glen Cannich in the east or by a long overland route from Glen Elchaig in the west. Further north, Glen Strathfarrar is entered via a locked gate at Struy, giving access to the four Munros which lie just north of the glen. All three glens are well wooded in their lower reaches, with the Caledonian pines of Glen Affric particularly splendid, but forestry and hydro electricity activities have spoiled the intimacy of these places, once reckoned to be the three finest glens in Scotland. But having said that, the hills tend to remain comparatively inviolate, and offer long days on high winding ridges well away from the signs of man's activities, big remote hills in a particularly beautiful corner of the Scottish Highlands.

Route Summary: From the car park near Dorusduain take the stalker's path which runs up to the Bealach an Sgairne (Route A). After crossing the stream which flows down from Coire an Sgairne take another path which runs up into the corrie and climb the slopes of Meall a' Bhealaich. Follow this ridge S to where it abuts on to the great summit plateau of Beinn Fhada known as the Plaide Mor. Continue SE along the edge of the plateau to the summit cairn. Return to the Bealach an Sgairne and climb directly to the summit of A' Ghlas-bheinn (Route B)

Beinn Fhada (Ben Attow) (100), 1032m/3386ft, A' Ghlas-bheinn (273), 918m/3012ft

Beinn Fhada has two distinct characters. Seen from Glen Affric it appears quite unremarkable – a long grassy ridge leading all the way from glen floor to summit. But, go west and see its finest features from that angle – steep cliffs, narrow ridges and wild corries and the best route of ascent. It's well named the 'long mountain' for it occupies much the same length as all of the Five Sisters of Kintail!

Take the track up Strath Croe from the Forestry Commission car park at Dorusduain. Cross the river by the footbridge and continue eastwards up Gleann Choinneachain below the steep north face of Sgurr a' Choire Ghairbh until you reach the zigzags near the foot of the little Coire an Sgairne. Follow a branch path up this corrie to the top. Finally, cross the summit plateau, the Plaide Mhor, and continue in a south-east direction to the highest point and the summit cairn.

The descent can be varied by going out along the ridge northwards to Meall a' Bhealaich which overlooks the narrow pass from Glen Affric, the Bealach an Sgairne. The descent to the pass is steep and some careful route selection is called for. From the path you can easily climb A' Ghlas-bheinn by its rather rough and rocky south ridge, past Loch a' Chleirich. Descend its west ridge to join the track through the forest to Dorusduain or continue north past the summit, down easy grassy slopes to pick up the path through the Bealach na Sroine. Follow this path, and later forestry tracks, back to Dorusduain.

Map: OS Sheet 33
Access Point: Strath Croe
Distance: 20km, 1260m ascent
Approx Time: 6-8 hours
Translation: long hill; the greenish/grey hill
Pronunciation: byn ata; a glash vin

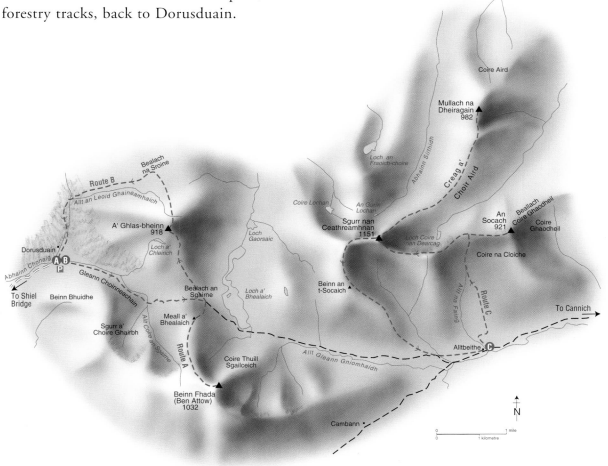

An Socach (269), 921m/3022ft, Sgurr nan Ceathreamhnan (22), 1151m/3776ft, Mullach na Dheiragain (167), 982m/3222ft

Sgurr nan Ceathreamhnan is a magnificent mountain of many peaks and ridges at the head of Glen Affric. It is fairly remote and all approaches to it tend to be long unless you happen to be staying at Alltbeithe Youth Hostel which conveniently lies right at the foot of the mountain. Otherwise you'll have to tackle Ceathreamhnan from Cluanie Inn or the head of Loch Duich over the Bealach an Sgairne. Probably the shortest approach is from Glen Elchaig in the north and this route has the added advantage of climbing up past the spectacular Falls of Glomach. Once above the falls you continue up the Allt Coire-lochain and on to the ridge on the west side of Coire Lochan which leads to the summit. Most Munro collectors will also want to climb Mullach na Dheiragain which lies about 4.5km north-east of Ceathreamhnan near the end of a long curved ridge and while both hills are in a sense connected, there is good justification in climbing Mullach na Dheiragain on its own from the north, from Glen Elchaig and the Iron Lodge to the head of Loch Mullardoch. Long grassy slopes up Coire Aird give easy access to the rockier north west ridge and a short distance after that the summit cone.

Another, longer, alternative is to tackle an entire horseshoe circuit of Gleann a' Choilich, the long and curved glen which separates the Beinn Fhionnlaidh/Carn Eighe/Mam Sodhail massif from the Ceathreamhnan/Dheiragain ridge. This entails about 25km of walking with about 2000m of climbing – and you still have to get to the start at the head of Loch Mullardoch! Alltbeithe Youth Hostel can be reached fairly easily through the An Caorann Mor from Cluanie Inn. The route tends to be fairly boggy both in its upper reaches and lower down in Glen Affric. A footpath follows the line of the Allt na Faing into the higher, rocky reaches of Coire na Cloiche and on to the bealach just west of An Socach (unnamed on the OS map). This hill is dramatically dwarfed by its bigger neighbours and it's hard to believe it's of Munro status. It is often climbed on its own from Affric Lodge via the Bealach Coire Ghadheil. The ridge, which runs west from An Socach, narrows appreciably and offers an interesting route over Stob Coire nan Dearcag, then takes you high above Coire nan Dearcag with its high-level lochan and over Ceathreamhnan's east top to finish eventually on the suitably rocky summit of Sgurr nan Ceathreamhnan – one of the great hills of the Western Highlands.

Route Summary: Reach Alltbeithe from either Loch Beinn a' Mheadhoin in Glen Affric (16km) or a shorter route through the An Caorann Mor from Cluanie. From Alltbeithe a footpath beside the Allt na Faing leads directly to the ridge just W of An Socach (Route C). Go E to the summit. Return to the ridge and follow it W again. Climb grassy terraces to the top of Stob Coire nan Dearcag. Continue on the gently rising ridge to the E top of Ceathreamhnan. Continue over rocky ground to the summit. Rough ground to the NE of the summit leads to a descent to a sharp rib above An Gorm Lochan. The ridge now broadens and offers an easy walk along the length of Creag a' Choir Aird to Mullach na Dheiragain. Return to Ceathreamhnan and descend to Alltbeithe by the S ridge of the W top

Map: OS Sheets 25 and 33

Access Point: Alltbeithe, GR080202

Distance: 26km, 1680m ascent

Approx Time: 9-12 hours

Translation: the snout; peak of the quarters; possibly summit of the hawk

Pronunciation: an sochkach; skoor nan keroanan; moollach na yerakan

Carn Eige, Mam Sodhail and Coire Lochan from Beinn Fhionnlaidh

Toll Creagach (77), 1054m/3458ft, Tom a' Choinich (41), 1112m/ 3648ft, Carn Eige (Eighe) (12), 1183m/3881ft, Beinn Fhionnlaidh (128), 1005m/3297ft, Mam Sodhail (Mam Soul) (14), 1181m/3875ft

Mam Soul and Carn Eige are the two highest hills in the area and both can be climbed in a fairly big hill day from the west end of Loch Beinn a' Mheadhoin, at the foot of Gleann nam Fiadh. A footpath runs up this glen and after 4-5km another footpath leaves the riverside and climbs steadily in a north-west direction to the Bealach Toll Easa between Tom a' Choinich and Toll Creagach. The latter summit can be easily reached from the bealach by a steep initial climb then a long pull on to Toll Creagach's summit dome. From the bealach Tom a' Choinnich is easily reached by a steep climb which threads its way through rocky outcrops. The summit gives access to a long and winding ridge with steep drops on either side. Cross the deep notch of the Garbh-bhealach and continue past the needles of Stob Coire Dhomhnuill (easily avoided on the left), round the head of Coire Dhomhain to Creag

Route Summary: From the car park near the head of Loch Affric a path runs N into Gleann nam Fiadh. As it turns W into the glen another path leaves the riverside and climbs NW over the Bealach Toll Easa. Toll Creagach can easily be climbed from the summit of this pass, and so can Tom a' Choinich. From here continue W over the undulating, and in places rough, ridge. Cross the deep notch of the Garbh-bhealach and continue past the needles of Stob Coire Dhomhnuill (easily avoided on the left), round the head of Coire Dhomhain to Creag na h-Eige and then to the great dome of Carn Eige itself. From the summit head N to Beinn Fhionnlaidh, a long pull involves a 305m drop and a pull up the other side. Return towards Carn Eige but the climb back to the summit can be avoided by a traverse up the W slopes to the pass between Carn Eige and Mam Sodhail. Continue to the summit cairn, a massive structure built round the OS pillar. Return to Glen Affric via the ridge which runs SE over Mullach Cadha Rainich and Sgurr na Lapaich avoiding the latter's craggy E cliffs.

Map: OS Sheet 25

Access Point: Glen Affric, GR215242

Distance: 37km, 2320m ascent

Approx Time: 12-14 hours

Translation: rocky hollow; hill of the moss; file hill; Finlay's hill; hill of the barns

Pronunciation: tow kraykach; towm a choanyeech; kaarn aya; byn yoony; mam sool

na h-Eige and then to the great dome of Carn Eige itself.

North of Carn Eige, way out on a sinuous limb, Beinn Fhionnlaidh sits proudly above Loch Mullardoch, mocking the Munro-bagger in its isolation and remoteness. It takes willpower, and lots of it, to turn your back on the easy ridge which runs south to Mam Sodhail and drop down the rocky slopes to the peaty bealach below Beinn Fhionnlaidh. The summit ridge is welcome after a steep climb from the bealach and you are suddenly aware of the comparative remoteness of this hill. Loch Mullardoch is at your feet and across the blue waters the slopes of An Socach, An Riabhachan and Sgurr na Lapaich rise steeply. Westwards, another long limb holds a Munro – Mullach na Dheiragain involves an even longer diversion to reach its summit cairn, all the way north from Sgurr nan Ceathreamhain. The summit of Carn Eige can be skirted on the return and a rising traverse soon reaches the ridge just north of Mam Sodhail. A rocky slope leads to the gigantic summit cairn. From here the best descent follows the excellent grassy ridge to Sgurr na Lapaich and down to Loch Affric or directly down Coire Leachavie to Glen Affric and a footpath back to your starting point.

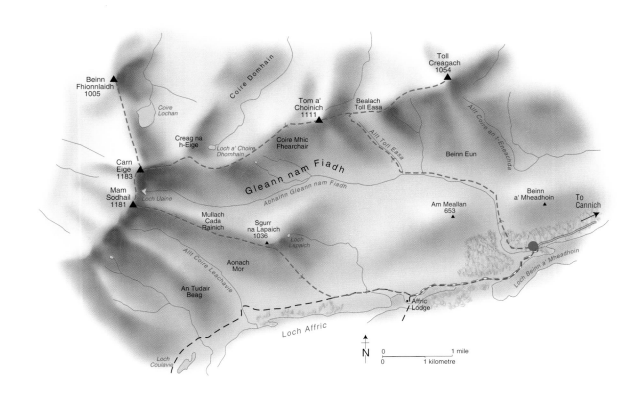

Sgurr na Lapaich from the slopes of Carn nan Gobhar

Carn nan Gobhar (152), 992m/3255ft, Sgurr na Lapaich (24), 1150m/3773ft, An Riabhachan (29), 1129m/3704ft, An Socach (67), 1069m/3507ft

North of Glen Affric, Glen Cannich also runs in an east/west direction and, like Affric, also boasts a loch. The lower reaches of Glen Cannich are beautifully wooded and the view up the glen is only marginally spoiled by the Mullardoch dam. Beyond it on the north side of the loch, a great ridge rises from Carn nan Gobhar and Sgurr na Lapaich and runs westwards to An Riabhachan and An Socach.

Route Summary: Follow the stalkers' path up the E bank of the Allt Mullardoch into Coire an t-Sith. Climb N up the steep slopes of Creag Dhubh to the ridge. Follow this WSW to the summit of Carn nan Gobhar. Follow the ridge NW over a wide saddle beyond which a steeper rib leads to the summit of Sgurr na Lapaich. Leave by the SW shoulder and descend steeply to the Bealach Toll an Lochain. Follow

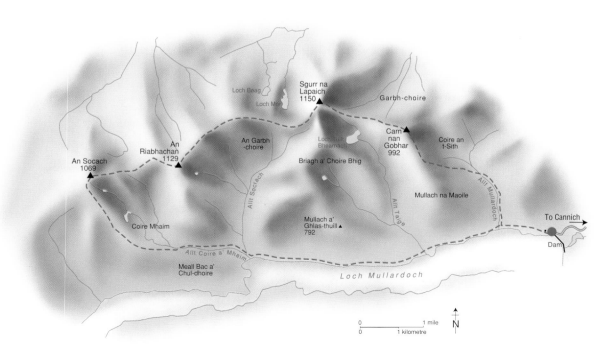

The Strathfarrar hills, looking west from Carn nan Gobhar

the rim of An Riabhachan's NE corrie to the NE top and then across to the summit. Cross to the SW top, here the main ridge turns NW towards the W top where a twist leads down to the bealach below An Socach. Climb easily to the summit. To return to Glen Cannich follow the S ridge which sweeps round to the SE and the indistinct path beside Loch Mullardoch

Map: OS Sheet 25

Access Point: Mullardoch Dam

Distance: 30km, 1890m ascent

Approx Time: 10-12 hours

Translation: hill of the goats; peak of the bog; the brindled, greyish one; the snout

Pronunciation: kaarn nan gower; skoor na lahpeech; an reeavachan; an sochkach

From the Mullardoch dam you can make a fairly straightforward circuit of Carn nan Gobhar and Sgurr na Lapaich returning by the south ridge of the latter. The other two hills of this group, An Riabhachan and An Socach, can be climbed from the west end of Loch Mullardoch after a long walk-in, or cycle in to Iron Lodge, but by far the best way to treat these hills is to walk along the north shore of Loch Mullardoch for 10km to the buildings at the foot of the Allt Socach and the Allt Coire a' Mhaim. Easy slopes climb out of Coire Mhaim and form the long curving south ridge of An Socach.

From the summit fine grassy ridges lead east, over the broad summit of An Riabhachan, through the rocky pinnacles of Sgurr na Lapaich and down over the bumpy afterthought of Carn nan Gobhar. It's a long walk, but a highly satisfying one. It can, as described in the route summary, be climbed from east to west, returning to the dam by the lochside footpath which is sketchy in places.

Sgurr Fhuar-thuill (82), 1049m/3442ft, Sgurr a' Choire Ghlais (60), 1083m/3553ft, Carn nan Gobhar (153), 992m/3255ft, Sgurr na Ruaidhe (151), 993m/3258ft

Glen Strathfarrar is the third of the three glens which join up in Strath Glas. It's almost as long as Glen Affric though much less popular, probably because the gate across the road at Struy may be locked and you have to ask permission to have it unlocked to allow you to continue up the glen. Once past this obstacle though, you can drive as far as the Loch Monar dam a distance of some 19km through the glen, one of the most beautiful in these Northern Highlands. The main interest for the Munro collector is the four hills which rise to the north side of the glen. The path up the Allt Toll a' Mhuic offers an easy ascent as far as the loch, beyond which it disappears. It can be picked up again higher in the corrie just below the first peak, Sgurr na Fearstaig. The traverse eastwards follows a well defined ridge as far as Sgurr a' Choire Ghlais but beyond this summit the last two peaks, Carn nan Gobhar and Sgurr na Ruaidhe, are rounded and rather featureless. The descent from the latter takes you down to the path by the Allt Coire Mhuillidh. The Glen Cannich mountains can also be climbed by Strathfarrar by the hydro road up the Uisge Misgeach, but this approach is probably longer than that by Loch Mullardoch in the south.

Route Summary: Access to Glen Strathfarrar is via a locked gate at Struy and is restricted to certain times. Pedestrian and bicycle access is unrestricted as the road up the glen is a right of way. At the time of writing, the arrangement is as follows: between the last weekend in March and the end of October the gate will be open from 0900 to 1300 and from 1330 to 1700 with last exit by 1800 on Mon, Wed, Thur, Fri and Sat. Sun opening is between 1330 and 1700. No vehicular access on Tues. At other times of the year access is only possible by car if the gatekeeper is at home. Tel. 01463 761260. Leave your car near Braulen Lodge. Further W, a stalkers' path climbs N into the corrie of Loch Toll a' Mhuic and on up the steep back wall of the corrie to finish just below the crest of Sgurr na Fearstaig. Continue E to Sgurr Fhuar-thuill. Follow the ridge E, over Creag Ghorm a' Bhealaich and down to the narrow saddle before Sgurr a' Choire Ghlais. Return to the main crest and descend to a saddle at the foot of Carn nan Gobhar, an easy 120m climb leads to the summit. Continue E, then SE, down into the Bealach nam Bogan, then the slopes to Sgurr na Ruaidhe. Descend via the path by the Allt Coire Mhuillidh

Map: OS Sheet 25

Access Point: Braulen Lodge, GR237387

Distance: 22km, 1520m ascent

Approx Time: 8-10 hours

Translation: peak of the cold hollow; peak of the greenish-grey corrie; hill of the goats; peak of redness

Pronunciation: skoor ooar hil; skoor a chor a ghlash; kaarn nan gower; skoor na rooy

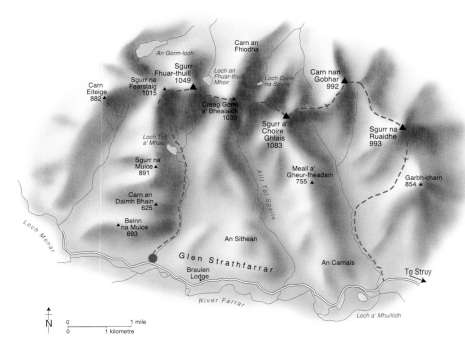

THE ACHNASHELLACH AND TORRIDON HILLS

The Munros:

Moruisg   Sgurr Choinnich   Sgurr a' Chaorachain
Maoile Lunndaidh   Bidein a' Choire Sheasgaich   Lurg Mhor
Beinn Liath Mhor   Sgorr Ruadh   Maol Chean-dearg Fionn Bheinn
Beinn Alligin (Tom na Gruagaich, Sgurr Mhor)
Liathach (Spidean a' Choire Leith, Mullach an Rathain)
Beinn Eighe (Ruadh-stac Mor, Spidean Coire nan Clach)

For many, this is the finest hillwalking area in the country – indeed there's a heart-strumming sound to the very name of Torridon. It's an evocative name, conjuring up an image of something unique, a symbolism of what fine mountains are all about. These are leviathan hills, ancient beasts which rise sheer from sea level with long lines of mural precipice, rounded and terraced bastions topped by sharp-pinnacled ridges, summits capped by grey Cambrian quartzite.

These great hills are possibly among the oldest in the world. Raised as a vast plateau, believed to be some 30 million years ago, it's now thought that the quartzite peaks, the rock of the original chain of mountains, could well be 60 million years old and if that's not old enough for you the sandstone below them is even older and the platforms of gneiss on which they stand could well be in the region of 2600 million years old.

If the enduring quality of these hills doesn't take your breath away, their appearance certainly will. All are individual, idiosyncratic, primeval – all are rugged, all are different. Beinn Alligin is elegant, shapely, bejewelled. Liathach is a monster and breathtakingly huge, while Beinn Eighe isn't so much a single hill as a chain of hills, a complex mini-range.

While Torridon is the jewel in the crown of Scotland's hills, the hills of the Ben Damph and Coulin Forests, to which ancient stalker's paths provide quick access, are also impressive. South of Glen Carron, Lurg Mhor is splendidly remote. Land-locked away beyond the head of lonely Loch Monar and girdled by trackless kilometres, it shares with its Munro neighbour, Bidein a' Choire Sheasgaich, the reputation of being one of Scotland's most isolated and inaccessible hills.

Liathach from the north-east

Moruisg (255), 928m/3045ft

Route Summary: Leave the A890 Glen Carron road at a car park about 1km W of the outflow of Loch Sgamhain. Cross the footbridge over the river (Route A) and take a stalkers' path which runs up the E bank of the Alltan na Feola. After about 2.5km leave the burn and climb E up grassy slopes. Continue until you reach the broad crest. Continue on the crest NE to the summit of Moruisg. Return and follow the broad ridge S over a subsidiary top and then descend more steeply SW to an obvious col. Climb W up a broad grassy ridge then SW after a distance to reach the flat summit of Sgurr nan Ceannaichean. The summit cairn overlooks the E corrie. Retrace your steps down the NE ridge then bear N down a steep ridge back to the Alltan na Feola

Map: OS Sheet 25

Access Point: Glen Carron

Distance: 13km, 1070m ascent

Approx Time: 4-6 hours

Translation: big water

Pronunciation: moarishk

Moruisg, and it's near neighbour Sgurr nan Ceannaichean, rise above Glen Carron and from their summits you can gaze north into the jumble of shapely hill features that make up the Torridon mountains. Until 2009 Sgurr nan Ceannaichean was also a Munro but it was demoted after a survey by the Munro Society found it to be slightly short of the three thousand foot mark. While you can climb Moruisg on its own Sgurr nan Ceannaichean is actually a more interesting hill and it's best to climb both hills together.

Leaving the best until last climb the long and relentless uniform slopes of Moruisg from a car park on the A890, just west of Loch Sgamhain.

The summit of Moruisg is flat and mossy and the ridge west offers easy walking with marvellous views both north, to the Torridons, and south to the Loch Monar hills. If you choose to climb Moruisg on its own you are best to return the way of ascent. Alternatively, cross a subsidiary top and drop down steeper grassy slopes to a col. To the right, Coire Toll nam Bian is a great rounded corrie, deep and steep with a headwall of broken crags. From the top of the corrie, a broad grassy ridge climbs westwards for about 500m before swinging south-west to climb the last few metres to the flat summit of Sgurr nan Ceannaichean.

Return the way you came for a short distance and then head north down the broad north ridge, the usual descent route back to the Alltan na Feola. Cross the burn at the first convenient spot to reach the stalker's path on the east bank.

Sgurr Choinnich (139), 999m/3278ft, Sgurr a' Chaorachain (78) 1053m/3455ft, Maoile Lunndaidh (125), 1007m/3304ft

Route Summary: Cross the railway and follow the forestry road up to a locked gate. Beyond the gate a path runs alongside the Allt a' Chonais (Route B). Continue on the track until a footbridge crosses the river and another track runs SW up and over the Bealach Bhearnais. Follow this towards the bealach and then head back E by way of the W ridge of Sgurr Choinnich. From the summit continue E and then down to the bealach before the long pull to Sgurr a' Chaorachain.

An excellent forestry road leads from Craig on the A890, 4km east of Achnashellach, up the Allt a' Chonais and makes a good approach to these hills, as well as for Lurg Mhor and Bidein a' Choire Sheasgaich. In fact the forest track is so good that I would strongly advise the use of a mountain bike for access to these hills. It can be ridden up as far as the bridge over the Allt a' Chonais, hidden in the heather, and picked up on your way back down. A long downhill freewheel through the forest is a fine alternative to a long footsore descent on forest tracks.

As you walk, or cycle, up the glen below the rocky west face of Sgurr nan Ceannaichean the mountains that appear in front of you are Sgurr Choinnich and Sgurr a' Chaorachain, divided by a steep col. It is possible to cross the river at Pollan Buidhe and climb up through the rough corrie to the col, but a more satisfying route follows a footpath south-westwards up to the Bealach Bhearnais to where Sgurr Choinnich's west ridge can be picked up. Climb this ridge which becomes increasingly rocky as you climb higher to the narrow level summit ridge.

Walk south-east along the summit ridge and descend for a short distance in the same direction before turning west-north-west where the corrie edge is followed down to the col below Sgurr a' Chaorachain. Follow the ridge directly to the summit where you can continue eastwards to Bidean an Eoin Deirg which can be descended steeply north-north-east to a col at about 600m. It is far better, though, to descend from Sgurr a' Chaorachain's north ridge for 500m before turning north east on to the Sron na Frianich above the waters of the dark Lochan Gaineamhach. Drop down the eastern slopes of the Sron to the peat-hag ridden bealach.

To continue to Maoile Lunndaidh, climb the long western ridge of Carn nam Fiaclan and follow the narrowing neck of ridge between the head of the impressive Fuar-tholl Mor in the north and Toll a' Choin in the south, to the huge, gravelly plateau of Maoile Lunndaidh.

Descend the broad heather-covered slopes of the north ridge into Gleann Fhiodhaig just east of the ruined Glenuaig Lodge. Follow the track back to the Allt a' Chonais and your awaiting bike.

Descend by the N ridge and the Sron na Frianich before dropping down E to the bealach at the foot of the W ridge of Carn nam Fiaclan. Ascend this ridge to a plateau at the head of Fuar-tholl Mor and cross in a NE direction to the summit of Maoile Lunndaidh. Descend N along the E rim of the Fuar-tholl Mor and down into Gleann Fhiodhaig

Map: OS Sheet 25

Access Point: Craig

Distance: 32km, 1680m ascent

Approx Time: 8-12 hours

Translation: moss peak; peak of the little field of the berries; hill of the wet place

Pronunciation: skoor choanyeech; skoor a choerachan; moela loondy

Route Summary: From the footbridge over the Allt a' Chonais follow the footpath to the summit of the Bealach Bhearnais. From the boggy summit leave the path and climb the NE ridge of Beinn Tharsuinn (Route C) crossing several undulations before reaching the summit. Descend SW to a small lochan and then WSW to an obvious col between the summit and the W top. From here drop down steep slopes for a considerable distance to reach the floor of the Bealach an Sgoltaidh. Steep and craggy flanks guard Bidein a' Choire Sheasgaich but an easier route can be found by traversing slightly to the right and so avoiding the steepest of the crags. A steep path zigzags its way up and you will top out beside a small lochan. Continue S to the pointed summit of Sheasgaich. From the summit descend S, then SE and follow the broad ridge to Lurg Mhor. To return you have to retrace your steps all the way to the Bealach Bhearnais and the Allt a' Chonais

Map: OS Sheet 25

Access Point: Craig

Distance: 29km, 1590m ascent

Approx Time: 8-12 hours

Translation: peak of the corrie of the milkless cattle; big ridge stretching into the plain

Pronunciation: beetyan a chora haysgeech; loorak voar

Bidein a' Choire Sheasgaich (224), 945m/3100ft, Lurg Mhor (163), 986m/3235ft

The remotest hills in the area, these are among the most isolated Munros in the country, and rise to the south-west of the head of Loch Monar in a wild and uncompromising setting. In effect, Bidein a' Choire Sheasgaich and Lurg Mhor form the southern arms of a horsehoe of big hills which enclose the western end of Loch Monar. Immediately to their north the long ridge of Beinn Tharsuinn, the Transverse Mountain, forms a continuation of this horseshoe with Sgurr Choinnich at the Bealach Bhearnais. Because of their remote position, you have to cross Beinn Tharsuinn, a Corbett, to reach Bidein a' Choire Sheasgaich and Lurg Mhor.

Follow the preceding route as far as the Bealach Bhearnais, and then climb the grassy ridge to the bumps and knolls of Tharsuinn's twisting summit ridge. Continue the traverse of this hill before dropping down its steep southern slopes to reach the narrow Bealach an Sgoltaidh at the foot of the rocky north ridge of Bidein. The way ahead looks forbidding, broken cliffs and rocky crags seem to bar the way, but there is a route through the hill's defences. Bear right, scrambling up through some crags and gullies – there is a path of sorts!

At the top of the steep section a fine ridge leads past a little lochan and tapers beautifully to the summit. The continuation to Lurg Mhor lacks the interest of what has gone before, descending around the head of a large corrie to a lochan before climbing a broad ridge to the rather featureless summit of Lurg Mhor.

It is possible to continue eastwards to Meall Mor over a narrow neck of ridge before descending to the head of Loch Monar and climbing back to the Bealach Bhearnais, but it is a lot of height to lose and a long pull up a wide corrie back to the Bealach. Alternatively, you can always try and head due north from Lurg Mhor to Bealach Bhearnais by a long traverse across the flank of Beinn Tharsuinn. Personally, I've always returned the way I came, and I suspect it's also quicker.

Route Summary: Take the path from Achnashellach station (Route A, p.180) through the pines above the River Lair. Climb above the forest on the path to a heathery hillside beneath the craggy terminal of Beinn Liath Mhor. Here the path separates, with one path running NW into Coire Lair and

Beinn Liath Mhor (258), 926m/3038ft, Sgorr Ruadh (195), 962m/3156ft

Coire Lair, north-west of Achnashellach, is dominated by three splendid mountains, Fuar Tholl, the Cold Hollow at 906m, Sgorr Ruadh and Beinn Liath Mhor. The traverse of these hills offers a rewarding outing in a wonderful situation with the hills of Torridon and the Damph and Coulin Forest dominant in the north.

Beinn Liath Mhor, summit

From Achnashellach Station a path weaves its way up through the forest and then the pine woods, latterly climbing up some steep slabs before straightening out as it enters Coire Lair. Some way ahead there is a junction of paths – one carries on to the head of Coire Lair and down into Torridon, another comes down from the bealach between Fuar Tholl and Sgorr Ruadh while the third bears off north eastwards over the south-east slopes of Beinn Liath Mhor and eventually joins up with the Coulin Pass to Glen Torridon. This is the one we want.

Enjoy the short walk up to the high point of the path, because you have a steep climb ahead of you. Take a breather before you leave the path and enjoy the view back to Fuar Tholl, a hill well known to climbers for the routes on its immense Mainreachan Buttress.

A long and steep slope of heather and boulders leads to the long curving ridge of Beinn Liath Mhor – the summit is at its northern end and comes after a lovely undulating, quartzite ridge walk. The descent to the Bealach Coire Lair is awkward. The slopes are made up of sandstone blocks and considerable care is required. Further down pass a small lochan and climb over a large knoll, well protected by sandstone blocks. On the south-west side of the knoll is another lochan which marks the Bealach Coire Lair. Climb out of the bealach towards the north-west ridge of Sgorr Ruadh, passing another small lochan before tackling the steep and rocky ridge to the summit. A path weaves its way through the crags and a bit

the other running NE into the Easan Dorcha. Take the latter for a short distance to its highest point, and then take the steep and unrelenting heather slopes of Beinn Liath Mhor. Climb to its E top and follow the stony quartzite ridge WNW to the summit. Continue on the ridge, narrow in places and descend to the Bealach Coire Lair, taking care as there are some crags to bypass and a prominent knoll either to cross, or circumnavigate. From the bealach climb S on to the NW ridge of Sgorr Ruadh and follow this ridge SE to the steep and prominent summit. The descent SE is via the Bealach Mhoir and wide open slopes back to the River Lair

Map: OS Sheet 25

Access Point: Achnashellach

Distance: 14km, 1140m ascent

Approx Time: 7-8 hours

Translation: big grey hill; red peak

Pronunciation: byn leea voar; skoor rooa

Maol Chean-dearg and An Ruadh-stac from the summit of Beinn Damh

of scrambling adds to the fun. The summit cairn is a wonderful viewpoint with the long jagged ridge of Liathach dominating the view to the north. The next hill, Fuar Tholl, although not a Munro, is probably the finest of the three. The mountain radiates three spurs, one north, one south and the other south-east, and it's on these spurs that the great rock features of the mountain are prominent.

Between the north and south-east spurs lies the Mainreachan Buttress, a magnificent mass of terraced sandstone which seems to be suspended above a tiny lochan below the north face of the mountain. Here lies some of the finest sandstone rockclimbing in the country.

From the wide pass between Sgorr Ruadh and Fuar Tholl a path drops down to the junction of paths at the foot of Coire Lair, but be warned, the River Lair can quickly rise in spate, making a crossing difficult. In such cases you'll have to follow the west bank of the river all the way back to Achnashellach.

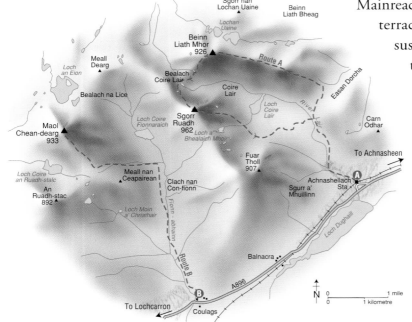

Maol Chean-dearg (247), 933m/3061ft

Along with Beinn Liath Mhor and Sgorr Ruadh, Maol Chean-dearg makes up the rocky trio of Munros that lies between Strath Carron and Glen Torridon. Because of the Coulags Pass running between Maol Chean-dearg and Sgorr Ruadh, the three Munros are rarely climbed in one outing and most folk treat Maol Chean-dearg as a single expedition, although it is best climbed along with its neighbouring rocky Corbett An Ruadh-stac.

It is the Coulags right-of-way that gives access to Maol Chean-dearg. From the little scattering of houses of the same name on the A890, make your way up the glen, which is fairly dull in its lower reaches but shows more promise as you climb higher. Cross the footbridge over the river, pass the bothy and the old stone of Clach nan Con-fionn to which the Celtic folk hero Fionn McCuill apparently used to tie his hounds. About 500m beyond the stone another path bears off to the left and begins to climb up to the high bealach between Maol Chean-dearg and Meall nan Ceapairean, with the rocky route to the Corbett An Ruadh-stac before you.

If you are intent only on Maol Chean-dearg turn north-west from the bealach and climb the broad scree-covered ridge over two large steps to the final summit slopes and the large cairn. The views from the summit are extensive with particularly good views of the very fine Corbett Ben Damh in the north west.

Route Summary: From Coulags follow the path on the E side of Fionn-abhainn (Route B). Cross the bridge to the W side after 2.4km or so and continue past the ruined cottage to the Clach nan Con-fionn. Shortly after this take the path which bears off W and climb to the col between Maol Chean-dearg and Meall nan Ceapairean. Turn NW here and climb the broad ridge to the summit

Map: OS Sheet 25

Access Point: Coulags

Distance: 13km, 910m ascent

Approx Time: 5-6 hours

Translation: bald red head

Pronunciation: moel chan dyerak

Fionn Bheinn (246), 933m/3061ft

Kenneth MacKenzie, the Brahan Seer, once predicted that 'the day will come when a raven, attired in plaid and bonnet, will drink his fill of human blood on Fionn Bheinn, three times a day, for three successive days.' I've no idea what this prophesy means, and neither am I certain that the Seer was referring to the same hill, but never mind – the hill doesn't have a lot else going for it!

Fionn Bheinn is an uninspiring hill, rising behind Achnasheen, which, since its hotel burnt to the ground, doesn't have a lot going for it either. Negatives aside, Achnasheen is on the road and the railway line to many more interesting places, so Fionn Bheinn can easily be visited en route to Torridon or the Achnashellach hills and shouldn't take more than three or four hours of your time.

The Allt Achadh na Sine is the usual line of ascent. Stay on its

Route Summary: Follow the Allt Achadh na Sine from Achnasheen and keep to its NE bank. Follow the burn high up into a corrie W of Creagan nan Laogh and climb grassy slopes N to the ridge. Follow the ridge W to the summit

Map: OS Sheets 20 and 25

Access Point: Achnasheen

Distance: 6km, 910m ascent

Approx Time: 3-5 hours

Translation: pale coloured hill

Pronunciation: fyoon vyn

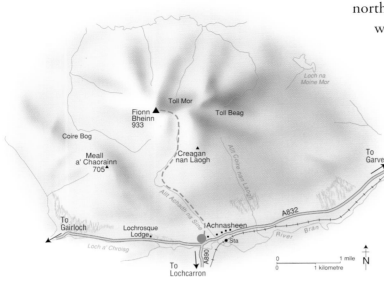

north-east bank and follow it high into a wide corrie west of Creagan nan Laogh. Climb the grassy slopes directly north to reach the broad summit ridge which is then followed westwards to the summit.

While it's easy to be disparaging about this hill there is no doubt that it stands on the edge of some superb country, with the Torridon giants to the west and the shapely Fannaichs, Sgurr nan Clach Geala and Sgurr Mor Fannaich to the north. Once you've drunk your fill of the views you can descend the way you came or vary it slightly by following the ridge above the Toll Mor for a short distance before descending the east side of the Creagan nan Laogh back to Achnasheen.

Route Summary: Cross the Torridon-Diabaig road from the car park and take the path which crosses the moorland towards Coir' an Laoigh of Tom na Gruagaich (Route A, p.187). Climb to the head of the corrie and ascend Tom na Gruagaich itself. Descend N down a rocky ridge to a col beyond where the ridge becomes broader. Climb NNE over a knoll, drop a little height to a bealach and then climb NE to Sgurr Mhor, the main summit of Beinn Alligin. From here descend steeply ENE then E down a narrow ridge to a col. Follow the well-marked path over the Horns of Alligin, using hands as well as feet in places. From the third 'Horn' continue the descent SE to the moorland and join the track in Coire Mhic Nobuil

Map: OS Sheets 19 and 24

Access Point: Coire Mhic Nobuil bridge car park

Beinn Alligin (Tom na Gruagaich (268), 922m/3025ft; Sgurr Mhor (162) 986m/3235ft)

The Torridon trio of Liathach, Beinn Eighe and Beinn Alligin must be one of the most magnificent groupings of small mountains anywhere, as well as being one of the oldest! Quartz-capped Torridonian sandstone offers an unusual mountain form, a landscape of ribs, buttresses and spires, intermingling with rounded battlements of immense bulk and while Liathach and Beinn Eighe are huge muscle-bound mountains in terms of visual mass, Beinn Alligin wears a more feminine robe – it's for good reason it's known as the Jewelled Mountain, or Mountain of Beauty.

Stretching in a gentle curve for almost five kilometres, the sandstone ridge of Beinn Alligin crosses four distinct tops, two of which are now Munros, and is split by a great natural cleft, the Eag Dubh. That great slash, along with Na Rathanan, the Horns of Alligin, are two of the most distinctive features of what is a very distinctive mountain.

A car park on the Torridon-Diabaig road makes a good starting point, and just across the road from it, at the right-hand side of the road bridge a fine footpath leads up through pine woods alongside the Abhainn Coire Mhic Nobuil and into Coire Mhic Nobuil itself.

Beinn Alligin from the Horns of Alligin

To the left of the bridge another path begins, a climber's path which is marked by cairns in a rough north-north-west direction across sandstone slabs to meet the Alltan Glas, which issues from the mouth of Coir' an Laogh. The effort of climbing the steep slopes of Coir' an Laogh is well rewarded by the views from the first Munro, Tom na Gruagaich, the hill of the damsel, a name which confirms the feminine quality of this mountain. As you pull up out of the dark confines of the corrie the abruptness of the view hits you unexpectedly. To the west, close at hand, lies the Trotternish Ridge of Skye and beyond it, the hills of Harris and the low-lying profile of Lewis. The Alligin ridge now lies before you. A careful descent from Tom na Gruagaich round the rim of Toll a' Mhadaidh Mor, over a slight bump, and then a steepish climb leads you to the main summit, Sgurr Mhor, just beyond the great gash of Eag Dubh na h-Eigheachd, the rubble of which litters the corrie floor below you. From the summit you have the option of re-tracing your route to the start, but a complete traverse of a hill is always much more satisfactory, especially over Torridonian sandstone pinnacles like the Horns of Alligin. A footpath avoids the difficulties on the right above steep grassy slopes but the Horns themselves pose little technical difficulty, just good exposed scrambling. From the third, and last, Horn continue the descent south-eastwards to the moorland below where a stalkers' path can be followed back to the Coire Mhic Nobuil footpath.

Distance: 10km, 1160m ascent

Approx Time: 6-8 hours

Translation: jewelled hill; hill of the damsel; big peak

Pronunciation: byn alligin; towm na groo-ageech; skoor vore

Liathach and Glen Torridon from Beinn Damh

Route Summary: Leave the road just E of Glen Cottage (Route B, p.187) and climb steeply up the craggy hillside into the Toll a' Meitheach. Higher up the corrie climb up to the right, NE, over steep ground to the col on the main ridge. Follow the ridge NW then W over two small tops to the cone of Spidean a' Choire Leith. Descend SW to a short and level grassy section. Continue over, or around the pinnacles of Am Fasarinen. An exposed path avoids the difficulties on the S side. Beyond the pinnacles it is an easy stroll on to Mullach an Rathain. From the summit the most interesting descent back to Glen Torridon is via the SW ridge, although there is a slightly quicker descent via the corrie of the Allt an Tuill Bhain

Map: OS Sheet 25

Liathach (Spidean a' Choire Leith (75), 1055m/3461ft; Mullach an Rathain (108), 1023m/3356ft)

A number of years ago I sat on a high sandstone block on the south side of Glen Torridon and gazed across the glen towards the grey bulk of Liathach. I was overwhelmed by the sheer size and bulk of this, the Grey One, and it frightened the life out of me. As I looked at it, tier upon tier of sandstone cliff, I was convinced there was no route up the mountain from Glen Torridon, or down it. It looked impossible. In time, I realised that it wasn't.

Liathach is essentially an 8km ridge which crosses eight separate tops. Two of those tops are credited with Munro status. The southern flank of the mountain appears to be impregnable, but on closer inspection several breaches in its defences are discovered, not least the usual route of ascent, just east of Glen Cottage and climbing up to the steep upper slopes of Toll a' Meitheach. Another possibility is up beside the Allt an Tuill Bhain at the western end of the mountain. This leads up steep sandstone slopes to another upper corrie where a steep headwall leads to the summit of Mullach an Rathain. A traverse of the mountain using these two routes of ascent/descent, makes a fine outing with all the difficulties in the latter half of the traverse, between the two Munro summits.

The footpath which leads up into Toll a' Meitheach follows the Allt an Doire Ghairbh over rocky steps, heather and steep grass and leads over a break in a rock band which seems to cross the face of the mountain. It's a steep scramble into the upper reaches of the corrie where a scree gully gives access to the ridge just west of Bidein Toll a' Mhuic.

Enjoy the views eastwards towards Beinn Eighe, then follow the ridge towards the first of the two Munros, Spidean a' Choire Leith. It's not particularly easy going, over loose scree and rock, first of all in a north-westerly direction, then west over a couple of subsidiary tops before the final bouldery slope of Spidean's cone.

Spidean a' Choire Leith is Liathach's highest point and the views on a good day are extensive, all the way from Ben Hope in the north to Ben Nevis in the south. Even more spectacular is the ridge that lies ahead. All 2km of it are extremely narrow and for much of its length it is broken and shattered into a series of spectacular spires, the Fasarinen Pinnacles.

These shattered quartzite teeth fall away dramatically into Coire na Caime on the north side, one of Liathach's magnificent northern corries which are hidden from the tourist in Glen Torridon. A scramble across the summits of the Pinnacles is far from impossible, and the walker who has a head for heights and some experience of rock climbing will love the airy traverse. Others are advised to follow an exposed, but well-trodden footpath, now very much suffering from erosion caused by over-use, which hugs the southern side of the pinnacles. This path leads to the second Munro of the hill, Mullach an Rathain, the aptly named hill of the row of pinnacles.

A wide, grassy ridge carries you on to the summit and the OS pillar. To the north a short, stony arête runs out to the highest of the Pinnacles and the lower peak of Meall Dearg, again overlooking the wonderful Coire na Caime. A long ridge runs westwards down to the subsidiary top of Sgorr a' Chadail, with fabulous views across Loch Torridon, but the descent route goes westwards and south of the summit cairn, a narrow ridge dropping towards a broadening slope of broken, scree-filled gullies and worn terraces and down towards the road alongside the Allt an Tuill Bhain. It's then only a short walk back to the car beyond Glen Cottage in Glen Torridon.

Access Point: A896, 800m E of Glen Cottage

Distance: 11km, 1310m ascent

Approx Time: 7-8 hours

Translation: grey one; peak of the grey corrie; summit of the row of pinnacles

Pronunciation: leeahach; speetyan a chora lay; moolach an raahan

Looking east along the main ridge of Beinn Eighe towards Sgurr Ban

Route Summary: Leave the car park and follow the broad track which leads up Coire Dubh Mor (Route C). At GR 934594 take another path which runs north round the prow of Sail Mor and traverses the hillside before climbing up into Coire Mhic Fhearchair. Cross the outflow of the loch and follow the east side of the loch before climbing screes and rough slopes SE to reach the ridge which leads to the summit, Ruadh-stac Mor. The traverse of Beinn Eighe can be continued by returning to the col and climbing in a SW direction up to a cairn at the E end of Choinnich Mhor. Continue SE over another col to reach a trig point at the top of the SSE spur that descends into Coire an Laoigh. Continue past the trig point for 200m to

Beinn Eighe (Ruadh-stac Mor (120), 1010m/3314ft; Spidean Coire nan Clach (150), 993m/3258ft)

Lying just south-west of Kinlochewe and Loch Maree, Beinn Eighe is separated from Liathach by Coire Dubh. It has seven peaks higher than 914m (3000ft), two Munros, and a clutch of remarkable north-facing corries, of which the finest, Coire Mhic Fhearchair, is arguably the most impressive corrie in Scotland. With its lochan reflecting the sandstone tiers of the Triple Buttress, it has the awesome atmosphere of a great cathedral, especially on a quiet, windless day when the waters are mirror still.

The traverse of all seven peaks involves a long expedition but the most straightforward route to Beinn Eighe's Munro summits, Ruadh-stac Mor and Spidean Coire nan Clach also has the advantage of being able to visit Coire Mhic Fhearchair en route. The starting point is the car park by the A896 in Glen Torridon just west of the Allt a' Choire Dhuibh Mhoir. A signpost points out the route, and the path is obvious as it takes its course up into Coire Dubh Mor, below the eastern ramparts of Liathach. Once past the obvious watershed, beyond a small lochan, a path peels off to the north around the great prow of Sail Mor. Follow it round, enjoying this great tract of wilderness landscape, as the path begins to climb again past some sparkling waterfalls, up a final rise and into the grand hall of Coire Mhic Fhearchair – one of the great mountain scenes of Scotland.

The route to the summit of Beinn Eighe's highest top is now straightforward, although it is made physically awkward by loose quartzite scree and boulder slopes. Ruadh-stac Mor is the end point of the ridge to your left, the eastern arm of Coire Mhic Fhearchair. Cross the outflow of the lochan and make your way round its eastern shores. A faint footpath weaves a route through the heather and jumbled boulders and eventually makes its way up the rough slopes towards the obvious col which separates the top from the main ridge of Beinn Eighe, and from there you'll find it an easy walk to the summit.

From there, return to the col and climb in a south-west direction up to a cairn at the end of the dome of Choinnich Mhor. The main ridge runs south-east over another col to reach a trig point at the top of the south-south-east spur that descends into Coire an Laoigh. Follow the main ridge past the trig point for 200m to the summit of Spidean Coire nan Clach. Return to the trig point and descend the south-south-east spur to Coire an Laoigh and the path to Glen Torridon.

Spidean Coire nan Clach. Return to the trig point and descend the SSE spur to Coire an Laoigh and the path to Glen Torridon

Map: OS Sheets 19 and 25

Access Point: Car park on A896

Distance: 16km, 975m ascent

Approx Time: 7-9 hours

Translation: file hill; big red peak; peak of the stony corrie

Pronunciation: byn ay; roo-a stak more; speetyan korra nan clach

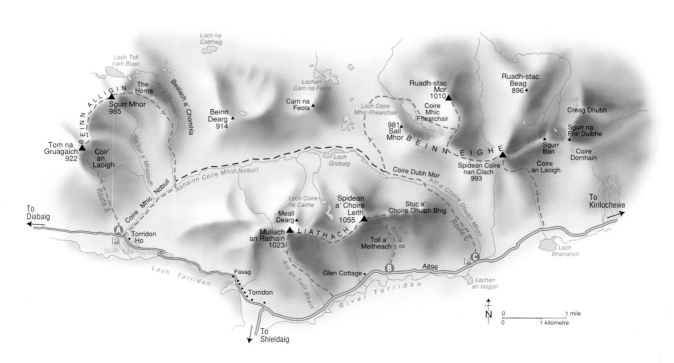

THE DUNDONNELL AND FISHERFIELD HILLS

The Munros:

Slioch   An Teallach (Sgurr Fiona, Bidein a' Ghlas Thuill)
Ruadh Stac Mor   A' Mhaighdean   Beinn a' Chlaidheimh   Sgurr Ban
Mullach Coire Mhic Fhearchair   Beinn Tarsuinn

Between the long arms of Loch Maree and Little Loch Broom in Wester Ross lies a great tangle of mountain country. Wild and remote, it boasts some of the most isolated Munros in Scotland, including An Teallach, arguably Scotland's finest mountain. In recent years there have been several attemps to discover which is Scotland's most popular mountain and in every published list this one hill, more than any other, stands aloof.

These days the word 'wilderness' tends to be over-used and often mis-applied, but the vast deer forests of Strathnashealag, Fisherfield and Letterewe have long been known to Scottish hill-goers as The Great Wilderness. The hills themselves are rocky, exposing the bare bones of the earth, folded into complex patterns and intermingled with a plethora of high-level lochans. A series of long sinuous lochs between Loch Maree in the south and Loch Broom in the north betrays the evidence of geological faults, subsequently carved out by massive glaciation. These basins, running from north-west to south-east, form the grain of the land, creating difficulties for those old travellers and drovers who wanted to move from north to south or vice versa. Ancient tracks avoid the lochs and the summits, weaving their way through glens and up over the bealachs at their heads. Even at that they have to cross rivers, which can be impossible when they are in spate, and make use of the man-made causeway between the Fionn Loch and the Dubh Loch.

Slioch (170), 981m/3218ft

Slioch, the Spear, is a real fortress of a mountain – steep rocky crags present an almost impregnable air as you view it from the road which winds its way along the south shore of Loch Maree.

But while it is violently steep on three sides, its great corrie, the Coire Tuill Bhain, or White Hollow, carves into its eastern extremity and offers a break in its defences. Every year, hundreds, if not thousands, of hill-walkers make use of that breach to gain one of the two summit ridges and enjoy far flung views across the incredible landscape of

Route Summary: From the car park at Incheril follow the path which runs along the N bank of the Kinlochewe River. After 5km cross the Abhainn an Fhasaigh by a footbridge and turn right on the path which runs up Gleann Bianasdail. After 0.8km branch left on the well-worn path which climbs N towards Slioch's SE corrie. Continue to gain the SE ridge and climb to the trig point summit. From

An Teallach – Sgurr Fiona from Sail Liath

here follow the ridge which leads to the N top which is the same height. Descend by the Sgurr an Tuill Bhain.

Map: OS Sheet 19

Access Point: Incheril, Kinlochewe

Distance: 19.2km, 1067m ascent

Approx Time: 6-9 hours

Translation: from Gaelic sleagh, a spear

Pronunciation: slee-och

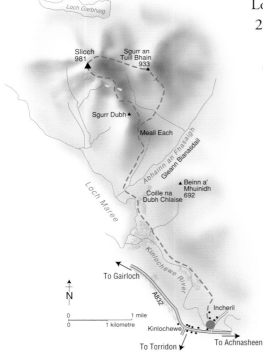

Torridon, up the length of an island-studded Loch Maree towards the sea and the Trotternish Peninsula of Skye, or across the slit trench of Lochan Fhada towards the jumble of remote mountains that make up the area known as the Great Wilderness.

But despite the panorama of mountains ranging out in all directions, it's Loch Maree which calls for attention. World famous for its beauty, this loch typifies all that is held in the phrase 'highland grandeur'. The largest loch north of the Great Glen, it covers 28 square kilometres with a backdrop that is as incredible as the Torridon hills on its south bank. Not only the mountains but the Caledonian pine forest which covers the slopes on those same southern shores is pretty ancient too, its generations of trees dating back some 8000 years. It's a miracle that these trees avoided the fate which befell other pine woods in the area, especially since 350 years ago local ironworks consumed 8 hectares of oakwoods daily for charcoal.

As you follow the path from Incheril along the riverbank to what is now the head of Loch Maree, you may well wonder at the size of the great flood plain, now scattered with broom and birch, which seems so out of proportion for an inland loch. This question runs alongside another – why is Kinlochewe (the Head of Loch Ewe) so named, since that particular sea-loch is some 24km to the west? Was it once connected to Loch Maree?

Loch Ewe is indeed the former name of Loch Maree, which suggests that the loch was once a great sea-loch, and that would explain the size of the flood plain at its head. Saint Maelrubha came to Eilean Maruighe, one of the loch's islands, in the seventh century and made it famous as a place of pilgrimage. In time the loch became associated with the island and the name of both were corrupted to Maree.

Once you've crossed the footbridge over the Abhainn an Fhasaigh, the path runs north-north-east up Gleann Bianasdail towards the mouth of Coire Tuill Bhain below Meall Each. The path is well worn but becomes fainter once the corrie is reached. The curving summit ridge which forms the corrie wall ahead of you may appear steep and intimidating, but the path breaches it just south of the main rise to the summit where twin lochans fill the ridge. Above the lochans the ascent steepens on rough and rocky ground before

Slioch and Lochan Fada

An Teallach from Sgurr Creag an Eich

it eases off. Pass a subsidiary knoll and climb to the trig point summit which is given the same height as the cairn immediately to the north.

While you could descend the same way, it's worth noting that the ridge between the summit and Sgurr an Tuill Bhain is a narrow and exhilarating traverse with superb views down to Lochan Fada below you. Continue over the summit and down steep slopes back into the corrie.

Route Summary: Leave the A832 road and take the track which runs up through the trees in Gleann Chaorachain and eventually crosses the Allt Chaorachain. Continue on the path across rocky slabs and heather towards Shenavall but before you begin the descent bear right and climb Sail Liath. From the summit follow the ridge of An Teallach to the Corrag Bhuidhe Buttresses (which can be avoided on the left).

An Teallach (Sgurr Fiona (73), 1060m/3478ft, Bidein a' Ghlas Thuill (72), 1062m/3484ft)

This mighty mountain virtually fills the Strathnasheallag Forest, with 10 tops above the magic 914m contour. Its rocky crest reaches a high point on Bidein a' Ghlas Thuill of 1062m and another of its peaks, Sgurr Fiona, at 1060m also boasts Munro status. But more important than mere Munros is the four-kilometre ridge around the mountain's eastern corrie, a sinuous, sharp edge which offers the hillwalker an exhilarating day's outing, without doubt one of the best expeditions in the country.

The best view of An Teallach is probably that from the old

THE DUNDONNELL AND FISHERFIELD HILLS

'Destitution Road' between Braemore Junction and Dundonnell. Three imposing ridges, Glas Mheall Mor, Glas Mheall Liath and Sail Liath form two corries, Glas Tholl and Toll an Lochain. The main summit, Bidein a' Ghlas Thuill, lies at the apex of the middle ridge and the main ridge, while Sgurr Fiona forms a bend on the main ridge as it curves round southwards and becomes a tight, pinnacled arête which ends on Sail Liath. This arête crosses a tall, leaning spire by the name of Lord Berkeley's Seat, a crumbling pile of sandstone which looks as though it could well topple over into Toll an Lochain below, and four high rock towers called the Corrag Bhuidhe Buttresses. The traverse of this arête is a fine one, but does call for some climbing experience.

The mountain can be traversed in both directions, from Dundonnell in the north, via the ridge of Meall Garbh and on to the high plateau north west of Glas Mheall Mor, or better still, from the A832 at the foot of Corrie Hallie. A track runs south-west through the trees of Gleann Chaorachain, crosses the Allt Gleann Chaorachain and climbs westwards over rocky slabs to the foot of the Sail Liath ridge.

Sail Liath eases you in gently. A rounded afterthought to the main ridge, her summit is dome shaped, and an eroded footpath leads down sharply to a high bealach from which the first of the ridge's summits is climbed. From here drop down to the Cadha Gobhlach where, unfortunately, evidence of An Teallach's popularity is all too clear. The soft sandstone of the hill has been ravaged by the passing of countless boots, not only an aesthetic problem but a practical one too. Secondary footpaths lead off in all directions and it's all too easy to follow the wrong track, especially in misty weather.

Most walkers avoid the Corrag Bhuidhe Buttresses, and that's a shame, for the traverse over these rocky

Scramble over the pinnacles to Lord Berkeley's Seat, descend and climb to the summit of Sgurr Fiona. Continue NNE to Bidein a' Ghlas Thuill.

Map: OS Sheet 19: GR064837, GR069844

Access Point: A832 Corrie Hallie

Distance: 22km, 1585m ascent

Approx Time: 6-10 hours

Translation: the forge; peak of wine; peak of the greenish-grey hollow

Pronunciation: an tyalach; skoor fee-ana; beetyan a ghas-hool

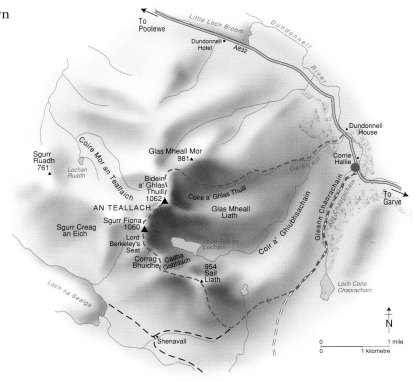

pinnacles is one of the great outings of the Scottish hills and is certainly the *pièce de résistance* of An Teallach. Ravaged footpaths skirt the Buttresses and Lord Berkeley's Seat before climbing Sgurr Fiona and the eroded state of these paths is a good enough excuse to take the higher, scrambling route.

From the Cadha Gobhlach a huge, terraced buttress seems to bar the way, but the route is clear enough, just follow the crampon scratches on the sandstone. A very steep slab, covered in good holds, marks the beginning of the scrambling. Higher still an awkward chimney marks the crux – an abseil sling decorates the top of it, and from there it's exposed ridge scrambling all the way to the top of the leaning, overhanging Lord Berkeley's Seat.

Descend the sandstone steps to the main footpath and climb the first of the hill's two Munros, Sgurr Fiona, the Peak of Wind. The route steepens again after Fiona as you descend north-north-east over some pretty rocky ground to the obvious col. There are no real obstacles left now, other than a long pull on to the highest summit, Bidean a' Ghlas Thuill. The normal descent route continues north from the summit to the obvious col and then drops down steep slopes eastwards into Coire a' Ghlas Thuill. Follow the north side of the stream to the Garbh Allt waterfalls from where a good path takes you back to the A832.

It's always a pity to traverse An Teallach and miss out on the cathedral-like grandeur of Toll an Lochain. On a recent visit the growing view down into the corrie encouraged us to find a descent route towards the lochan and after some slipping and sliding on loose sandstone and quartzy scree we hit the top of a great snow chute which gave some of the best glissading I've had for a long time. Within ten minutes we were standing by the lapping waters of the loch itself, exhilarated by our long glissade, having descended about 400m.

The prospect of the long walk back out to Corrie Hallie was overshadowed by the splendour of the surroundings, with the great riven cliffs above us rising to a stormy sea of rocky, sharp crests and bare, blank buttresses, possibly the finest corrie in Scotland.

Route Summary: A private road from Poolewe (Route A, p.197) runs along the E side of the River Ewe to Inveran and Kernsary. From Kernsary go E then SE through woods to the path on the N bank of the Allt na Creige.

Ruadh Stac Mor (276), 918m/3012ft, A' Mhaighdean (187), 967m/3173ft

Stand on the summit of Slioch and look north across Lochan Fada towards the great complexity of hills and deep glens that make up the heart of this, the most wonderful wilderness area in Scotland.

Looking west across Fionn Loch and Dubh Loch towards Ruadh Stac Mor and A' Mhaighdean

There, in the centre of this heartland, lie the rock-bound twin peaks of Ruadh Stac Mor and A' Mhaighdean, arguably the remotest of all Scotland's 283 Munros. In many ways it's a shame to try and climb these hills in a single day – far better to carry a rucksack with tent and food and wander them at leisure over several days – this is backpacking country par excellence. My own first introduction to this area was a long walk from Dundonnell in the north to Poolewe, over all the Munros. We enjoyed a superb high camp on A' Mhaighdean and I will never forget the view down the length of the Dubh Loch, the Fionn Loch and Loch Ewe out to sea and the long limb of Trotternish Ridge of Skye. More recently, during another long walk for television, from Kinlochewe to Dundonnell, we failed to see any view from A' Mhaighdean because of mist, but the experience of remoteness and rocky splendour was almost as great. These are special hills indeed.

From Poolewe, a private road runs alongside the River Ewe to Inveran and Kernsary. From here a track runs through woods and eventually runs alongside the Allt na Creige. It continues across flat and boggy terrain in a south-east direction, makes a slight divergence to cross the Strathan Buidhe, and continues across more flat ground to the causeway at the south-eastern end of the Fionn Loch.

Now this may sound, on the face of it, a fairly dull walk on featureless terrain, but all the time the great rocky bastion of the western faces of A' Mhaighdean grow in height and presence, and with the rocky buttresses of Beinn Lair filling the view to the south there is a feeling that you are approaching a very special place. And you are.

From the north side of the causeway a very good path continues

Follow it past Loch an Doire Chrionaich then S to cross Strathan Buidhe. Go E over causeway between Fionn Loch and Dubh Loch and follow stalkers' path to Carnmore. Continue E, make a rising traverse across slopes of Sgurr na Laocainn. Turn N to follow the Allt Bruthach an Easain for almost 1km. At a path junction turn right and follow the path over slabs and pavements to Fuar Loch Mor. Continue on this path up into the rocky corrie to the bealach below the screes and crags of Ruadh Stac Mor. Thread your way up through the cliffs to the summit. Return to the bealach and climb the NE ridge of A' Mhaighdean to its summit plateau. Continue SSW for a final climb through gneiss boulders to the summit. Return to the earlier path junction, back to Carnmore and Poolewe by the outward route.

Map: OS Sheet 19

Access Point: Poolewe

Distance: 40km, 1189m ascent

Approx Time: 10-14 hours

Translation: big red peak; the maiden

Pronunciation: roo-a stak more; ah-vatyin

past Carnmore and makes a rising traverse across the slopes of Sgurr na Laocainn. At its high point it turns north to follow the Allt Bruthach an Easain for almost 1km before turning south-east again to make the rocky climb up over great slabs and pavements to Fuar Loch More, a dramatic stretch of water enclosed in a tight grip of craggy cliffs.

From the lochside, continue on this path up into the rocky corrie to the bealach below the sandstone screes and crags of Ruadh Stac Mor and it takes little time, or effort, to thread your way up through the cliffs to the summit. Return to the bealach where there is a fine rocky howff and climb the north-east ridge of A' Mhaighdean to its summit plateau. Continue in a south-south-west direction for a final climb through gneiss boulders to the summit and some of the best mountain views in the country.

An alternative route of ascent follows the stepped north-west ridge of A' Mhaighdean from the west end of Fuar Loch Mor. There are plenty of crags on the ridge, but all the real difficulties can be avoided. For those who don't mind a bit of exposure, this is the recommended route to the summit.

Beinn a' Chlaidheimh (280), 916m/3005ft, Sgurr Ban (157), 989m/3245ft, Mullach Coire Mhic Fhearchair (115), 1018m/3340ft, Beinn Tarsuinn (238), 936m/3071ft

Route Summary: From the bothy at Shenavall (GR 066810) cross the Abhainn Strath na Sealga (Route B). (Take care; the crossing of this river when in spate is not advisable and there is no bridge.) Climb the steep heather-covered slopes of Beinn a' Chlaidheimh to the SW. The slope becomes steeper as you reach the summit ridge and the final pull is up the ridge just E of the summit. Descend to the S on long scree slopes towards Loch a' Bhrisidh and follow the corrie rim to the summit of Sgurr Ban over white quartzite scree. Continue to another scree-filled col just S of Sgurr Ban where another steep climb takes you to the summit of Mullach Coire Mhic Fhearchair. Continue S to a prominent knob where the mountain's S ridge suddenly turns W to Beinn Tarsuinn. This can be turned by easy slopes to the E and S. Continue over rocky

The traverse of these hills is a serious undertaking, and the best base for climbing them is Shenavall, although Sgurr Ban, Mullach Coire Mhic Fhearchair and Beinn Tarsuinn can be climbed in a fine, if long, circuit from Incheril near Kinlochewe, leaving Beinn a' Chlaidheimh to be climbed another day from the north.

Beinn a' Chlaidheimh lies south of the Abhainn Strath na Sealga. Once safely across it's best to tackle the steep heathery slopes in a south-west direction and so avoid the craggy north slopes of the hill. Gain the Creag Ghlas ridge and follow it to the fields of white quartzite which cap the summits of so many of these hills.

Beinn a' Chlaidheimh sits just above the 914m Plimsoll line. Below, to the south, Loch a' Bhrisidh is set in a craggy cirque before a dazzling white slope of quartzite stretches up to the summit of Sgurr Ban. Although splendidly quartz capped, Sgurr Ban can be ascended on grass for much of the 300m climb from the bealach to its broad plateau summit, but immediately to the south Mullach Coire Mhic Fhearchair presents a contrasting image

– steep and bouldery, its slopes riven and seamed with long scree gullies and protuding crags running upwards to its narrow top and large cairn. The western face of the hill is of pink sandstone, split by great searing gullies. The summit cone, like Sgurr Ban, is of Cambrian quartzite. The main feature of Mullach is a 1.6km long ridge of gneiss which extends south-eastwards into the head of Gleann an Nid, terminating in a series of spiring pinnacles. Between Mullach and Beinn Tarsuinn is an intermediary top, Meall Garbh, but this can be avoided by following a very good path which runs along the foot of its north west-facing slopes. A boggy bealach leads on to the grassy slopes of Tarsuinn.

This mountain forms the red sandstone tiered headwall of Gleann na Muice and forms a marvellous curving ridge cradling a high lochan in its clench. From the summit the views northwards are superb, towards the castellated ridge of An Teallach. The narrow, sandstone crest of Beinn Tarsuinn is an interesting one, dropping from the summit on to a flat topped table, then a series of pinnacles, weathered and seamed. Follow the ridge almost to its end then drop down grassy slopes to a peat hag riven bealach. From here head north below the crags of Stac a' Chaorruinn and follow the infant waters of the Abhainn Gleann na Muice down grassy slopes into the glen where a stalker's path eventually meets up with the Gleann na Muice Beag path to Shenavall.

platforms to the summit of Beinn Tarsuinn. To return to Shenavall take a line across the N slopes to reach the stalkers' path in Gleann na Muice

Map: OS Sheet 19

Access Point: Shenavall

Distance: 20.8km, 1768m ascent

Approx Time: 8-12 hours

Translation: hill of the sword; light-coloured peak; summit of the corrie of Farquhar's son; transverse hill

Pronunciation: byn a' shleev; skoor bawn; moolach corrie veechk erachar; byn tarshin

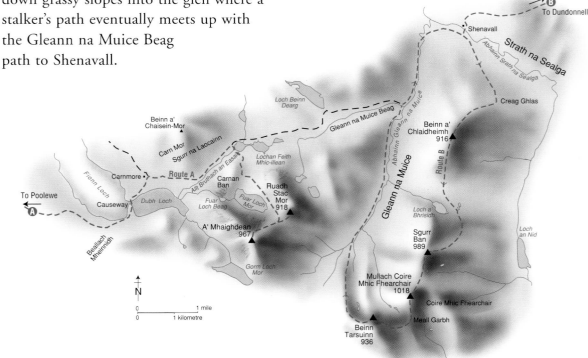

THE FANNAICHS
AND ULLAPOOL HILLS

The Munros:

Meall a' Chrasgaidh   Sgurr Mor   Beinn Liath Mhor Fannaich
Sgurr nan Clach Geala   Sgurr nan Each   Sgurr Breac   A' Chailleach
An Coileachan   Meall Gorm   Ben Wyvis (Glas Leathad Mor)
Am Faochagach   Beinn Dearg   Cona' Mheall   Meall nan Ceapraichean
Seana Bhraigh   Eididh nan Clach Geala

These hills make up two hill groups of very different character, with Ben Wyvis lying out on a limb to the east. Both groups have a splendid wilderness quality to them and although fairly close to the Garve/Ullapool road they offer a fine feeling of remoteness. To the north and north-east lie great chunks of wild country, roadless and without habitation. The best of the Fannichs undoubtedly lie to the west, with Sgurr nan Clach Geala in particular appearing almost Alpine in feature when viewed from Sgurr Mor.

To the north of the Dirrie More, the Beinn Dearg group introduces the walker to the vast watery landscape of the north-west, especially Seana Braigh, which lies in isolated splendour in the midst of this wilderness. One of the remotest Munros, its ascent demands a considerable expedition, although it is probably more easily climbed, if by a less attractive route, from Oykel Bridge in the north-east.

Route Summary: Cross the dam and follow the track beside the pipeline (Route A). This track eventually ends at a small dam on the Allt a' Mhadaidh. Just before it a footbridge crosses the stream from where another track climbs in a SW direction towards Loch A' Mhadaidh. Pass the loch on its N shore and climb to the bealach between Meall a' Chrasgaidh and Carn na Criche. Climb Meall a' Chras-gaidh, return to the bealach and follow the ridge over Carn na Criche. Climb the steep slopes of Sgurr Mor to the summit, descend SE then E to follow the ridge to Beinn Liath Mhor Fannaich. From the summit descend due N, then NE down steep

Meall a' Chrasgaidh (243), 934m/3064ft, Sgurr Mor (43), 1110m/3642ft, Beinn Liath Mhor Fannaich (209), 954m/3130ft

The track that runs up towards the Fannaichs from the A835, Garve to Ullapool road, follows an enormous pipeline that diverts the water flow over the watershed to Loch Droma and the big Glascarnoch hydro-scheme. It always reminds of the sacrifices that Scotland has made in the name of hydro-power.

Scotland's contribution to the national grid is a generous one, but the concrete dams do little to enhance the landscape quality of the Highlands. Many bulldozed tracks have been gouged into the wild places and electricity pylons still march their way across some of the most spectacular landscapes in Europe.

Thank goodness we still have some wild places left. The track from Loch Droma leaves the pipeline at a little dam and sub-station and follows the Allt a' Mhadaidh, the stream of the fox, up over the peat hags to Loch a' Mhadaidh. Away to the right lies Beinn Liath Mhor Fannaich, rising at the end of the craggy ridge that connects it to Sgurr Mor, the highest of the nine Munros of the Fannaichs deer forest. On the other side of the loch lies Meall a' Chrasgaidh, easily reached by the grassy corrie that rises behind the loch.

At the cairn on Meall a' Chrasgaidh (which can also be climbed along with Sgurr nan Clach Geala and Sgurr nan Each) it's easy to see why this Highland landscape is so special. To the west the castelled form of An Teallach, perhaps the most magnificent of our mountains, stands in isolation. Further north lies a complete chain of mountain icons – Ben More Coigach, Stac Pollaidh, Cul Mor and Cul Beag, Suilven, Canisp, Quineag and the hills of Assynt. This is surely a landscape without equal – anywhere.

The twisting ridge from Meall a' Chrasgaidh, over Carn a' Criche and onto the steep slopes of Sgurr Mor is notable for the views across to Sgurr nan Clach Geala, the finest of the Fannaichs, with its high, hanging corrie and steep buttresses. Another high ridge, the Am Blachdaich, connects it to the Chrasgaidh/Sgurr Mor ridge, and yet another ridge runs south from its summit to another Munro, Sgurr nan Each.

Two other Munros, An Coileachan and Meall Gorm, lie south-east of Sgurr Mor and are best climbed from Loch Fannich in the south but Beinn Liath Mhor Fannaich is the final top of this superb 17km high-level circuit of Loch a' Mhadaidh. A stalkers' path runs across the western flanks of the hill and from there it is a short, steep climb to the rocky summit.

heather slopes back to the Allt a' Mhadaidh and the earlier hydro-board track

Map: OS Sheet 29

Access Point: Loch Droma on the A835, GR253754

Distance: 20km/1020m ascent

Approx Time: 7-9 hours

Translation: hill of the crossing; big peak; big grey hill of Fannaich

Pronunciation: myowl a kraaskee; skoor more; byn leea voar faanich

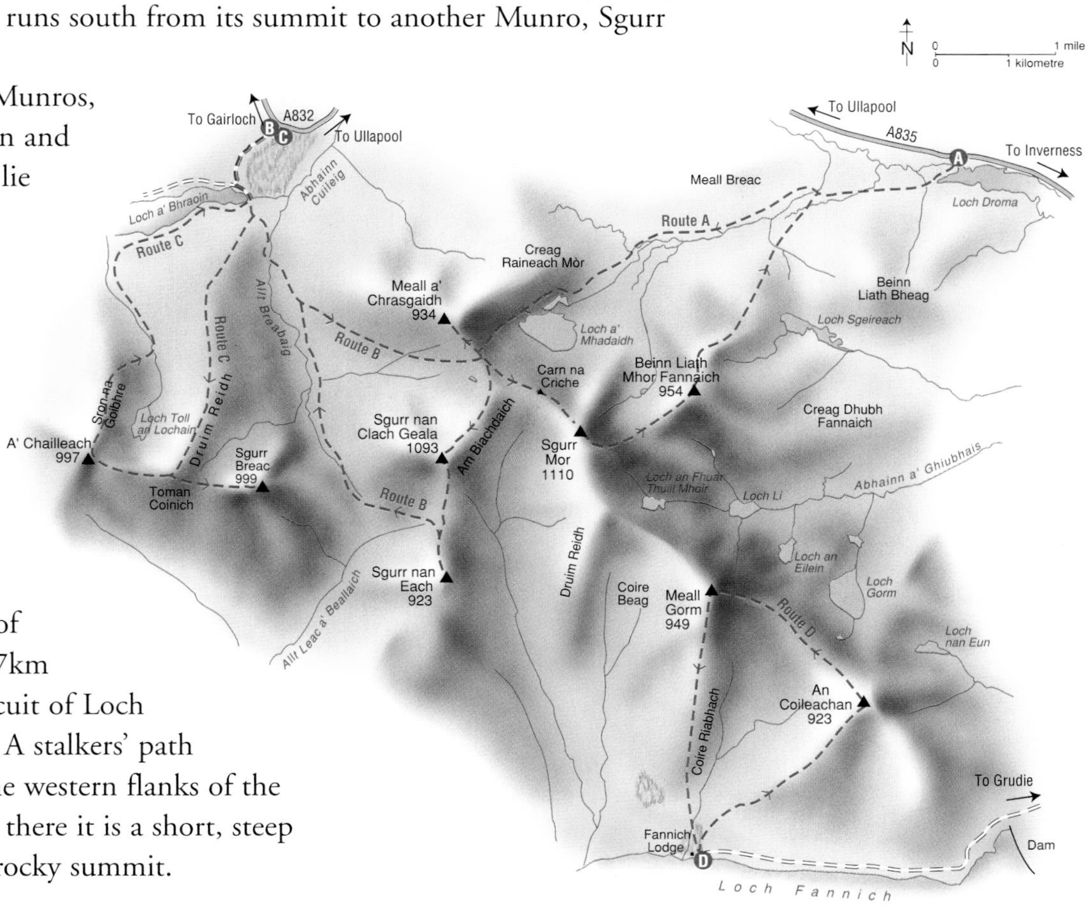

The western Fannaichs from Sgurr nan Each

Sgurr nan Clach Geala (53), 3586ft/1093m, Sgurr nan Each (267), 3028ft/923m

Route Summary: From Loch a' Bhraoin cross the outflow and follow the footpath S (Route B). Cross the Abhainn Cuileig, leave the footpath and strike diagonally across the SW slopes of Meall a' Chrasgaidh to the bealach between that hill and Sgurr nan Clach Geala. You could also climb Meall a' Chrasgaidh, then return to the bealach, and climb to the high saddle SW of Carn na Criche. Climb the NE ridge of Sgurr nan Clach Geala, descend S and continue to the rocky ridge of Sgurr nan Each. Return to the bealach S of Sgurr nan Clach Geala and drop down W to the path which runs back to Loch a' Bhraoin

Map: OS Sheet 20

Access Point: A832, near Loch a' Bhraoin

Distance: 20km, 220m ascent

Approx Time: 7-9 hours

Translation: peak of the white stones; peak of the horses

Pronunciation: skoor nan klach gee-ala; skoor nan yaach

The most attractive of the Fannaichs is Sgurr nan Clach Geala. With its near neighbours, Sgurr nan Each and Meall a' Chrasgaich, it lies on the east side of the footpath which runs through from Loch Fannich to Loch a' Bhraoin, a stalkers' path that offers a fine exit from Sgurr nan Each after a traverse of the Munros.

Take the private road to Loch a' Braoin, cross its outlet and continue on the stalkers' path beside the Allt Breabaig. After 1km cross the burn and take the steep heathery west slopes of Meall a' Chrasgaich. As its name, the rounded hill of the crossing, would perhaps suggest, it lacks the ruggedness of some of its neighbours but its summit is most certainly a viewpoint par excellence and can be included in this walk or in the Sgurr Mor/Beinn Liath Mhor Fannaich route.

From Chrasgaidh a long slope leads to a wide bealach. One ridge heads off to the north-east to climb Sgurr Mor while another becomes the rough north-east ridge of Sgurr nan Clach Geala. Follow the graceful curved ridge to the narrow summit ridge and then descend to another bealach, the Cadha na Guite, before climbing the slopes to the shapely summit of Sgurr nan Each. Return to the Cadha na Guite, down the slopes to the west-north-west and the stalkers' path back to Loch a' Bhraoin.

Sgurr Breac (138), 999m/3278ft,
A' Chailleach (144), 997m/3271ft

The most westerly of the Fannaichs, these two hills are joined to the rest of the ridge by a high col at the head of the Allt Breabaig. A footpath runs south from Loch a' Bhraoin to this col where Sgurr Breac can be climbed by its eastern ridge. A good high-level ridge runs west from Sgurr Breac over the subsidiary top of Toman Coinich and onto A' Chailleach. This ridge is like the upright of a letter F with two projecting spurs, Sron na Goibhre and Druim Reidh running out in a northerly direction forming the arms of the corrie of Toll an Lochain.

One of these spurs, the Druim Reidh, rises steeply from the eastern end of Loch a' Bhraoin and once the initial height is gained, runs gently southwards towards Toman Coinich and its central position between the two Munros.

Climb both Munros from this top and return by way of the Druim Reidh.

Route Summary: At Loch a' Bhraoin, cross its outlet, soon leave the path to climb the NE nose of Druim Reidh (Route C). Follow ridge to Toman Coinich. Descend SE to a high bealach, and a short climb to Sgurr Breac. Return to the bealach, re-ascend Toman Coinich and descend WSW to another high bealach. Climb A' Chailleach. Descend via spur of Sron na Goibhre to the outflow of Loch Toll an Lochain and the shores of Loch a' Bhraoin
Map: OS Sheets 19 and 20
Access Point: A832 near Loch a' Bhraoin
Distance: 16km, 1140m ascent
Approx Time: 6-8 hours
Translation: speckled peak; the old woman
Pronunciation: skoor brechk; a chalyach

An Coileachan (266), 923m/3028ft, Meall Gorm (215), 949m/3113ft

These two Munros, at the eastern end of the Fannaichs, can be climbed either from the north or the south and both routes have advantages and disadvantages. Hillwalkers coming from the north tend to link these two Munros with the ascent of Beinn Liath Mhor Fannaich and Sgurr Mor. The usual approach is the same as Route A as far as the small power station on the Allt a' Mhadaidh. From the power station take to the heather-covered slopes on the south side of the river and climb onto the north ridge of Beinn Liath Mhor Fannaich. Descend steeply to the upper rim of Coire a' Mhadaidh and follow the ridge as it curves gently round to Sgurr Mor with steep craggy ground falling away to your right and more open slopes to the left. The final slopes are steep and lead to a huge summit cairn. Retrace your steps back down and continue south-south-east over the slabs of Meall nam Peithirean and around the crest of Coire Fhuar Thuill Mhoir to pick up a stalkers' path on Creachan Rairigidh. Follow this south-east to the summit of Meall Gorm. The wide ridge continues east, then south-east as it drops down to the Bealach Ban, before rising to An Coileachan.

Now comes the chief disadvantage of this northern approach. It's a long, long way back to the A835, over very rough and boggy ground. The best line is from the Bealach Ban, taking a diagonal line

Route Summary: At time of writing it isn't possible to drive from Grudie Bridge to Fannich Lodge, a distance of 11km, but you can use a mountain bike. From Fannich Lodge climb the slopes of An Coileachan by its SW ridge (Route D). From the summit a broad ridge stretches NW to Meall Gorm and its two small tops. The true summit is the one with a windbreak shelter built near it. By backtracking from the summit for a short distance you'll find a stalkers' path descending the S ridge of Meall Gorm. This path goes all the way back to Fannich Lodge. Fannich Estate: 01997 414318
Map: OS Sheet 20
Access Point: Fannich Lodge, GR218660
Distance: 11km, 670m ascent
Approx Time: 4-6 hours
Translation: the little cock; blue hill
Pronunciation: an kilyachan; myowl gorram

to reach the col between An Coileachan and its northern outlier, Meallan Buidhe. Head north down easy slopes to the Abhainn a' Ghiubhais Li and follow rough, tussocky and boggy ground back to the A835. Follow the road back to the west end of Loch Droma.

The approach from the south is shorter and significantly easier, but you'll need to get permission to drive the 11km from the Strathbran/Achnasheen road, the A832, to Fannich Lodge as the gate at Grudie Power Station is normally locked. You could, of course, use a bike! This road is often blocked by snow in the winter.

From Fannich Lodge an excellent stalkers' path runs up the south ridge of Meall Gorm and gives easy access to An Coileachan. Sgurr Mor is also within easy reach and it's not a lot further to climb Beinn Liath Mhor Fannaich as well.

Ben Wyvis (Glas Leathad Mor) (85), 1046m/3432ft

Route Summary: From the A835 just S of Garbat follow the footpath that runs alongside the Allt a' Bhealaich Mhoir. Continue past the forest plantation into the Ben Wyvis National Nature Reserve and leave the stream to climb the slopes of An Cabar. The path improves the higher you climb. From An Cabar the summit, Glas Leathad Mor, lies 1.6km away in a NE direction over a rolling mossy ridge. Continue past the

It's not the most dramatic mountain in Scotland, nor the prettiest, but it can throw down a challenge which can cause problems for the unwary. Ben Wyvis is Inverness's mountain, just as Ben Lomond is Glasgow's and just as generations of hillwalkers from the Central Belt have first scuffed their boots above the bonnie, bonnie banks, so many local folk have battled up the heather-clad slopes of Tom a' Choinnich, Glas Leathad Mor and An Cabar, the tops which collectively make up Ben Wyvis.

The flat summit skyline and rather featureless western slopes, those seen from the Garve-Ullapool road, don't immediately suggest any sense of threat, but when Martin Moran from Lochcarron was climbing all the Munros during the winter equinox a few years ago it was here that he came closest to getting the chop – he was avalanched off Glas Leathad Mor.

My own first attempt on Ben Wyvis wasn't quite as dramatic, but didn't lack excitement. We had struggled up on to An Cabar, only 2km from the summit and 96m lower, but gale force winds had us, literally, on our knees, and from time to time sudden gusts threatened to lift us off the ground. Swallowing our pride, we made a

Map labels:
To Ullapool
Tom a' Choinnich
Garbat
Allt a' Gharbh Bhaid
Ben Wyvis 1046
An t-Socach
Glas Leathad Mor
Coire na Feola
Allt a' Bhealaich Mhoir
An Cabar 950
Bealach Mor
Tom na Cailich 706
To Garve
Little Wyvis 764
N
0   1 mile
0   1 kilometre

Looking south from the summit of Ben Wyvis

hasty retreat and left the summit for another, more benevolent, day.

The main physical features of the hill are the two great corries which are gouged out of the eastern flanks of the hill, the dark side of the mountain which is relatively unseen, and unfrequented. Here the snow lies late into the summer and mountaineer John Mackenzie, Earl of Cromartie, told me that his ancestors used to rent their land from the Crown on condition that they could gather a snowball at any time of the year.

The popular route begins at the foot of the Allt a' Bhealaich Mhoir near Garbat on the Garve-Ullapool road and follows a well-constructed footpath for 2km to the boundary with Scottish Natural Heritage's nature reserve. In the late 1990s the Footpath Trust created a marvellous route over the lower slopes of the hill, and now the areas beside the trail have grown over and the footpath, once a muddy scar on the landscape, has literally been healed. Once into the Nature Reserve the path approaches An Cabar and climbs to a high-level 2km ridge walk across huge swathes of green mosses and sedge, a breeding ground for dotterel, to the cairn on Glas Leathad Mor.

summit, descend, then climb the slopes of Tom a' Choinnich. Descend in a SW direction to the Allt a' Gharbh Bhaid, and follow the forestry edge back to the footpath beside the Allt a' Bhealaich Mhoir

Map: OS Sheet 20

Access Point: Small car park just off the A835 at Garbat

Distance: 22km, 1310m ascent

Approx Time: 6-8 hours

Translation: from Gaelic fuathas, possibly hill of terror; big greenish grey slope

Pronunciation: byn wivis; glas lehat moar

Am Faochagach (210), 954m/3130ft

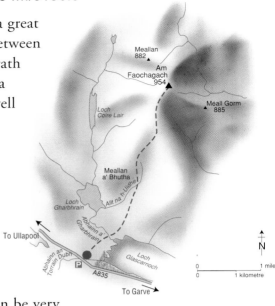

This is the high point of a great tangle of hills which lie between Loch Glascarnoch and Strath Vaich. Am Faochagach is a big, bluff, rounded hill, well protected by big walk-ins from the Glascarnoch Dam or from Strath Vaich in the east. The obvious approach, from the A835 at Loch Droma, is both pathless and exceedingly wet and crossing the Abhainn a' Gharbhrain can be very difficult in wet weather. In such conditions it's worth trying to cross above Loch a' Gharbhrain, but you'll have two burns to cross – the Allt a' Gharbhrain and the outflow from Loch Coire Lair. This hill is best kept for a period of dry weather.

Once over the waterways the ascent is easy. A north-easterly line climbs steep heather-covered slopes on the south bank of the Allt na h-Uidhe, then more easterly up steeper slopes to the summit spine. Follow the broad ridge northwards, over a rounded subsidiary top to the final summit slopes. Two cairns adorn the flat summit dome.

Beinn Dearg (57), 1084m/3556ft, Cona' Mheall (176), 978m/3209ft, Meall nan Ceapraichean (177), 977m/3205ft

You notice the great bulk of Beinn Dearg as you drive over the A835 Ullapool road from Garve. It rises beyond the foot of Loch Glascarnoch beside Cona' Mheall. It's a straightforward walk to climb the two hills from this approach and perhaps also Am Faochagach, slightly to the east, but beware. The flat area between the foot of Loch Glascarnoch and these hills is very wet and boggy indeed and the river which flows into the loch can often be difficult to cross. A few hundred metres north of Inverlael House, a private forestry track runs up through the Lael Forest into the lower part of Gleann na Sguaib. I would strongly recommend using a mountain bike for the first 3km up through the forest. The long downhill freewheel at the end of a hard hill day is delightful.

Beinn Dearg and Cona' Mheall from Am Faochagach

The path through Gleann na Sguaib takes you on to a high and broad pass, a stony place with scattered lochans. To climb Beinn Dearg, on your right, follow the line of a massive dry stone dyke that runs up virtually all the way to the summit. Near the top, where the dyke bears west, go through the gap in the wall and follow a south-south-west bearing for about 300m to cross the bald dome of the summit slopes and find the summit itself.

Directly east of Beinn Dearg's summit, the slopes steepen, eventually to form the sheer western wall of the spectacular Coire Ghranda, with its high-level lochan and Cuillin-like atmosphere. The north-east wall supports the flat-topped ridge of Cona' Mheall which can be reached either by a long and wet walk-in from Loch Droma on the A835, or from the Bealach Coire Ghranda at the head of Gleann na Sguaib. The first route involves a spectacular scramble up the south-east ridge, probably the mountain's finest feature. From the Bealach Coire Ghranda it is a straightforward walk to the summit cairn on the north-east corner of the summit ridge. Back at the Bealach it's an easy climb up the south-east ridge of Meall nan Ceapraichean.

Beinn Dearg col and the path back down Gleann na Sguaib.

Map: OS Sheet 20

Access Point: Inverlael (If there are no parking places here you'll find a small car park a short distance to the S on the A835.)

Distance: 24km, 1520m ascent

Approx Time: 7-11 hours

Translation: red hill; hill of the joining; possibly from ceap, meaning a rounded hilltop

Pronunciation: byn dyerak; konival; myowl nan kyapreechan

Seana Bhraigh (262), 927m/3041ft,
Eididh nan Clach Geala (257), 927m/3041ft

Route Summary: From Inverlael follow the forest track as far as Glensguaib (Route B). Continue up the glen for about 3km to where a small cairn marks the start of a stalkers' path (unmarked on the OS map) which climbs NE to Lochan a' Chnapaich. Climb the heathery slopes NW of the loch to the summit slopes of Eididh nan Clach Geala. From the top, easy-angled slopes lead NW to the top of Coire an Lochain Sgeirich. Continue across boggy terrain towards Loch a' Chadha Dheirg from where a N direction will take you around the head of the Cadha Dearg to the easy slopes of Seana Bhraigh. Follow the cliff edge to the summit. Return via the footpath which runs W down Coire an Lochain Sgeirich, across the Allt Gleann a' Mhadaidh and down the nose of Druim na Saobhaidhe

Map: OS Sheet 20

Access Point: Inverlael

Distance: 28km, 1130m ascent

Approx Time: 7-10 hours

Translation: old upper part; web of white stones

Pronunciation: shena vry; aydyee nan klach gyala

Since Seana Bhraigh lies very much in isolation to the north of the Beinn Dearg group it makes a lot of sense to climb it as a solitary peak. This also gives a fair choice of approach – from Glen Achall near Ullapool or Strath Mulzie in the north, from Gleann Beag in the south east, or from Inverlael in the south west. The first three approaches involve a considerable walk-in, although mountain bikes can be used, but perhaps the best option for the day walker is from Gleann na Sguaib near Inverlael.

If climbing Seana Bhraigh only, climb up through the forest to Glensguaib and then ascend the long nose of Druim na Saobhaidhe which forms the northern wall of Gleann na Sguaib. A footpath follows the ridge, crosses over the Allt Gleann a' Mhadaidh and runs up the length of Coire an Lochain Sgeirich to the vast plateau north-east of Eididh nan Clach Geala.

Alternatively, Seana Bhraigh can be climbed fairly comfortably with Eididh nan Clach Geala to make a fine round which makes the most of some very good stalkers' paths, one of which isn't

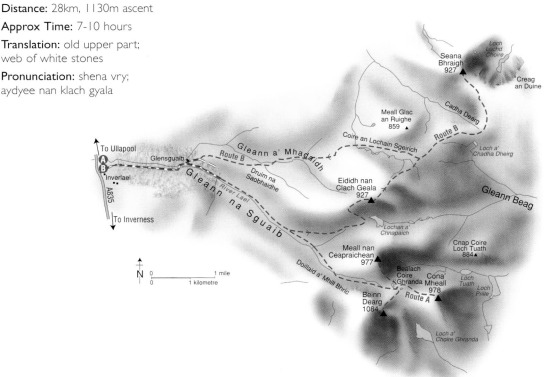

shown by the OS. Walk up
the length of Gleann na
Sguaib as far as the Eas Fionn
waterfall where a cairn by the
side of the track marks the
beginning of a very good
stalker's path which climbs
the hillside to Lochan a'
Chnapaich. Just before you
reach the lochan, climb
northwards on to the broad
spur which emanates from
Eididh nan Clach Geala, pass
a small lochan tucked away in
the heathery folds, and follow
the broad ridge to the quartzy
summit.

From there, broad grassy
slopes lead north-east past
the head of Coire an Lochain
Sgeirich (your eventual descent
route) and small lochans to
the rim of the impressive
Cadha Dearg, the Red Pass.
I once sat here enthralled
watching a golden eagle
quarter the air space *below*
me. This is a wild place of
tremendous atmosphere, rich
in botanical interest, with

Seana Bhraigh and Loch Luchd Choire from Creag an Duine

great crags forming its eastern and northern extremities. The
walking is easy around the great rim and then up grassy slopes,
skirting the 906m bump and up final stony slopes to the summit –
a breathtaking point with the windbreak cairn sitting on the very
edge of nothing! The view across the void of the Luchd Choire
to Seana Bhraigh's eastern top, Creag an Duine, is one of immense
spaciousness with the whole of the North West arrayed before
you in all its mountain glory.

Return by the rim of the Cadha Dearg and the footpath down
Coire an Lochain Sgeirich.

ASSYNT AND THE FAR NORTH

The Munros:

Conival   Ben More Assynt   Ben Klibreck   Ben Hope

If there is one area in Scotland which truly exposes the pointless nature of Munro-bagging it is this vast area north of Ullapool. Within a collection of smaller hills of the character of Stac Pollaidh, Suilven, Cul Mor and Cul Beag, Canisp, Quineag, Foinaven, Arkle and Ben Loyal we have some of the finest mountains in the country, and I'm afraid the Munros, fine as they are in their own right, very much stand in the shadow of their less-high neighbours.

So many Munro-seekers drive huge distances to climb these hills in quick bagging raids – many will climb Klibreck and Ben Hope in a day with a drive in the car in-between. I remember driving all the way north from Glasgow to climb Conival and Ben More Assynt and immediately driving all the way south again, looking out of the car window on the return drive just wishing I could stay in this incredible area for a bit longer.

Geologically, the area is predominantly gneiss, on top of which sandstone hills have weathered to create some of the weird and magnificent mountain shapes that are so typical of the region. From Inchnadamph the bare quartzite screes of Conival's upper tier contrast with the rich green of Gleann Dubh below, the bold greenness indicating the predominance of limestone. Below this surface lie caves, pot-holes and water courses and the well-known caves of Traligill in Gleann Dubh.

Further north Ben Hope and Ben Klibreck are isolated hills surrounded by vast moorlands, a factor which greatly enhances their appearance, particularly the former.

Route Summary: Take the farm track, just N of the Inchnadamph Hotel, which runs alongside the River Traligill. Follow the path to the Traligill Caves, but stay on the NE bank. Opposite the caves leave the track and take to the slopes on the SW face of Beinn an Fhurain. Aim for the obvious col between Beinn an Fhurain and Conival. From the col the final slopes lead to a level ridge and the summit. Continue E along the rough ridge of scree and quartzite boulders to the summit of Ben More Assynt. The summit cairn is on the N top.

Conival (158), 987m/3238ft, Ben More Assynt (141), 998m/3274ft

From Inchnadamph the grey quartzite screes of Conival tend to hide the bulk of Ben More Assynt, a rather secretive hill which is unusual in this area of normally bold mountains. These two hills are invariably climbed together, although a fine ridge walk over Conival and Breabag to the south offers great views of the superb corrie between Conival and Ben More Assynt which is ringed by sheets of grey quartzite screes and holds a sparkling green lochan. A diversion to Ben More and back to Conival involves only another 3km of ridge walking.

The normal route of ascent leaves the road a couple of hundred metres north of the Inchnadamph Hotel and follows the farm track along the north bank of the River Traligill beyond the cottage at

Conival and Ben More Assynt from the south-east

Glenbain to a prominent copse of trees. Just beyond this point, a footpath crosses the river by a wooden bridge and continues towards the Traligill Caves but unless you want to visit them, and they are worth the short diversion, stay on the north side of the glen and after a short distance follow a rising traverse up the south-west face of Beinn an Fhurain towards a col between Beinn an Fhurain and Conival.

From the col it's a straightforward climb up the broad north ridge, initially up quartzite screes and then through some small outcrops to the fairly level summit ridge and the cairn. A crest of broken quartzite blocks and boulders stretches east from the summit of Conival to the north top of Ben More Assynt, a distance of 1.5km. Although the walking is rough, there is a sense of spaciousness, with wide views both north and south. The ridge narrows dramatically in places, here and there it is very steep sided but there are no technical difficulties. In wet weather the quartzite blocks can be slippery, though!

The summit of Ben More is comprised of two rough bumps, the north one is the true summit.

Map: OS Sheet 15
Access Point: Inchnadamph
Distance: 17.6km, 1128m ascent
Approx Time: 4-7 hours
Translation: hill of joining; big hill of Assynt
Pronunciation: konivaal; byn moar assint

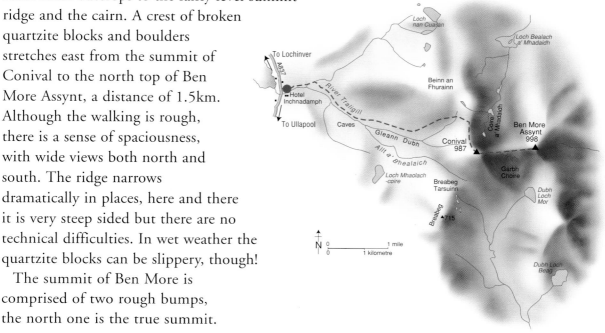

Ben Loyal (left) and Ben Klibreck (on the right in the distance) from the summit of Ben Hope

Route Summary: Cross the river and go E across the moorland towards Loch nan Uan. From the N end of the loch go SE up steep grassy slopes to the main ridge. Follow the easy ridge to a bouldery slope which leads to the summit

Map: OS Sheet 16

Access Point: A836 Lairg/Tongue road, GR545303

Distance: 11.2km, 792m ascent

Ben Klibreck (Meall nan Con) (194), 962m/3156ft

Another isolated hill rising high from the bare Sutherland moors, Beinn Cleith Bric, to give it its old name, is an 11km long, sinuous spine between Loch Naver and Loch Coire. The western aspects of the hill are in the most part steep and heathery with one prominent line of crags displayed just below the summit, Meall nan Con. The eastern side, overlooking Loch Coire, has more character, with the great grassy corries enclosed by bulging shoulders.

A number of expeditions can incorporate the ascent of Klibreck, from either the Crask Inn in the south or from Altnaharra in the north but the easiest approach, and the shortest, starts from the A836 road through Strath Vagastie. There is a good parking spot beside the river at GR545303 and once across the river, rough moorland rises towards the western slopes of the hill. Head for Loch nan Uan and from its northern shore the grass and heather slopes steepen quite dramatically towards the lowest point of the ridge above. From the outflow of the loch it's best to head south-east and so avoid the craggy ground below Meall nan Con.

Once the ridge is reached, a short ascent on good underfoot conditions lead to the summit boulderfield and the cairn.

Approx Time: 4-6 hours
Translation: hill of the speckled cliff
Pronunciation: byn kleebreck

Ben Hope (256), 927m/3041ft

The most northerly of all our Munros, Ben Hope is most often climbed from Strath More up the burn north of the broch of Dun Dornaigil, which leads to the upper southern slopes. The western cliffs are a clear marker on the left and the summit is reached in a couple of hours. While it's an easy enough walk there is a fine feel of isolation, particularly since the eastern and southern slopes ease off into a watery wilderness and northern views follow the long thin arm of Loch Hope and the open spaciousness of the sea.

From the north the hill appears as a crag-girt wedge, but a long ridge gives easy access from the south from either one of two starting points.

Beyond the farm at Alltnacaillich, just north of the Dun Dornaigil (well worth visiting this ancient beehive-shaped building), the Allt na Caillich offers a line up past some fine waterfalls on to the ridge of Leitir Mhuiseil. Follow this northwards by an obvious cliff edge, all the way to the summit cairn.

Alternatively, a signposted route starts from an old shed a couple of kilometres north of Alltnacaillich and points a way to a breach in the western escarpment which offers a more direct, if steeper, line onto the broad terrace which runs up the hill to the east of the crags. Higher up the hill a line of cairns marks the route to a large cairn, and then the summit.

The more adventurous scrambler may wish to climb Ben Hope from the north. This route involves a walk-in from the head of Loch Hope towards the Dubh-loch na Beinne, a lochan which is situated just below the mountain's north-western crags. Above the dark waters you can climb fairly easily to the mountain's north ridge where a section offers some exhilarating scrambling to the summit. The most difficult section can be avoided on the left (east) by climbing a gully which leads to the ridge higher up.

Route Summary: From the farm at Alltnacaillich go N for 1.6km and leave the road by a shed. Follow the stream and head NE to make for an obvious break in the crags which takes you on to a wide terrace above the escarpment. Turn N and follow the cliff edge which buttresses the mountain's summit
Map: OS Sheet 9
Access Point: Alltnacaillich
Distance: 6.4km, 914m ascent
Approx Time: 2-4 hours
Translation: hill of the bay
Pronunciation: byn hope

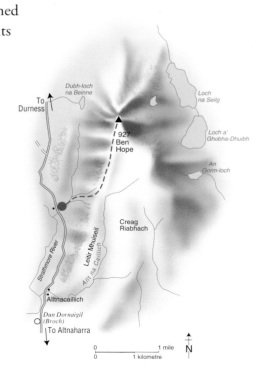

SKYE AND MULL

The Munros:

Ben More (Mull)   Bla Bheinn (Blaven)   Sgurr Dubh Mor
Sgurr nan Eag   Sgurr Alasdair   Sgurr Mhic Choinnich
Inaccessible Pinnacle (Sgurr Dearg)   Sgurr na Banachdich
Sgurr a' Ghreadaidh   Sgurr a' Mhadaidh
Bruach na Frithe   Am Basteir   Sgurr nan Gillean

The islands of Mull and Skye are, somewhat surprisingly, the only two Scottish islands which can boast Munros. Ben More on Mull is an attractive hill and many Munroists keep it as their 'last Munro', making a celebration weekend out of it, sailing out across the Sound of Mull to Craignure from Oban, driving around to Loch na Keal for the walk and celebrating later in the evening in Tobermory. There have probably been more Munro celebrations in the restaurants of Tobermory than anywhere else.

There are regular celebrations in Skye's Glenbrittle and Sligachan too, celebrations that are tinged with a certain amount of relief. For many walkers, the Skye Cuillin is the dark side of their Munro ambitions, the fears that wake them up in the middle of the night with sweaty palms have much to do with exposure, knife edged ridges, steep scrambles and of course the In Pin, the most technically difficult of all the Munros. These are the Munros that require not only fairly advanced rock scrambling, but some rock climbing skills too, and the Inaccessible Pinnacle requires knowledge and experience of how to abseil. Hence the relief for many walkers once they've successfully completed the Cuillin Ridge – they can get on with the rest of their life without the Cuillin nightmares!

But in essence all that is required is an experienced companion – preferably a mountaineer with a rock climbing background, someone who is happy to belay you, and encourage you on the steeper sections.

Because of the unique nature of the main Cuillin Ridge, I've taken a different approach to describing it from the rest of this book. While the ridge breaks down naturally into four separate expeditions, I'm well aware that many may want to walk the entire ridge in one go, while others may wish to climb single Munros, depending on time available and the weather, which can be fickle to say the least. I've therefore described the ridge in one main essay, while describing a logical break-down of the ridge into four expeditions in the route summaries. I hope this gives a clearer picture of the options available.

Sgurr na Gillean (sunlit on the right) from the south-east

Ben More (Mull) (189), 966m/3169ft

Route Summary: Start at the foot of the Abhainn na h-Uamha and follow the S bank up the grassy Gleann na Beinne Fada to reach the col between Beinn Fhada and A' Chioch. Turn S and climb towards A' Chioch. Continue on the ridge over A' Chioch to Ben More. Descend by the broad NW ridge

Map: OS Sheet 48

Access Point: The B8035 beside Loch na Keal, near the outflow of the Abhainn na h-Uamha

Distance: 13km, 950m ascent

Approx Time: 5-7 hours

Translation: big hill

Pronunciation: byn moar

This hill seems to be gaining the reputation of the 'final Munro', as more walkers keep this hill as the last of their Munro round than any other. There are a number of reasons for this, the major one being the difficulty of access. You have to make a weekend of Mull's Ben More and if you're going to make a weekend of it you might as well make it a celebratory one. That's exactly what I did. I deliberately kept Ben More as my final Munro, took my wife with me, climbed the hill with her on a wet and cloudy day and retreated to Tobermory for a slap-up celebration dinner.

Other than those collecting the island's only Munro the Isle of Mull is curiously ignored by hill walkers, which is a pity for there are a couple of grand Corbetts and a lot of fine walking, albeit mostly on rough ground. If nothing else, Ben More offers a taster of what the island has to offer.

Perhaps another reason why walkers leave Ben More as their last Munro is to give them a chance to save up for it – it can be a costly weekend. Positioned near the west of the island it is a fair distance from the ferry at Craignure and you either have to take a car on the ferry from Oban, and drive to the starting point, or take a local bus to Salen from where you still have an 11km walk to Loch na Keal. A bike would be useful, and cheaper to transport on the Oban-Craignure ferry!

From the roadside at Loch na Keal follow the Abhainn na h-Uamha up the length of Gleann na Beinne Fada to the obvious col in the ridge between Beinn Fhada on your left and A' Chioch on the right. From the col turn south and climb increasingly steep and rocky slopes to the summit of A' Chioch. The ridge to Ben More continues in much the same way, a steep and rocky descent to the narrow bealach then another steep, rocky climb to the summit wind break of Ben More. This final climb to Ben More looks difficult from the bealach but don't be discouraged, it's easier than it looks.

A word of warning – the summit of Ben More has much magnetic rock and compasses are notoriously unreliable. The best descent is down the broad and straightforward north-west ridge.

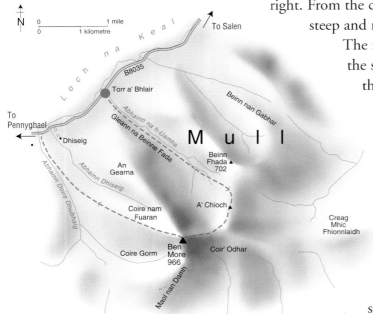

The A' Chioch ridge from the summit of Ben More

Bla Bheinn from across Loch Slapin

Route Summary: Leave the Elgol road at the Allt na Dunaiche just S of the head of Loch Slapin on its W side. Take the path that runs alongside the N bank of the stream through a wooded gorge, and then more steeply into Coire Uaigneich. Here the path becomes indistinct in places, but turns NNW up a steep slope just right of an obvious gully and soon reaches a distinct shoulder. Once this shoulder abuts on to the main ridge follow it in a WSW direction, following the rim of the ridge. As you climb closer to the summit dome there are one or two rocky obstacles to be scrambled over before more scree slopes lead to the summit

Map: OS Sheet 32

Access Point: Head of Loch Slapin

Distance: 8km, 950m ascent

Approx Time: 5-7 hours

Translation: possibly blue hill, or possibly warm hill

Pronunciation: blaa-vin

Bla Bheinn (Blaven) (252), 928m/3045ft

In many ways Blaven is even more impressive than its celebrated cousins, the Cuillin. Standing at the head of Loch Slapin, Blaven and its Corbett neighbour, Clach Glas (the traverse of both mountains is a rock scrambler's delight) are set apart by the gulf created by Glen Sligachan and Strath na Creitheach. As such, the views are finer than any you'll see in the Cuillin, indeed on a stormy day of dark shifting clouds the views west and north-west from the summit of Blaven are distinctly Tolkienesque! Sherrif Alexander Nicolson, a local man and one of the early mountaineering pioneers on Skye, suggested Blaven was the finest mountain on the island. It has twin summits with the south-west top only a couple of metres lower than the main one.

Blaven is often climbed from Camasunary up the Coire nan Leac, or, less often, from the Am Mam between the A881 Elgol road and Camasunary. This route is less attractive as it involves a long haul up the mountain's stony south ridge. The 'trade route' is undoubtedly the often wet footpath which leaves the road near the head of Loch Slapin and follows the course of the Allt na Dunaiche into Coire Uaigneich.

Follow the path on the north side of the burn through some woodland and pass some lovely wooded waterfalls. Just past the falls, cross the stream and continue west. Soon the path steepens as you take more of a south westerly line up heather, then grassy slopes and into the secret corrie, Coire Uaigneich.

In the upper reaches of the corrie where the slope flattens out considerably start climbing in a north-north-west direction on the south flank of the east ridge. A rough path takes a zigzag line and

Clach Glas and the 'Red Cuillin' from the summit of Bla Bheinn

becomes clearer on the higher screes as it passes the top of the
Great Prow, which appears on the right before reaching a small top
on the hill's eastern shoulder.

The ridge is straightforward from here, as it
narrows and weaves gently to the left and
then to the right before becoming less
steep as it broadens out to the summit
trig point.

Descend southwards along the
summit ridge to a col. From here the
Great Scree Gully offers a fairly rapid
descent back to Coire Uaigneach. An
alternative descent is to head south
from the south-west top, which is
easily reached from the col, and then
follow the broad south-east ridge to
the upper slopes of Coire Uaigneach
and the footpath back to Loch Slapin.

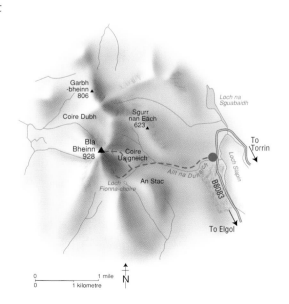

217

The Cuillin from the north-west, across Loch Bracadale

The Cuillin Ridge: Sgurr Dubh Mor (228), 944m/3097ft, Sgurr nan Eag (265), 924m/3031ft, Sgurr Alasdair (154), 992m/3255ft, Sgurr Mhic Choinnich (217), 948m/3110ft, Inaccessible Pinnacle (Sgurr Dearg) (164), 986m/3235ft, Sgurr na Banachdich (190), 965m/3166ft, Sgurr a' Ghreadaidh (185), 973m/3192ft, Sgurr a' Mhadaidh (277), 918m/3012ft, Bruach na Frithe (200), 958m/3143ft, Am Basteir (242), 934m/3064ft, Sgurr nan Gillean (191), 964m/3162ft

Without doubt the finest way to climb the 11 Munros of the Cuillin is in one continuous expedition, starting at the south end of the ridge on Sgurr nan Eag, or even better Gars-bheinn, the most southerly top on the Cuillin ridge, and working your way north through the most spectacular mountain scenery in the British Isles to finish on the airy peak of Sgurr nan Gillean. The expedition is made up of 18 individual tops, 14 of which are over 914m, 11 of which are classed as Munros. Never dropping under 760m in its 11km, this is the longest ridge walk in Britain.

Most hillwalkers take about 12 hours for the trip, from Gars-bheinn to Sgurr nan Gillean, bivvying out somewhere on the Gars-bheinn to Sgurr a Choire Bhig ridge before setting off at daybreak. The record between the two tops is currently just under three-and-a-half hours!

Bruach na Frithe is most easily approached from the Sligachan end of the Bealach a' Mhaim track which crosses over boggy moorland between Sligachan and Glen Brittle. At a point about 1km short of the summit of the pass a cairned line diverts up to the Fionn Choire, from where a line can easily be worked out to the summit. Alternatively, the north-west ridge can be easily followed to

Sgurr Dubh Mor, 944m/3097ft, Sgurr nan Eag, 924m/3031ft

Route Summary: From the camp site in Glen Brittle follow the track towards Coire Lagan but after 800m or so leave the path and cross the moorland in an ESE direction towards Sron na Ciche (Route A). Make for the edge of Coir' a' Ghrunnda by contouring around the foot of Sron na Ciche, and then climb into the corrie to reach the lochan. Climb to an obvious col on the main ridge between Sgurr Dubh na Da Bheinn and Sgurr Thearlaich. Climb easy slopes to Sgurr Dubh na Da Bheinn and from there follow the ridge E to Sgurr Dubh Mor. Return to Sgurr Dubh an Da Bheinn and descend S along the main ridge, traversing below the steep-sided Caisteal a' Garbh-choire on either its W or E side. Continue along the main ridge to Sgurr nan Eag

Map: OS Sheet 32

Access Point: Glen Brittle House

Distance: 14km, 1190m ascent

Approx Time: 5-6 hours

Translation: big black peak; peak of the notches

Pronunciation: skoor doo moar; skoor nan ayg

Sgurr Alasdair, 992m/3255ft,
Sgurr Mhic Choinnich, 948m/3110ft,
Inaccessible Pinnacle (Sgurr Dearg),
986m/3235ft

Route Summary: Known as the Round of Coire Lagan the easiest approach is by the Great Stone Shoot in Coire Lagan (Route B), which takes you into the gap between Sgurr Alasdair and Sgurr Thearlaich. Alasdair is easily reached from the gap by an easy scramble, while the best way onto Sgurr Thearlaich is to descend for a short distance to the E of the gap and climb an obvious crack on your left. This takes you on to Thearlaich's S rib, which can then be followed to the slabby summit.

Descend rocky grooves to an obvious bealach and from here move up a little and then traverse round the W face by Collie's Ledge (moderate difficulty). A much more direct route for climbers takes the obvious corner of King's Chimney (difficult) on the S side. Walkers who don't wish to climb are best descending to Coire Lagan by the Great Stone Chute between Sgurr Alasdair and Sgurr Thearlaich, regaining the ridge by the An Stac screes.

From the summit of Sgurr Mhic Choinnich descend NNE to the col above the An Stac screes. It will be necessary to drop down a little to reach a cairned path in the scree that leads up below the west edge of An Stac's tower. Staying close to the base of its wall climb to easier ground. Continue on the main ridge and climb the Inaccessible Pinnacle by its E ridge (moderate difficulty - rock climbing). On the tiny summit a convenient boulder provides an anchor for an 18m abseil off the W side of the pinnacle. Descend to Glen Brittle by Sgurr Dearg's W ridge

Map: OS Sheet 32

Access Point: Glen Brittle

Distance: 14km, 1680m ascent

Approx Time: 8-9 hours

Translation: Alexander's Peak (named after Sheriff Alexander Nicolson who made the first ascent in 1873); Mackenzie's Peak (named after John Mackenzie, the first Skye guide); red peak

Pronunciation: skoor alastar; skoor veechk chunyeech; skoor jerrack

Sgurr na Banachdich, 965m/3166ft,
Sgurr a' Ghreadaidh, 973m/3192ft,
Sgurr a' Mhadaidh, 918m/3012ft

Route Summary: Take the path above the Eas Mor waterfalls to the upper basin of Coire na Banachdich (Route C). From here a cairned route takes a devious line beneath the crags of Sgurr Dearg eventually turning left to reach screes which lead to a gap in the ridge N of Sgurr Dearg. To the N, across the Bealach Coire na Banachdich, steep rock and screes lead to Sron Bhuidhe, then two more 'tops' before the final pull to Sgurr na Banachdich. From the summit a short dip leads to the foot of Sgurr Thormaid. This is climbed by scrambling over large blocks and boulders. From the summit continue to the NE avoiding the 'three teeth' by traversing easy angled slabs on their left. Follow the short narrow arête which leads to a 120m scramble on good holds to the S top of Sgurr a' Ghreadaidh. Follow the very narrow ridge crest to the summit. Continue on the narrow ridge down into the gap known as the Eag Dubh. This is followed by another descent to a second gap, the An Dorus. From here scramble to the SW summit of Sgurr a' Mhadaidh, the only 'top' which is given Munro status. Follow the ridge NW which runs out to Sgurr Thuilm and drop down into Coir a' Ghreadaidh from the obvious col, returning to Glen Brittle

Map: OS Sheet 32

Access Point: Glen Brittle

Distance: 14km, 1340m ascent

Approx Time: 6-8 hours

Translation: possibly smallpox peak; peak of torment; peak of the fox

Pronunciation: skoor na banachteech; skoor a ghraytee; skoor a vaady

Bruach na Frithe, 958m/3143ft,
Am Basteir, 934m/3064ft,
Sgurr nan Gillean, 964m/3162ft

Route Summary: From the hotel at Sligachan follow the road W for a short distance to where a footpath crosses the moorland to reach the Allt Dearg Mor (Route D). Stay on the N bank and follow the footpath past Alltdearg House. Leave this path as it begins to bend S towards the Bealach a' Mhaim and take to open grassy slopes which lead into the mouth of the Fionn Coire between Sgurr a' Bhasteir and the NW ridge of Bruach na Frithe. Climb increasingly rocky slopes to reach the crest of the Cuillin Ridge at the Bealach nan Lice. Head W from the bealach up easy slopes to the summit of Bruach na Frithe. Return now to the Bealach nan Lice and follow the scree path round the N side of Am Basteir to the Bealach a' Bhasteir. From here follow the E ridge of Am Basteir to an awkward scrambling descent, which has been made even more difficult by a rockfall. You might have to abseil into the gap, or alternatively, descend a sloping ledge in the S side of the ridge to gain a lower ledge that can be followed back to the ridge close to the summit. From the summit of Am Basteir return to the Bealach a' Bhasteir the way you came and follow a gravel path ENE to the foot of Nicolson's Chimney which, after a steep scramble on good holds (moderate rock climbing) gives access to the W ridge of Sgurr nan Gillean. Scramble up this ridge to the summit. Descend the steep and very narrow SE ridge to a col and follow the well-worn path down Coire Riabach and back across the moors to Sligachan

Map: OS Sheet 32

Access Point: Sligachan

Distance: 15km, 1160m ascent

Approx Time: 7-8 hours

Translation: slope of the deer forest; meaning obscure; peak of the young men

Pronunciation: brooach na freea; am bastar; skoor nan geelyan

reach the summit. This is certainly the easiest of the Skye Cuillin and the view from the summit will give a fine taster of the rest of the ridge. The Fionn Choire path leads to the Bealach na Lice, an easy pass, but the continuation into the Harta Corrie and Glen Sligachan involves a long, awkward walk.

Sgurr na Banachdich is the easiest Munro from the Glen Brittle side of the ridge, and utilises a well-worn approach up Coir' an Each to gain the western slopes which run out to Sgurr nan Gobhar. Sgurr Alasdair, at 992m, is the highest of the Cuillin and the easiest approach is by the tiresome Great Stone Shoot from Coire Lagan. Unless you are a climber, forget the other routes, which are invariably barred by crags.

Sgurr nan Eag is probably the remotest of the Cuillin Munros, and can be reached by its bouldery south slopes after a long walk across boggy moorland from Glen Brittle. It's well worth traversing the ridge to Gars-bheinn, the most southerly top on the Cuillin ridge, but avoid Coire nan Laoigh for descents.

The Inaccessible Pinnacle from Sgurr Alasdair

Coir' a' Ghrunnda is a fascinating place geologically but can be difficult to enter unless you're prepared to scramble a bit. If you are, then it's worthwhile linking Sgurr nan Eag with Sgurr Dubh Mor. This summit can be immensely difficult to find, never mind climb – it's positioned amid a great jumble of rocks and boulders and involves a fair bit of awkward scrambling to reach it. Try and keep it for a clear day. From Sgurr Dubh Mor a rocky ridge leads to Sgurr nan Eag, a route which is fairly straightforward, but the descent from Sgurr nan Eag westwards back to the Glenbrittle path is incredibly rocky and knee-jarring. My knees have never been the same since.

Sgurr a' Mhaidaidh and Sgurr a' Ghreadaidh can be climbed with some moderate scrambling from Coire a' Ghreadaidh. Being multi-topped, or, more accurately, multi-toothed hills, route finding can be extremely difficult. Sgurr Mhic Choinnich is a serious scramble, it is exposed and the rock can be extremely slippery when wet, especially on the summit slabs. It's usually climbed as part of the round of Coire Lagan, along with Sgurr Alasdair and the In Pin and involves an exposed route called Collie's Ledge, a marvellous rocky promenade which appears to be carved from the rock face – it's actually a lot easier than it looks.

From its position just south of Sligachan, Sgurr nan Gillean is to most folks the epitome of the Cuillin. It is reached by a well maintained path from near the Sligachan Inn which weaves its way over and round low moorland hillocks, eventually crossing Coire Riabhach and curving round on to the south-east ridge of the hill. Higher up some scrambling is involved and the summit is extremely airy. Despite the scrambling this is the easiest route up the mountain. Am Basteir is usually climbed along with Sgurr nan Gillean and can be difficult in misty weather. The summit crest is exposed and a rock fall has made one particular descent even trickier than it was before. To continue to Bruach na Frithe you are best to return to the Bealach am Basteir and follow the path that skirts above the scree slopes to the Bealach nan Lice. From there it's an easy scramble to Bruach na Frithe.

Without doubt the Inaccessible Pinnacle (Sgurr Dearg) is by far the most difficult of all the Cuillin hills, indeed of all the Munros. A narrowing blade of rock leaning against the summit crest of Sgurr Dearg, this impressive feature will either delight you, or scare the pants off you. It can be reached either by the path up Coire na Banachdich or from Coire Lagan, or from the ridge from Sgurr Mhic Choinnich.

There are two routes up the In Pin – the short steep western face which involves a rock climb of about V. Diff standard and the longer, east ridge, a moderate rock climb in technical terms but one which is seriously exposed. If you're an experienced climber then you'll romp up this eastern ridge, exhilarated by the position and exposure. If you've never climbed and are unhappy using your hands then you'll need a rope, climbing gear and an experienced companion. However you climb it, you have to abseil from the top, a 24m drop to Sgurr Dearg.

Far too many Munro collectors are put off by the In Pin which is a great shame for while it may be exposed it is not technically difficult and it's well worthwhile swallowing your pride and asking some climbing acquaintance for help. The ascent of the Inaccessible Pinnacle is without question one of the highlights of any round of the Munros.

'In wildness is the preservation of the world'
Henry David Thoreau
1817-62

Bla Bheinn and Clach Glas from the Allt na Dunaich

Mountain Safety

Appropriate safety precautions should always be taken when venturing on to the Scottish hills. The number of serious injuries and deaths on the mountains has greatly increased in recent years, so it is very important to ensure that you are properly equipped whilst on a climb. There are a number of items which are essential for all climbers tackling a hill. Don't set off without packing waterproofs and spare inner clothing, food, a map, a compass, whistle and torch. It is also advisable to carry a survival bag for emergencies. Before you undertake a climb, make sure you have alerted someone of the route you are taking and always report back when you are finished.

Remember that Scottish winter conditions can often be Arctic, and as severe as those on higher European mountains. They should therefore be treated with the utmost respect: an ice axe, crampons and specialist winter gear are necessary when climbing during the winter months, as is an understanding of any potential dangers such as unpredictable and severe snow conditions (particularly avalanches and snow cornices). When planning your outing make sure to pay attention to the weather forecast, and even if the likelihood is for fine weather it is important to be prepared for all outcomes, even during the summer months. Patches of snow left over from the winter are often still around in the summertime and should be avoided as they are likely to be hard, icy and slippery.

Anyone who is climbing in the Scottish mountains should be able to navigate accurately especially as tracks and paths are rarely signposted and can be difficult to trace on a map. The mountain weather can be extremely fickle and change very suddenly from bright sunshine to wicked storms, so consideration must be given to the possibility of routes becoming difficult or impassable due to variation of terrain and rising water levels in rivers and burns.

Scottish hillwalking and climbing courses are offered by numerous qualified instructors and guides and there are many such organisations operating in the Highlands. Guidance can also be found in the many magazines, pamphlets and other books published on the subject of mountaineering. To obtain information on mountaineering clubs and means of getting in touch with them you can contact:

The Hon. Secretary of the Mountaineering Council of Scotland
The Old Granary, West Mill Street,
Perth PH1 5QP.   www.mountaineering-scotland.org.uk

Sportscotland,
Caledonia House,
South Gyle,
Edinburgh EH12 9DQ.

ACCESS

Early in 1996, a Concordat on Access to the wild areas of Scotland was published[1] following an earlier review of access to Scotland's hills by Scottish Natural Heritage. The opening paragraph said:

> 'There is a longstanding tradition of access to hill land in Scotland – cherished by those who use the hills and long accepted by landowners and managers where this freedom is exercised with responsibility. As more people go to the hills, there is a growing need to encourage sensitive management and recreational practice. The Concordat aims to ensure that people can continue to enjoy access to the open hill in a way which shows consideration for the interests of others.'

That Corcordat eventually paved the way for new legislation on access in Scotland, which followed on from devolution and the creation of a Scottish Parliament. A land reform agenda was set out by the new Scottish Executive, which included the creation of national parks in Scotland, and new access legislation. The Land Reform (Scotland) Act 2003 now gives the public statutory access rights to most land and inland water in Scotland, including hills, mountains, moorland, woods and forests. Wild camping is included amongst the rights. It means that walkers can climb hills and wild camp, out of sight of road or houses, without any threat from land managers. But bear in mind that hillwalkers only have these rights if they exercise them responsibly by respecting the privacy, safety and livelihoods of others as well as caring for the environment. Equally, land managers have to manage their land and water responsibly in relation to access rights.

In conjunction with the new access legislation, a Scottish Outdoor Access Code has been published (www.outdooraccess-scotland.com) to provide detailed guidance on the responsibilities of those exercising access rights and of those managing land and water. The Code provides a practical guide to help everyone make the proper decisions about what best to do in everyday situations. However, many estates in Scotland are involved in deer stalking and ask hillwalkers to respect the stag shooting season which runs from about mid August until 20 October. Some estates may extend this season for a couple of weeks or so and some may begin slightly earlier. During this time there are many upland areas in Scotland that are unaffected by deer stalking, like those reserves operated by Scottish Natural Heritage and the National Trust for Scotland.

To help hillwalkers find out where stalking is taking place the Mountaineering Council for Scotland and SNH jointly operate a website (www.hillphones.info) and Hillphones system. By using Hillphones intending visitors can obtain information about stalking and plan their outings accordingly. Recorded messages are updated by 8.00am each day and calls are charged at normal rates. Wherever possible, Hillphone messages contain a forecast of stalking activities for the next few days.

The service is supported by the Access Forum, and has been organised by the Mountaineering Council of Scotland, Scottish Natural Heritage and the participating estates. The service aims to improve communications between stag hunters and hillwalkers and so far has been a huge success.

[1] *Scotland's Hills and Mountains: A Concordat on Access* (The Access Forum, SNH, Battleby, Nr. Perth, 1996)

INDEX